Moving
off the
Map

Moving
off the
Map

A Field Guide to Changing
the Congregation

Thomas G. Bandy

ABINGDON PRESS
Nashville

MOVING OFF THE MAP: A FIELD GUIDE TO CHANGING THE CONGREGATION

Copyright © 1998 by Abingdon Press

Library of Congress Cataloging-in-Publication Data

Bandy, Thomas G., 1950–
  Moving off the map: a field guide to changing the congregation /
Thomas G. Bandy.
    p.   cm.
  ISBN 0-687-06800-2 (pbk.)
  I.Church renewal.   I. Title.
BV600.2.B33   1998
250—dc21   98-40758
                                                                                    CIP

99 00 01 02 03 04 05 06 07—10 9 8 7 6 5 4 3 2

MANUFACTURED IN THE UNITED STATES OF AMERICA

To my wife, my family, and all those who are committed to ministries of transformation

PREFACE

This book is the result of the courageous experiments and explorations of transforming congregations and visionary congregational leaders. It has emerged from consultations in a wide diversity of social and cultural contexts in the United States and Canada. Small and large churches . . . rural, urban, and suburban churches . . . English, Hispanic, French, Chinese, and numerous other cultural churches . . . all these have helped shape the tools for transformation presented here. I honor and appreciate their courage to take the risks of systemic change, and I celebrate with them the abundant harvest of ministry that has been the result.

I am deeply grateful for the continued support of my wife and family, whose prayers and patience have allowed me the time and energy to continue the ministry of congregational systemic change. When I see the future in my children's eyes, the quest to change the systems of congregational Christian experience becomes ever more urgent.

CONTENTS

—— PART III ——
FREEING THE FAITHFUL!
THE BASIC BOUNDARIES OF CONGREGATIONAL LIFE

Contents

— PART I —

GROWING THE LEADERS

WHAT CHANGE MEANS FOR CHURCH LEADERS

— 1 —
THE CHALLENGE FOR THE TWENTY-FIRST CENTURY

Martha died in the Cincinnati Zoological Gardens in 1914. She was the last passenger pigeon. With her death, the species became extinct. Just a century earlier, passenger pigeons darkened the skies of North America. The great naturalist Audubon wrote in amazement at the flocks of hundreds of thousands of birds that would pass overhead. Their primary nesting grounds were in Michigan, and the town names of *Pigeon Lake* and *Pigeon River* were gained for that notoriety. The passenger pigeon was about the size of a chicken. It was a beautiful, friendly, wonderful bird indigenous to North America, and it thrived in enormous numbers. No one—including the great Audubon himself—would have ever predicted that in a few short years the species would die.

What happened? Some scientists blame the fact that the passenger pigeon did not seem to create enough young. Birth rates declined among the pigeons, and the enormous flocks could not be replaced. Most environmentalists blame capitalism. The birds were extensively hunted for their meat, and barrels of pigeon meat were sold through Chicago markets until the turn of the century. At that time, the market was so glutted with pigeon meat that the bottom fell out and no profits could be gained. However, the bird was still hunted and killed, straight to the breeding grounds in Michigan.

The real cause of the extinction of the passenger pigeon lies in the nature of the species itself. First, *passenger pigeons were preoccupied with families.* They were strictly monogamous, and both male and female shared parenting responsibilities. Although this sounds wonderful, this preoccupation caused them to spend less time adapting to the environment and more time perpetuating the habits of the passenger pigeon among the young. Because they were unable to welcome unattached new birds, the genetic pool became weaker and weaker, until they could no longer give birth to the young birds that they wanted to love so dearly. They handed down a heritage, and in the end it killed them.

Second, *the heritage handed down by the passenger pigeon included incredible friendliness.* These birds were so gregarious that thousands of them would nest in a single tree. Even when the tree became overloaded and threatened to collapse, all the birds remained in the tree. No entrepreneurial groups of birds could leave the nest and form a new nesting place. They loved each other, welcomed new birds into the nest, and in the end, collapsing nests would kill them by the thousands.

Third, *this gregarious nature made the passenger pigeon vulnerable to a hostile environment.* As the world became less safe for their species through hunting, the passenger pigeons could not adapt to the new world. The primary trick of the hunter was to capture a passenger pigeon, tie its feet with a string, and place it on a stool or rail in the middle of a field. As flocking birds passed over, the hunter would jiggle the string and make the captured pigeon dance. Those gregarious passenger pigeons would immediately land and swarm around their leader—and the hunters would simply walk into their midst and club them to death.

Thus, the real reason the passenger pigeons all died is that they relied upon the wrong model of leadership. They trusted an *enabling leader.* The *enabling leader* would fly ahead to find a tree in which to nest. The rest of the flock would gather around him. He would help all the little young ones find a place on the branches, assist all the pigeon families to find a place in the tree, and one-by-one help every passenger pigeon enjoy the greatest harmonious fellowship possible. Even if the tree proved to be rotten and dying, even if the tree became overcrowded and threatened to collapse, and even if food sources became depleted and the flock was threatened by starvation, the *enabling leader* could do nothing. The flock dared not venture forth to find a new home for fear that even one of the birds might be lost. Unable to move forward, adapt, or grow in the face of a changing environment, pigeons became the easy victims of natural disasters and the easy prey of thoughtless boys with BB guns.

All final extinction required was the tethering of the *enabling leader.* Just as the *enabling leaders* became bound to the flock and the nesting tree due to gregariousness, tradition, and the fear of losing a single member of the flock, so also they were manipulated to bring ultimate destruction to the very flock that they loved. Hunters learned to tie them down by a string. All the pigeons would gather. Together they would die. The *enabling leader* was called a *stool pigeon*. Here, then, is the lesson for the church on the brink of the twenty-first century.

Preoccupation with children and youth in the church may sound admirable, but it ultimately leads to heritage protection. The more churches understand themselves as "family churches," the less likely they are to include unattached singles, couples, or families from other cultures (or "species") in the "gene pool" of the congregation. The congregation becomes increasingly homogeneous, less adaptable to the changing environment, and less likely to be open to radical creativity. Tradition becomes all-important.

The heritage of friendliness is expressed in many churches through their gregariousness around the coffee urn following worship or during fellowship gatherings. All churches pride themselves on being friendly, and they are! This is precisely the source of the danger. Everybody loves the roost. Everybody knows everybody by first name. Therefore, no second worship service can begin, no new congregation can spin off from the parenting nest, and no entrepreneurship can pioneer new territory— because everyone values friendliness, fellowship, unity, and harmony too much.

The real reason churches are dying in the midst of a changing cultural environment is that they are relying on the wrong model of leadership. The clergy and the church are caught in a vicious circle of ultimate destruction. Family churches value gregariousness, heritage, and homogeneity—and they nurture leaders who find personal satisfaction in prioritizing gregariousness, heritage, and homogeneity. Often these church leaders do not even recognize the vicious circle in which they are trapped. They may not even recognize that the church "roost" is rotten and in imminent danger of collapse, that the worship center is overcrowded and cannot accept more people, or that community demographics have shifted and the mission field has moved on. If they recognize it, they may not care. "We are the righteous remnant," they tell themselves. "Our way of life may be endangered, but that is only because our way of life is the only way to live. At least we will die nobly." If they recognize it and care about it, they are helpless to do anything. Any attempt to move the congregation physically or spiritually runs the risk of losing someone, and that is a risk the congregation dares not take; it is a risk for which the *enabling leader* simply cannot accept the guilt.

Thus, the most bitter lesson for the church upon the death of Christendom is that *enabling clergy* are in fact the "stool pigeons" of the twenty-first century. Imagine their agony as they watch more and more parishioners flock around them, knowing that they are doomed! And yet also knowing that, due to their inclination and training, they can do nothing else than be what they are, stool pigeons! All you need to do is tether the enabling clergy. Tether them by pensions, limited training, codependent "needs to be needed," addictions to maintain lovely cathedral buildings, or addictions to preserve a great denominational heritage as certified officers of the church. Allow some *controllers* (dysfunctional elders, lay leaders, board members, matriarchs, or patriarchs) to pull on the string so that the "stool pigeon" clergy dance—and the Christian people will flock to their ultimate destruction.

Poor Martha! The last stool pigeon died in 1914. How lonely she must have felt. Do you think she even realized her fault? Or did she just excuse herself by saying that she was "faithful to the end"?

The time required for the passenger pigeon to transition from being one of the most abundant species in North America to virtual extinction was only about 50 years. At the close of the twentieth century, environmentalists estimate that an entire species of animal or plant life is becoming extinct every single day. Christendom has been sick unto death for well over 100 years. We began to recognize this clearly during the past 50 years. Yet the actual death of congregations is happening suddenly, quickly, and with an odd sense of surprise on the part of church leadership. It is as if the stool pigeons never really thought it would come to this. The death of Christendom was a theological exercise in probability, a theoretical conversation, and (for some) an obstacle in career development. It is as if they saw the rotten tree overburdened by contented birds but never really believed the tree would collapse! It is as if they fluttered their wings, tethered by the strings of controlling denominations, watching their mates flock about them with cooing pleasure—and never truly believed the hunters would step out of the shadows and club them all to death.

This is precisely what is happening, and will happen, over the next decades. Although the timeline will vary in different regions of North America, we will see entire pigeon roosts collapse, congregations close, entire presbyteries and dioceses disintegrate into chaos, and whole denominations declare bankruptcy and merge with other declining churches, only to die in the end. It will happen suddenly, quickly and will take both church leadership and the media by surprise—not because they had not been warned but because they never really believed God would let it happen to them. After all, for years Chicken Little (or, in this case, "Pigeon Little"!) has been crying, "The sky is falling! The sky is falling!" and we seem to have paid the church utility bills one more year. Perhaps it is all a false alarm.

Yet the forces of change have mounted, and the hunters are gathering in the shadows. The next decades will bring killing stress to the church:

• Governments and municipalities will change the laws and find ways to tax church property and clergy benefits, exploding congregational budgets beyond repair.

• Veteran church members over age 55, who compose the largest portion of the congregation, will retire, enter nursing homes, or die. Their energy and financial contributions will be lost. They will leave behind bequests, which they hope will preserve the church institution but which, in fact, will be just one more tether to make the stool pigeon dance.

• The spiritually yearning public will continue to be institutionally alienated. The younger public will simply stop coming to traditional churches altogether, and veteran church leaders will rapidly move to the margins of congregational life, burned out and disenchanted.

• Immigration and wholesale cultural migration will transform North American society. Not only will ethnic peoples refuse to participate in the homogeneous churches of North American Christendom, the cultural revolutions of the next decade will lead their own second and third generations to refuse to participate in the homogeneous churches of their own ethnic heritage.

• Fewer and fewer potential Christian leaders will feel called to be a stool pigeon. They will not find personal fulfillment in being a stool pigeon and will refuse to be trained as stool pigeons. The quality of church leadership will rapidly drop. Denominational control to certify and influence the hiring of salaried staff will weaken. Seminaries and denominational learning centers will either radically diversify curriculum or be closed.

• Litigation, liability for past institutional injustices, and urgent competition for the charitable funding of unpopular causes will deplete the reserve funds of denominations and congregations. Credit from the bank for further capital improvement or development will cease. Congregations that saw utility and pension expenses surpass mission in the budgets of the 1960s will now be unable to provide adequate salaries and heat the building.

• Generic mission funds of the denomination will suddenly bottom out, and denominational responsibilities to maintain and insure heritage property that no one else wants will multiply exponentially. Denominational mission grants and capital funding will be slashed, denominational offices will be cut, denominational publishing and resource development will be abandoned, and denominational influence on public affairs will not even be acknowledged by the media or governments.

All these hunters have gathered in the shadows of the next few decades. Meanwhile, the stool pigeons continue to dance, tethered by the strings of control, gathering the gregarious flock (who love the youth, prize the family, value tradition, and enjoy contented potluck suppers) to the killing fields.

This is not a theoretical death of Christendom. It is a real death of Christendom—and of all those Christendom churches and other ecclesiastical machines. It is the immediate future . . . un-less . . . *unless the Christian congregations of North America change.* This same period can be a window of opportunity to transform the church into a new species of Christian community that can flourish in the twenty-first century.

Given the crisis that confronts congregations and church leaders on the brink of the twenty-first century, and given the sweep and scope of that crisis, the change demanded for church transformation can be characterized in four ways:

1. Change must be *systemic.* This change must alter the very

nature of the species. It cannot simply change a single behavior pattern or personality trait. For example, it would not have helped the passenger pigeon to learn to roost only in maple trees, rather than elm trees, or to choose stool pigeons with pure white feathers and advanced academic degrees as their leaders, rather than stool pigeons with gray feathers and basic academic degrees. The problem lay in the nature of the species. The whole sweep and flow of the system of congregational life and mission must change.

2. Change must be *owned by the congregation*. The fate of the congregation is independent of the fate of the denomination. Ultimately, the death of the denomination will not destroy the congregation, nor will the survival of the denomination rescue the congregation. Their fate is in their own hands. Denominations can only help or hinder; they cannot ultimately force or block congregational transformation. Ministers can be helped by mentoring colleagues who are similarly striving for transformation and by parachurch organizations that can provide guidance for planning and resources. However, in the end, the local congregation alone must do it.

3. Change must be *concentrated*. Change cannot be diluted by irrelevant goals like the survival of a community, the preservation of a heritage, the maintenance of historic or sentimental property, the perpetuation of an institutional polity, the observance of specific ceremonies and rites, or the guaranteed salaries of authoritative officers. When it comes to systemic change, all that matters is the Gospel. Either the system helps people experience the transforming power of God and walk daily with Jesus, or it does not. If it does not, then no matter how daring, fun, intriguing, or socially beneficial it might be, it does not fulfill the New Testament purpose of the church. If it does, then congregations can flourish and bear fruit (spiritual, social, and economic) to benefit all humankind.

4. Change must be *anchored in the experience of the congregation with Jesus*. The real issue before the church is not merely theological. It is christological. The key question that I first articulated in *Kicking Habits: Welcome Relief for Addicted Churches* (Nashville: Abingdon, 1997) remains the key question for church transformation: *What is it about our experience with Jesus that this community cannot live without?* Bill Easum and I sought to elaborate

upon this theme in *Growing Spiritual Redwoods* (Nashville: Abingdon, 1997). No enduring change can happen in the church, no matter how large or small, without it being linked to continuing spiritual growth in one's relationship with Jesus.

These four characteristics of the change demanded for church transformation will bring extraordinary stress to the congregations and church leaders of dying Christendom. It will be stressful:

- to acknowledge the legitimacy of these demands;
- to understand the full scope and intensity of these demands;
- to persuade others to address these demands;
- and to develop strategies to accomplish what is demanded.

In order for the church to address the four characteristics of change for a post-Christendom and pre-Christian age, they will need to prepare themselves to overcome all four dimensions of stress.

First, there are the stresses that lie behind the demand for *systemic* change. Many congregations and church leaders cannot accept the demand to literally change the nature of the species. If they change the nature of the species of passenger pigeon, then they will no longer truly be passenger pigeons! The identity they have long celebrated; the denominational ethos they have struggled to preserve; and the traditions and idiosyncrasies they have laughed at, struggled with, but always cherished must disappear. Indeed, congregational identity in the sunset of Christendom has been defined less by "what we are" than by "why we're different from them." Passenger pigeons are different from other birds of the forest, and they would rather die than be like the sparrows of the field.

Even when congregations and church leaders acknowledge the legitimacy of the demand for systemic change, they often fail to understand its full scope. They talk about systemic change but in fact implement only programmatic change. They declare an initiative to develop small spirituality cell groups and mission teams—and then locate the initiative in a committee of the church. They celebrate a plan to multitrack worship—and then harness all the tracks to the Christian year. The power of transformational strategies is abruptly curtailed by controlling organizations and denominational demands for uniformity. They may be gathered in alternate worship or assembled onto a different branch of the roost, but they are, in the end, still passenger pigeons.

Even if the legitimacy and scope of systemic change is understood, congregations and church leaders find it difficult to convince others of the need. In part, this is because ownership for systemic change cannot be achieved by a congregational vote, but only through one-to-one faith sharing. It is as if one of Jesus' listeners were to say: "Let me get this straight, Jesus. You're saying that if I want to save my life, then I will inevitably lose it. And if I lose my life for your sake and the Gospel, then I will somehow save it? Come on, man! Talk sense!"

Attempts to convince other passenger pigeons of the need for systemic change are often met with gales of laughter and a phone call to ask the clergy to go offer pastoral counseling. On a deeper level, however, those who would convince others of the need face a more profound barrier. It is not an enjoyable task. It is rarely appreciated by the flock. And stool pigeons who have a need to be needed will find it exceptionally difficult to do. It is the nature of passenger pigeons to love each other too little and to like each other too much.

Finally, even if the legitimacy and scope of systemic change is understood, and even if congregational readiness for change is achieved, leaders will have difficulty developing strategies to achieve transformation. Christendom leaders have all been trained to bring change through programmatic strategic planning. However, the world is changing so swiftly that, even in the business sector, programmatic strategic planning no longer works. By the time the program is in place and the master plan has been developed, the opportunity is lost and the world has moved on. The key to systemic change is *opportunistic initiative*. It is the ability to seize the moment, create and liberate mission teams, and surf the chaos of change. This requires high trust and absolute clarity regarding the values, beliefs, vision, and mission of corporate life. It also requires profound spirituality and integrity for leadership. In other words, Christendom leaders who have been trained to be professionals with skills suddenly discover that transformational strategies depend on personal authenticity and vision! Stool pigeons cannot merely be retrained—they must themselves be transformed.

Second, there are the stresses that lie behind the demand for *ownership by the congregation*. Many congregations simply refuse to take responsibility for their own growth. They insist that the denomination must provide them with guaranteed resources, continuous financial subsidies, and certifiably correct strategic plans. Even though they may dislike denominational bureaucracy, they are nevertheless dependent upon denominational permission giving. They assume that congregational mission can be identified by a denominational committee, that congregational vision can be handed down from denominational officers, and that workable congregational strategies can best be developed by the "experts at the head office." If things go awry in the congregation, they appeal to the hierarchy to discipline or remove leadership. They manipulate the electoral process to take control of denominational committees. They restructure the national denominational assembly. Passenger pigeons always want to check with the home nesting grounds in Michigan before relocating to another tree.

Even if congregations accept the legitimacy of the demand for the ownership of change, they often fail to understand its full scope. It means that congregations take responsibility for self-sufficiency in all things. They may borrow resources from many places, but they must customize them for their own core values, beliefs, vision, and mission. They may borrow money for capital development from many sources, but they must manage debts well and cannot expect a kindhearted denominational "parent" to forgive those loans in the course of time. They must take responsibility to wisely choose their own leadership, train their own leadership, and hold accountable their own leadership. Church growth is solely the responsibility of the congregation. Yet, when anyone points out that the flock is declining, passenger pigeons are inclined to shrug their feathers and declare that it is the inevitable fate of the species.

Even if congregations accept the legitimacy and scope of the demand for ownership of change, they may have a hard time convincing their denominational middle judicatories. Most middle judicatories continue to believe they have a duty to oversee the life and mission of the congregation. At best, they build communication networks and encourage congregational ownership in all things. At worst, they build processes of inquisition and censorship. They enforce institutional rules, curtail creativity, correct any perceived doctrinal or ideological "errors," and burden congregational leadership with gathering statistics and additional bureaucracy. Transforming congregations almost inevitably become the misfits of the middle judicatory. Passenger pigeons are supposed to behave like passenger pigeons—or else!

Even if congregations accept the legitimacy and scope of the demand for ownership of change and convince their middle judicatories to be facilitators rather than blockers, they may have a hard time developing strategies to achieve their goals. This is because congregations have become so dependent on professional clergy that lay leaders have rested content with mediocrity. No strategy for change will work in the twenty-first century *unless it is accompanied by an expectation for excellence!* In fact, it is the excellence of the strategy, rather than the precise content of the strategy, that will have the most profound impact for transformation. Many congregations *buy* excellence rather than *build* excellence. They identify a strategy and then acquire salaried staff to implement it. Unable to afford the staff, they then abandon the strategy. Lay leadership development is the key to congregational ownership, but it is the perceived role of the average passenger pigeon to merely enjoy the fruits of gregariousness!

Third, there are the stresses that lie behind *concentrated* change. Many congregations experience stress for transformation because their goals have been diluted by other expectations. They cannot accept the legitimacy of concentrating their energies on the Gospel. Municipal or regional governments persuade them that the perpetuation of their institution is crucial to the survival of a community or a neighborhood. They are preoccupied with the maintenance of a tradition or a property. It may be that the demands and expectations that dilute their goals are in fact of genuine social or economic significance. It may also be that people have joined the church, not because of their allegiance to the Gospel, but because of their commitment to these other goals that dilute the purpose of the church. The fact remains that passenger pigeons tend to peck away at everything and anything.

Even if congregations accept the legitimacy of concentrated change, they may fail to understand its true scope and intensity. This is because the core values of passenger pigeons are almost entirely relational. They love families and youth, harmony and fellowship, good relationships and inclusiveness. They love group building processes, table groups, redundant management, and meetings. Unfortunately, this also means they have trouble setting strategic priorities. *Input* is always more important than *outcome.* It is less important to choose a particular tree in which to roost and more important to ensure that everybody will roost there.

Even if congregations accept the legitimacy and scope of concentrated change, they may find it difficult to convince others of the need. Middle judicatories and denominational assemblies are as easily swayed by emerging regional and world issues as congregations are swayed by emerging local pressures and as congregational leaders are swayed by individual crises. They move from one urgent issue to another—and take the whole flock with them. Priorities are set in one national assembly, and before the budget can be effectively shifted and the programs effectively implemented, priorities are rearranged in the next national assembly. The church takes responsibility for everything except the one thing that has been given to its charge by Christ: the Gospel. Passenger pigeons constantly flock from one field to another.

Even if congregations accept the legitimacy and scope of concentrated change and convince others of the urgency, they may experience stress in developing strategies to achieve their goal. The key problem is that they fail to make intentional connections between faith sharing and beneficial action. They believe that "actions will speak louder than words." Yet in a post-Christendom world in which do-gooders are regarded with remarkable suspicion, *they have to share the motivation that lies behind the action.* Beneficial action, without intentional spiritual growth, never achieves long-term societal solutions. Professional church leaders have been implementing beneficial programs to change human behavior for decades, and the world is still a mess. Leaders must simultaneously become authentic spiritual guides, facilitating transforming experiences with God, which change the human heart. This is hard to do if the leader, congregation, or denominational judicatory is dancing on strings pulled by unseen forces in the world.

Fourth, there are the stresses that lie behind the demand for change to be *anchored in the experience of the congregation with Jesus.* Many congregations cannot accept the legitimacy of this demand. This is true for both stereotypically liberal and conservative churches. The experience of Jesus is an incarnational mystery of immanence and transcendence, but churches of every brand name have surrounded the original formula of Chalcedon with dogmatic and ideological interpretations to which they demand uniform assent. The last thing they want to accept is the essential mystery of the experience. That encourages personal discovery, invites diversity, and links faithfulness to experiential ambiguities, rather than rational certainties. Passenger pigeons all coo the same way.

Even if congregations accept the legitimacy of this demand, they may fail to understand its true intensity and scope. The experience of relationship with Jesus is actually more like *eros* than *agape*. It is a rush of fulfillment, rather than sacrifice. It is a joyful creativity. It is an ecstasy of union. It is constant preoccupation with "the Beloved" through every minute of the day. It is the irrational passion articulated in Song of Songs and the love that is "to die for" articulated in Romans 14:8. Such an experience of the divine is an alternate thread running through the history of Christian thought and one that has been recovered by many feminist theologians today. Passenger pigeons tend to be frightened by such talk. Flying with the wind is less important than flying with the flock.

Even if congregations accept the legitimacy and scope of this demand, they may find it difficult to convince others of the need. Such strong, focused passions make people worry about religious bigotry. The specter of fanaticism, intolerance, judgment, inquisition, and violence frightens the church to moderate its enthusiasm. Christians fail to discern that the fanatics and inquisitors of history have actually been intensely rational people. The intolerance lay in their refusal to accept mystery and their insistence that propositional interpretations of mystery could convey the whole truth. True mystics, on the other hand, have usually been the most passionate and peaceful of God's creatures. Passenger pigeons claim to live in mutual respect with the other creatures of the forest, but with an attitude of condescension and pity that, after all, those other creatures are not passenger pigeons.

Even if congregations accept the legitimacy and scope of this demand and gain the support of others, they may find it hard to develop the strategies to achieve their goal. Oddly enough, when it comes to helping others experience Jesus, congregations make too much of strategic planning. It is as if they would help people fall in love by organizing a computer dating service. Yet evangelism is not a program, but a way of living. People never plan to fall in love with Jesus, nor can churches plan to enable others to experience the transforming power of God. It happens. It happens through the spontaneous action and the unrehearsed word. Church leaders must train themselves to be *opportunists,* not *strategic planners.* Passenger pigeons always have a confirmation class and a membership assimilation program.

Systemic change is easy to discuss, and difficult to do. Church transformation is exciting to contemplate, and more painful than anyone expects to accomplish. Church leaders have begun to confess openly . . . often with tears . . . that they were never trained to do this.

TOP TEN TETHERS
Holding Back the Clergy

10. We were trained for modesty,
    not honesty
9. We were trained to preach,
    not midwife.
8. We were trained to organize large groups,
    not multiply cell groups
7. We were trained to assimilate members,
    not transform persons.
6. We were trained to fight culture,
    not use it.
5. We were trained to do ministry,
    not equip others to do ministry.
4. We were trained to give judicious permission,
    not risk getting out of the way.
3. We were trained to fear the irrational,
    not celebrate its transforming power.
2. We were trained to encourage self-sacrifice,
    not self-fulfillment.
1. We were trained to obey the judicatory,
    not surrender to biblical visions.

TOP TEN TETHERS
Holding Back the Laity

10. We were encouraged to be loyal,
    not take risks.
 9. We were encouraged to read responsively,
    not pursue spiritual disciplines.
 8. We were encouraged to serve offices,
    not shepherd people.
 7. We were encouraged to go to church,
    not shape a lifestyle.
 6. We were encouraged to analyze,
    not synthesize
 5. We were encouraged to manage institutions,
    not multiply ministries.
 4. We were encouraged to build strategic plans,
    not seize emerging opportunities.
 3. We were encouraged to explain bad things,
    not overcome gratuitous evil.
 2. We were encouraged to be faithful,
    not transformed by joy.
 1. We were only encouraged,
    but never seriously trained.

The cultural hunters of the twenty-first century have learned to use this antiquated training, which has been inbred in the leadership of the church, for the ultimate destruction of the congregation. Church leaders and congregations may shake their heads with despair. Can leadership be transformed? Is it possible? Can the passenger pigeon be transformed into a whole new species of bird?

And the answer is *YES!* It can be done. It is being done. Your congregation can do it. God will help you do it. However, it cannot be done without *LEADERSHIP!* Church leaders of the twenty-first century must themselves become a new species.

— 2 —
TRANSFORMING CHURCH LEADERS

The whole purpose of church leadership in the twenty-first century is to birth new leadership. It is to grow self-starting disciples of Jesus capable of imagining possibilities and seizing opportunities, implementing creative tactics and learning from failure, and operating within clearly articulated core values and bedrock Christian beliefs. Authenticity in the twenty-first century means that the superiority of leader over follower is abandoned entirely. The experience of being healed and healing are one.

In *Growing Spiritual Redwoods,* Bill Easum and I described the "midwifing" leadership of the twenty-first-century church. Authentic leaders speak out of their own experience of life struggle and spiritual victory. They are visionaries, synthesizers, and motivators.

The Four Depth Dimensions for Spiritual Leadership in the Twenty-First Century

1. *The ability to learn and apply new skills:*
Spirit-filled conversation with culture;
motivational faith-sharing;
small-group spiritual growth;
equipping lay initiative.

2. *The ability to celebrate wholeness:*
healing and being healed;
pursuit of spiritual life and spiritual calling;
communication of essential joy.

3. *The ability to discern hope:*
recognition of hidden potential in persons;
recognition of hidden possibilities in situations;
recognition of hidden resources within oneself.

4. *The ability to trust God:*
humility within a larger mystery;
risk and reliance on a web of interrelationships;
courage to simply exist.

The ability to learn and apply new skills is more than simply the courage to take risks and learn from mistakes. It is the commitment to experience life itself as constant change and growth. It is the willingness to surrender ego and admit that one might be wrong. Passenger pigeons learn only from fellow passenger pigeons, but the church leaders of the future will learn from all the creatures of the cultural forest. The tools to motivate, nurture, and equip others will not be gained simply from seminaries or denominational retreats, but from corporate business, nonprofit organizational training, and the public sector—and from the religious experiences of other denominations, traditional faiths, and emerging spiritual movements. These learning opportunities will rarely be listed in a continuing education catalog. They will be sought out by leaders with an insatiable need to learn.

The ability to celebrate wholeness is more than a bundle of eclectic tastes and interests. It is the intuition that makes unexpected connections between popularly perceived polarities. It is the daring vulnerability that places mutual brokenness side by side and invites communion. The tools for healing, spiritual discipline, and communication are not professional, but authentic. They convince others because they are clearly working effectively in the life of the leader. Faith and lifestyle are one. Such tools are rarely gained through pursuit of advanced academic or professional degrees but are refined through simultaneous meditation and experimentation. They will be sought out by leaders with an insatiable need to bridge every boundary.

The ability to discern hope is more than optimism that good will triumph in the end. It is the perceptiveness that identifies potential and teases it out of the fabric of life. It is the ability to shift back and forth from the macro to the micro and to see the smallest detail as a fulcrum that can shift the course of history. The tools for recognizing hidden potentials are not taught in books or obtained over the Internet. They are grown through mentoring relationships with other leadership midwives providentially discovered in the midst of life. These relationships are rarely designed or certified, but they will be sought out by leaders with an insatiable need to grow.

The ability to trust God is more than the confidence that a denominational authority or judicatory will look out for your best interests. It is the irrational *faith* described by Kierkegaard—or the radical *"courage to be"* described by Tillich. It is the conviction that participation in a greater divine purpose is more valuable than stability in daily life—and that participation with the divine is all that gives stability to daily life. It is the power to endure. The tools that help one live out a multitude of roles in daily living, through unity with the "God who is above all gods," will not be provided through psychotherapies or self-help processes. They will be discovered through spiritual disciplines that are shared in partnerships with others who are distinctively different in personality, temperament, culture, language, or lifestyle. Such disciplines will be sought out by leaders with an insatiable need to explore the fullness of grace.

The following exercises can be used to help congregations and traditional clergy explore the four depth dimensions for spiritual leadership. Score each category for the degree of relevance to congregation or clergy: 1 (no significance) to 5 (very significant). Compare the results and discuss. Each obstacle and opportunity for the congregation is paralleled by the obstacle or opportunity for church leadership. Because leadership is an event involving a unity of team participants, rather than a manipulation involving an authority figure with obedient servants, congregation and clergy can act in ways that either trap or empower each other. The destructive codependencies that exist between traditional leaders and followers are allowed to continue because each side is free to complain about the other without unmasking its own parallel needs.

Church leadership cannot be transformed until the shared addictions common within Christendom have been broken. One does not first send the clergy away to be retrained and then expect transformed leaders to transform the church. The addictions of the congregation will either draw the clergy back into the old addictive patterns or fracture the pastoral relationship. Similarly, one cannot first transform a congregation through the employment of interim or temporary church leaders and then call or appoint a permanent pastor for the church. Either the addictions of the new pastor will draw the congregation back into the old addictive patterns or the pastoral relationship will end within three years. Church leadership is an event, and the transformation of leadership will be a team effort.

Leadership Obstacles

1. Ability to learn and apply new skills

Congregation
Management blocks ministry:
  Budget and funding woes
  Property maintenance demands
  Denominational controversy
    blocks congregational
    sensitivity
  Control replaces trust

Clergy
Clergy need the institution:
  Salary and pension needs
  Identity dependent with place
  Career advancement and
    entitlements block clergy
    sensitivity
  Duty replaces daring

2. Ability to build and celebrate wholeness

Congregation
Conformity masquerades as
  unity
  Fear of deep intimacy
  Judgment between minorities
  Insistence on agreement
  Reluctance to build consensus

Clergy
Self-denial masquerades as
  servanthood:
  Fear of serious vulnerability
  Servicing institutional insiders
  Dependence on popularity
  Reluctance to risk contradiction

3. Ability to discern and proclaim hope

Congregation
Nostalgia masquerades
  as tradition:
  The one-day-a-week church
  Obsessions with children
    and youth
  Presentational worship
  Fear of failure

Clergy
Personal agenda masquerades
  as ministry:
  The 7-day-a-week chaplaincy
  Resolving issues of one's
    childhood
  Props for self-esteem
  Fear of looking foolish

4. Ability to trust God absolutely

Congregation
Spiritual contentment over
  spiritual restlessness:
  Fear of creativity
  Prescriptive accountability
  Preoccupation with trivialities
  Limiting the Holy

Clergy
Celebration of success over
  birthing potentials:
  Fear of taking initiative
  Preservation of "comfort zones"
  Preoccupation with generalities
  Mediating "The Holy"

Church leadership cannot learn and apply new skills until the leadership event is freed from the domination of program management and institutional preservation, on the one hand, and preoccupation with career advancement and retirement guarantees, on the other.

Church leadership cannot truly build and celebrate wholeness until the leadership event embraces true diversity and surrenders guilt and obligation as primary motivators for ministry.

Church leadership cannot effectively discern and proclaim hope until participants in the leadership event have come to terms with their past and no longer seek either to recapture what is lost or to correct history.

Church leadership cannot trust God absolutely until the leadership event stops trying to control the Holy.

The emergence of a whole new species of church, and of a whole new species of church leadership, can only happen simultaneously.

The next exercise helps congregation and clergy assess the degree to which their shared leadership event builds healthy participation. The opportunities in each column parallel and mutually reinforce each other. Once again, congregation and clergy estimate the degree to which each opportunity is present for the other. Rank items from 1 (no significance) to 5 (very significant):

Healthy Congregation . . . Healthy Leadership		
Depth Dimension	*Congregation*	*Clergy*
Learn and apply new skills	Laughter	Honesty
	Quest for quality	Personal excellence
	Value creativity	Model risk-taking
	Multiple tastes	Readiness to grow
Build and celebrate wholeness	Affirmation and Recognition	Shared ownership
	Energy for consensus	"Both/And" synthesis
	Learn from failure	Coach through defeat
	Spontaneous caregiving	Self-care

Discern and proclaim hope	Recognition of injustice	Compassion for victims
	Generosity	Large vision
	Hospitality	Attention to detail
	Joy	Spontaneous emotion
Trust God absolutely	Witness to redemption	Personal experience of grace
	Positive attitudes	Visible spiritual disciplines
	Reverence	Humility
	Intercessory prayer	Patience

Church leadership *can* be transformed when the patterns of congregational life and individual initiative display healthy qualities. In such a climate the behavior of the congregation and the behavior of the clergy are synchronized and mutually reinforcing. No unhealthy division of labor is created as one side intervenes in the behavior of the other, and no hidden "moral superiority" or spiritual dependency is fostered in which one side condescends to assist the other. Instead, healthy congregations display the unity of a single "leadership event" in which all participants share responsibility for personal transformation, growth, ministry, and witness.

The leadership event learns and applies new skills because the clergy personify the humor, risk taking, openness, and quest for quality that the congregational participants themselves reveal in daily living.

The leadership event builds and celebrates wholeness because the salaried staff are a microcosm of the inclusive synergy that dominates both the program and spontaneous activity of the congregation, and they mirror the congregation's value for personal health.

The leadership event discerns and proclaims hope because the clergy illustrate to the public the same compassion for the least of the brothers and sisters of Jesus that the congregational participants demonstrate in their homes, neighborhoods, and workplaces.

The leadership event trusts God absolutely because the salaried staff all confess to the same need for grace and prioritize the same

*yearning for spiritual discipline that congregational participants
build into both corporate and private worship.*

The emergence of a whole new species of church, and of a whole
new species of church leadership, changes the character of leadership itself. Eventually, there are no distinctions between leaders
and followers. The clergy as an entitled, privileged, authoritarian
class of leadership simply disappear. There is only the leadership
event, which embraces everyone equally.

In *Growing Spiritual Redwoods*, my colleague and I presented the idea that the spiritual leaders of tomorrow will not be
born or created—they will be grown. They are spiritual midwives because they themselves have experienced the pain and
joy of giving birth facilitated by another. They know what it is
like to give birth, and they have experienced personally the
blessing of midwife support. Yet if the spiritual leaders of
tomorrow are neither born (with leadership abilities part of
their personality) nor created (with leadership abilities
obtained through seminaries or certification processes), many
clergy eager to transform themselves are left wondering how to
go about it.

Sue Monk Kidd has helped me see a simple typology in her
small article "Birthing Compassion" (in *Communion, Community,
Commonweal: Readings for Spiritual Leadership*, ed. John S.
Mogabgab [Nashville: Upper Room Books, 1995]). What follows
is my own interpretation of it for the transformational process of
traditional clergy.

COMMIT TO AN UNPREDICTABLE PROCESS OF CHANGE

The difficulty in leadership transformation is that it cannot
take place in a predictable pattern or period of time. One cannot
conclude the process in a sabbatical leave. The process that works
for one will not work for another. The transformational outcome
for one cannot be imitated by another. Therefore, clergy eager for
the transformation of their leadership must commit themselves to
a process that includes the following:

Prayer: An intense spiritual discipline of daily and weekly conversation with God through scripture, meditation, and silence.
Partnership: Intentional and regular communication with congregational participants and other spiritual seekers beyond the congregation, who may or may not be professional colleagues but who are also committed to a similar quest for leadership transformation.
Opportunity: Openness to irrationality, or the unexpected and unexplainable in-breaking of grace that heals, changes, and visibly reshapes your own attitudes and personal relationships.
Acceptance: An experience of serenity within oneself and shared among one's spiritual partners in which one is reconciled to the worst, aware of the best, and conscious of the ongoing ambiguities that together compose your leadership potential.

Such a process touches upon all four depth dimensions for spiritual leadership. It is best undertaken in the context of overall systemic change for the congregation. It will require patience: *You cannot force the heart!*

FACE THE COLLECTIVE THEY

Sue Monk Kidd identifies the *collective they* as the "scripts written by culture, friends, family, church, job, and tradition" that we consciously or unconsciously enact in our daily lives. The process of prayer and scripture reading will only be the beginning. The quality and diversity of your partnerships in the spiritual journey will significantly impact the honesty and speed of transformation. The in-breaking of revelation may cause you to shiver with anxiety, or tremble in fear, as it did for Biblical leaders before you.

Resist manipulations: Discover the ways in which guilt, low self-esteem, fear, and institutional or cultural obligations dictate your use of time and energy.
Unravel illusions: Identify the fantasies that you consciously or unconsciously play out in daily life or that shape the expectations of significant others with whom you are in frequent relationship.
Face Addictions: Address the habitually self-destructive behavior patterns that rob life of meaning but to which you spontaneously return in times of stress or confusion.

The partnerships you have made in the process of transformation can give your insights a reality test and provide personal support in times of stress.

RECOGNIZE THE *AUTHENTIC ME*

One's true identity as a person, as well as one's true potential as a leader, lies beyond the social roles that we play in life. It is this truth that empowered the great monastics of the past to make transitions among seemingly contradictory occupations or social roles. The monastic could be hermit, politician, revolutionary, pastor, tent maker, military leader, scholar, explorer, and friend— all in a single lifetime! It was all possible because their true identity as persons, and potential as leaders, transcended the obligations and expectations of any particular social role.

Unity with God: Build a daily consciousness that your identity is tied to your relationship with Jesus as a branch is joined to the vine. Personal fulfillment lies not in what you do or in who you are, but in the core relationship in which you participate.
Recognition of Gifts: Look behind the activities that fill you with joy and that you seemingly do with excellence, to discern the gifts that God has given you.
Discernment of Call: Surrender the call to play an institutional role, and rediscover the call to be in ministry, which was likely your original, "naive" motivation for church leadership in the first place.

The profound self-affirmation that can emerge from the recognition of authentic leadership potential can appear to some as sheer egotism. It is the openness and flexibility of spiritual leadership for *multiple* roles, linked to the absoluteness of a relationship with God, that reveals the essential humility of leadership.

AWAKEN THE *COMPASSIONATE WE*

This is the final step that moves beyond distinctions between leader and follower to create the leadership event. The partnerships begun in the spiritual process not only form deeper bonds of mutual support but are expanded to include more and more people. In a sense, it is the constant expansion of the process of leadership transformation that in itself is the leadership event. Leadership is the process of including more and more people, with an infinite diversity of gifts and skills, within a single leadership event.

Enlarged Vision: Reorient your leadership energies from prioritizing church insiders to prioritizing the lost, who have no experience of connection with God. Discover in detail the real diversity of individual needs and potentials.

Shared Emotion: Share the suffering, as well as the celebration, of the world. Reveal the spectrum of emotion within you to the public, even if it leaves you vulnerable for criticism.

Motivated Action: Anchor every activity in your unity with God, gifts, and callings. Simultaneously do good and share the faith motivation for the deed. Let the passion for justice and the joy of relationship to Jesus become a single, seamless flow of energy.

Recognition of authentic leadership potential may have unexpected and unsettling implications. Some clergy may discover that professional ministry is an unauthentic response to the manipulations of culture or the illusions of their personal needs—and resign. Others will reassess all that they are doing, begin to do things differently and do different things, and discover a joy in leadership that escapes previous burnout. However, beware! Unless the congregation is also involved in systemic change, transformed clergy may be asked to resign!

Transformation of church leadership and systemic change in congregational life and mission always happen simultaneously. The speed of the one may be faster than the other in different stages of transformation, but the leadership event that lies at the core of the twenty-first-century church cannot be achieved unless change is happening in both directions. This is what will give leaders and congregational participants the courage and patience to endure the stresses of church transformation. So long as leaders and participants can see that change is happening, progress is being made, and the vision of a transformed church continues to be celebrated even when the obstacles are immense, they will continue their journey together. However, if either the transformation of leadership or the systemic change of the congregation comes to a halt or is reduced to mere rhetoric, the pastoral relationship will likely fracture.

The tools for change provided in the following pages integrate systemic change for the congregation and transformation of congregational leadership.

All Systems Go! provides a congregational mission assessment process that explores all eleven subsystems of congregational life. Your answers to the questions raised will help you identify strengths, weaknesses, and hidden corporate addictions. Congregational leaders can then customize a long-range plan for their unique context.

Freeing the Faithful! provides a practical discernment tool to identify the core values, bedrock beliefs, motivating vision, and key mission, which together form the boundaries beyond which no individual or group can go—but within which they are free to do anything instantly. This umbrella becomes the foundation of future permission-giving organizations; small group and mission team development; and leadership accountability.

Drawing a New Ministry Map! provides an alternative to traditional strategic planning processes that recognizes the ever-changing dynamism of the mission field and the need to link mission development to spiritual growth and calling rather than program and property. Congregational leaders can plan ahead with confidence that motivation can be maintained and new opportunities can be seized with integrity.

These processes address the four characteristics of change demanded in the twenty-first century. Change must be *systemic, owned by the congregation, concentrated, and anchored in the experience of the congregation with Jesus.* Time, patience, and creativity are all required.

Remember, the window of opportunity is brief, and the need for transformation is urgent. Before your "pigeons come home to roost," equip yourself to fly! Let go, and take off!

> Look at the birds of the air; they neither sow nor reap nor gather into barns, and yet your heavenly Father feeds them. Are you not of more value than they? (Matthew 6:26)

— PART II —

ALL SYSTEMS GO!
CONGREGATIONAL MISSION ASSESSMENT

— 3 —
INTRODUCTION TO
SYSTEMS ANALYSIS

Church leadership in the pre-Christian (post-Christendom) world must ask the right questions if they are ever going to solve the puzzle of congregational growth in the twenty-first century. The Congregational Mission Assessment is designed to assist congregational and regional mission planners in evaluating their progress toward becoming a thriving church. It helps uncover strengths and weaknesses in the system of congregational mission and identifies future directions to build a thriving church with a balanced mission program. It asks the right questions in all eleven subsystems of the thriving church.

Each question is itself a window into a wider range of spiritual and practical issues of church transformation. Some of the questions here may not be relevant to your local church context, but it is not uncommon for the seemingly least applicable questions to reveal the most significant challenges for church transformation. Questions leaders believe to be unanswerable are really questions leaders do not want to face! The Congregational Mission Assessment is intended to go beyond the identification of strengths and weaknesses to the identification of hidden corporate addictions. The addictions are habitually self-defeating behavior patterns that run like threads among all eleven subsystems of church life. Congregations habitually return to these patterns in times of confusion or stress. These addictions sabotage the very best strategic plans and render the congregation impotent for change.

For churches that are just beginning to consider church transformation, it may be helpful to first use the Church Addiction Test, which is included at the end of this chapter. This will help you anticipate areas of change that may be most stressful for your congregation. Following the Congregational Mission Assessment,

I will provide examples of threads of corporate addictions from actual experience.

It is important that the congregation fully support the process of the Congregational Mission Assessment. In most cases, the official board of the congregation will organize the use of this tool. In some cases, the congregation itself may appoint a distinct planning group. Planning group members should familiarize themselves with the resource. A variety of different research teams and focus groups will be needed at each stage of the process, and these are described in this resource as each stage is introduced. The systemic models for declining and thriving churches should be studied by those planners who use this tool. Complete descriptions of these models are found in my book *Kicking Habits: Welcome Relief for Addicted Churches.*

The Congregational Mission Assessment leads planners through "The Thriving Church System" in three major stages. All together, there are eleven different subsystems of the thriving church that need to be examined.

FOUNDATION
Congregational Identity
Congregational Mission
Congregational Organization
FUNCTION
Experiencing God
Growing in God
Listening to God
Serving God
Sharing God
FORM
Property
Funding
Communication

In our book *Growing Spiritual Redwoods*, Bill Easum and I discussed ministry in the twenty-first century, pre-Christian era using the metaphor of a topographic map and explorers discovering the unknown. Imagine that the explorers have done their work. A rudimentary map of the new territory has been made. Now you are about to build a railroad into the new land.

The first three subsystems are *foundational*. This stage leads planners to assess *the basic umbrella of congregational life* (core values, bedrock beliefs, motivating vision, and key mission) that pervades all congregational life. The roots and aims of congregational behavior, as well as the organization that seeks to make that behavior intentional, are then examined. All together, the church is guided to examine its deepest assumptions and expectations. Leaders bring to consciousness their most profound hopes and perceive the contradictions between their dreams and their daily behavior.

This process is like picturing the track plan and laying the roadbed of a future railroad into the unknown. The right-of-way is surveyed, stones and gravel are poured, wooden ties are laid, and the appropriate gauge iron rail is spiked to the ties. If this foundation is well laid, future trains will reach the appropriate destinations on time, without accident, and loaded with all that is helpful to feed the spiritually hungry people of the new world.

The next five subsystems are *functional*. This second stage leads planners through the pentagon-shaped model of the thriving church. It examines the flow of church life in the process of being changed, gifted, called, equipped, and sent. It places the focus of attention on living out the fullness of Christ, rather than living out the fullness of an institution. All together, the church is guided to examine the content of its message and the methods by which the Gospel is shared with others to transform individuals and society.

This process is like taking an inventory of the freight that this future railroad will be required to haul. Solids, liquids, and gas—in varying sizes, configurations, and quantities—must all be appropriate to the indigenous needs of the people in the new world. The nature of the freight and the methods of delivery will determine the concrete and visible forms that will be created to deliver the Gospel effectively and tranformationally to the public.

Therefore, the last three subsystems are *formal*. This third stage leads planners to assess the vehicles through which congregational mission is implemented. Location, buildings, and space can now be assessed for their viability. Strengths and weaknesses in funding attitudes and strategies can be determined. Advertising, marketing, public relations, grievance procedures, and general communications can be evaluated for effectiveness. All together, the church is guided to examine the structures, customs, and processes that may have stood for centuries but that today may need to be radically renovated, relocated, upgraded, or simply replaced.

Most churches from dying Christendom do strategic planning backwards. They start by debating issues of property and finance. Unable to gain consensus for change, they scramble to improve communications. Only after everyone is really involved in the conversation about the future do they study the various programs of congregational life and mission. They usually limit themselves to the study of what exists and miss altogether key subsystems necessary for a thriving future. Once mere programmatic change fails, and subsequent financial crisis grows, they are finally forced to examine the foundations of congregational life. They painfully arrive at the place where they should have begun—only now they are so exhausted, pressured, and bruised that they can hardly bear the challenge. It is this bitter experience of backwards planning that makes veteran church leaders cringe at the mere thought of strategic planning.

It is as if a pioneering corporation precipitately purchased millions of dollars worth of railroad equipment. The equipment included a variety of locomotives, freight, and passenger cars—all purchased from a variety of geographic and cultural contexts and all purchased at bargain prices. The reasons for purchasing such equipment may have been that most of the shareholders had a sentimental attachment to steam locomotives or that they liked European-style coaches or that they were all light eaters and believed no passengers would ever require dining cars. Whatever the motivation, the railroad now has a fine assortment of structures, vehicles, and processes.

Only now does the "Christendom, Topeka, and Santa Fe" Railroad consider what kind of freight it will carry. They discover that the size, configuration, quantity, and character of the freight does not fit well into the cars they have purchased, and the freight is too heavy to be hauled by the locomotive power they have leased. They decide, therefore, to modify, squeeze, and force the freight into the existing cars that they have. Passengers who prefer to dine have no choice but to stand in line at the snack bar. The freight they will carry is only that which fits into their particular train, and it may or may not be valuable to feed the spiritually hungry people waiting at the end of the line. A large pile of desperately needed material is left at the station because it is too expensive or too unwieldy, and it just does not fit into the train. It will wait there until some other entrepreneurial church figures out a way to move it.

Finally, this railroad belatedly considers the foundations along which the now loaded train will run. They never really considered where the tracks needed to go or how the tracks needed to be laid. The antiquated nature of the railroad cars and the oddly selective freight loaded on the train both limit the track plan to fairly level terrain. This train does not go over mountains! It takes the long way around. The gravel on the roadbed is not deep enough, the ties are not weatherproofed sufficiently to sustain rough use, and the gauge in the iron rails is too narrow and too light. When accidents happen and the train derails, the shareholders blame the locomotive engineer, reduce the freight on the cars even more, or buy a better steam engine.

The end result of such backwards planning is that many Christendom churches deliver inappropriate and irrelevant freight to the spiritually hungry public at the end of the line. Plans are designed to suit the needs of the institution, rather than the needs of the public. Freight is delivered too slow and frequently never arrives at all. Such institutions are considered quaint and traditional, and the "steam era" pipe organs, wooden pews, and other antiquated technologies give the illusion of eternal solidity. Nevertheless, ridership drops, alternative ways to deliver needed spiritual support are developed, and the denomination eventually abandons the line.

The point is that it does not have to be this way! The Congregational Mission Assessment guides church leaders toward systemic transformation that eventually can help you overcome mountains, increase ridership, and deliver spiritual fruits that are celebrated with enthusiasm by the twenty-first-century public. You can do it—if you have the desire and the courage for systemic change.

The planners who use this tool should read through all stages and decide how questions can be answered with the greatest accuracy. The questions in each section are divided into three groups:

Data Recovery: statistics and other quantifiable or concrete information that can be gathered from congregational records.

Ministry Review: insight into trends, perceptions, goals, and processes related to programs or ministries of the congregation. *Leadership Audit:* review of leadership responsibilities, competencies, cooperation, style, and credibility.

Some questions may be assigned to particular individuals, committees, or focus groups. Other questions may require some form of survey within the congregation. Users must keep in mind that the perceptions of church leaders may not reflect the reality of congregational mission and life. Therefore, seek to include people from the margins of congregational life, as well as core participants. The exact strategy of research will vary from congregation to congregation. The goal, however, is to build as truthful a profile of congregational life and mission as possible. As you seek volunteers for the process, care should be taken to select individuals for their relevant talents or experience and not simply for the committee they happen to serve.

• Try not to burden a few veteran leaders with all the research. The more people involved in the process, the more accurate the assessment becomes.

• Intentionally include both veteran church insiders, and marginal members and fringe participants. The latter groups can both reality check and fine tune the perceptions of core participants.

• Deploy volunteers in teams of two or more. Even in small churches, two people can offer valuable mutual support to one another. Larger churches should add volunteers to the teams to reflect their congregational diversity.

• Emphasize *short-term* commitments. Individuals may serve on more than one team in the process, but when the goals of a section are finished, that team has come to an end.

• Make research commitments pointed, intentional, and time-limited. When you have achieved your goals or completed the timeline, STOP! Research can go on forever, but avoid exhausting yourselves. After all, you need future energy to do the strategies for change that emerge!

The planning group should anticipate the work for each section and develop a timeline that fits with the activities of the church.

Timelines will vary from section to section. Some teams can be gathering data for a future section while other teams are completing earlier sections. If the planning group anticipated approximately *one week* of intensive work for each of the eleven sections, for example, the entire Congregational Mission Assessment could be completed in eleven to twelve weeks. On the other hand, some congregations may find that it is more helpful, both to care for volunteer energies and give opportunity to assimilate information, if the process is implemented in stages through an entire year.

The planning group can assume the following general process for each section of the Congregational Mission Assessment:

● Introduce volunteer teams in Sunday worship with prayer. Recognize the time-limited service of individuals in the team.

● Divide responsibilities among teams and volunteers. Each individual may work with a specific task or with specific people.

● Gather the data, or dialogue with people. Team members intentionally gather information.

● Collate responses as a team. The teams compile their report. Usually it is most helpful if data or insights can be keyed on computer disk with a common software.

● Present the report to the planning group. Team reports are added to the cumulative assessment. The accumulating assessment can be printed as hardcopy and placed in binders for ease in assimilation.

● Thank teams during worship. Celebrate the short-term service of team participants.

The information gathered by the research teams should be organized as answers to the questions provided. Each team will collate its research and provide the planning group with the completed report for its limited piece of work. A final report that answers all questions will gradually be compiled.

The interpretation of the complete Congregational Mission Assessment will require serious study. This study should not be limited to the planning group, to a single "strategic planning committee," or even to the official board. Study should be as broad and inclusive as possible. Remember that the thriving church system and the old bureaucracies of Christendom do not correspond directly to each other. A section of the Congregational Mission

Assessment cannot simply be given to a standing committee for evaluation. The entire official board, all staff, and all groups and committees will need to devote significant agenda time to digest all the information gathered. Focus groups that include marginal members and fringe participants, and that intentionally reflect the full demographic diversity of the community surrounding the church, will be vitally important. The congregation may also seek the insight of its denominational judicatory or of neighboring congregations. Finally, the congregation will find it valuable to share the finished Congregational Mission Assessment with an independent church consultant.

Most volunteers will have been gaining insight into the congregation as the process unfolds. There will be moments of excited discovery—and also moments of deep consternation. Be sure to be patient, and allow opportunities for informal dialogue to share feelings and questions. Do not leap to initiate any strategic plans until the full Congregational Mission Assessment is completed. Discovery of areas of strength or weakness in the system of the thriving church is only one goal. The more challenging task is to discern the hidden addictions of congregational life. These addictions are the self-defeating behavior patterns to which the congregation habitually returns in times of confusion or stress. These addictions sabotage the best-laid strategic plans. These addictions run like a thread through the whole system of congregational life and mission—affecting the foundations, functions, and forms of the church all at once. These addictions will be the most painful, and the most crucial, learnings from the Congregational Mission Assessment. The following Church Addiction Test may help prepare the congregation to look for certain key themes as the Congregational Mission Assessment unfolds.

THE CHURCH ADDICTION TEST

Get a grip on your hidden institutional addictions! Score your anxiety in response to each of the "Top 20 Shocking Truths Thriving Churches Have Learned." Then turn the page to learn the positive discoveries thriving churches have made, and identify those areas where you will find the greatest difficulties or best opportunities for church transformation.

Top 20 Shocking Truths Thriving Churches Have Learned

No Anxiety   High Anxiety
1   2   3   4   5   6   7   8   9   10

1. The youth are *not* the future of your church!
2. Nobody really cares about the mere presence of God!
3. "Merely friendly churches" are the dinosaurs of the twenty-first century!
4. Accepting whatever volunteers offer is *not* good enough!
5. Most people do not listen to organ music during the week!
6. Debt freedom *always* leads to church decline!
7. Bureaucratic, organizational consensus *kills* churches!
8. It does *not matter* what people *know* following the service!
9. It is *not* the pastor's job to visit the hospitals!
10. Elders have *no business* managing the church!
11. Church membership is *unimportant!*
12. If you want action, *never* form a committee!
13. Self-sacrifice is the *wrong* message!
14. God and the Holy Spirit are *not enough* for the donut shop public!
15. Church insiders are the *least able* to predict the church future!
16. Sunday school is *no longer* the cornerstone of Christian education!
17. Finance committees *should not* talk about money!
18. *Nobody has time* to hold church offices!
19. Strategic planning is *over-rated!*
20. When it comes to mission, if you can say it all with words, *you have missed the point!*

Top 20 Positive Discoveries Thriving Churches Have Made

Compare these top 20 positive discoveries with the previous shocking truths that revealed your institutional church addictions. Then discern your areas of greatest difficulty or opportunity for church transformation.

1. *Transformed adults (ages 18-40) are the future of your church.* Adults who are changed, gifted, called, and equipped will take care of the kids—and everything else!

2. *Everybody wants to be touched by the healing power of God.* The public is desperate to be changed, different, and liberated from their hurts and addictions.

3. *Churches that provide multiple opportunities for intimacy are the new species.* People want to go beyond the coffee urn to bare their souls with a deeply trusted few.

4. *God expects every Christian to be on a constant crusade for excellence.* Training one's God-given gifts to a high standard of performance is both fulfilling and effective.

5. *Most people like contemporary music with strong melody and lots of rhythm.* Percussion, guitar, creative instrumentations, and small group ensembles get people's attention.

6. *Sound debt management is the key to thriving church development.* People will maximize their small investments and service the debt of motivating missions.

7. *Streamlined, high-trust organizations grow churches.* Church management is best done by a trusted, gifted, and equipped few.

8. *What matters most of all is how people feel following the worship service.* People want to "feel better" for worship and be motivated to do, learn, and serve through the week.

9. *It is the pastoral leader's job to train gifted laity in pastoral care.* Clergy are trainers, motivators, and visionaries who equip others to do ministries.

10. *It is the elders' business to actually do ministry.* Every layperson is called to discover and exercise the spiritual gifts God has given them.

11. *Participation in any aspect of congregational life and mission is everything.* Doing hands-on mission, and involvement in ministry, is more meaningful that mere belonging.

12. *If you want action, find a gifted and called individual and turn that person loose.* Trained laity who are free to take initiative will find whatever help they need.

13. *Self-affirmation is the right message.* People seeking self-worth give generously to express and celebrate their inner value.

14. *Christ is that revelation of the Trinity which directly addresses transformation.* The church best engages the public when it talks about their experience of Jesus Christ.

15. *People on the fringe of church life are key to discerning the future.* Biblical visions are most often perceived among those who have been marginalized.

16. *Small groups are the cornerstone of Christian education.* Groups in any configuration, meeting during the week in homes, promote Christian growth.

17. *Finance and administration leaders talk mostly about mission.* Church boards only exist to empower people to walk in mission with the risen Lord.

18. *People make time to deepen self-awareness and exercise spiritual gifts.* In the rat race of daily life, people will take the time to do things that are really meaningful.

19. *The anticipation of the unpredictable is the art of thriving church life.* Spontaneity, flexibility, and planned stress management are part of authentic visions.

20. *Motivating visions are always a "Song in the Heart."* They are best shared without words, to get the blood of church participants and total strangers pounding.

Adding Up Your Addictions and Counting Your Opportunities

Add your scores in each of the following areas. Higher numbers indicate areas where you will find it difficult to understand or implement change. Lower numbers indicate possible "entry points" to initiate church transformation. *Remember, the statements overlap, because from one direction or another, sooner or later, transformation touches the whole system of church life.*

Organization and Structure
   Statements 7, 12, 15, 18 total:
Worship and Spirituality
   Statements 2, 5, 8, 13 total:
Vision and Systemic Clarity
   Statements 1, 11, 14, 20 total:
Leadership Expectations
   Statements 4, 9, 10, 19 total:
Education and Nurture
   Statements 1, 3, 11, 16 total:
Stewardship
   Statements 6, 13, 17, 18 total:

— 4 —
FOUNDATION

CONGREGATIONAL IDENTITY

Congregational identity is like an umbrella under which all aspects of local church life and ministries are embraced. It is not a heritage. It is the living identity, both intentionally and unintentionally revealed, which newcomers will perceive and evaluate.

Your goal is to discern:

- what that "basic umbrella of congregational life" *really is*.
- how that identity is *celebrated, articulated, and tested*.
- to what degree your congregational leaders *demonstrate* that identity.

The *Data Recovery* questions may be answered by 2 or 3 volunteers. The *Ministry Review* questions may be best answered with several focus groups. A good rule of thumb is one focus group for every 50-100 church participants (members, adherents, worship attenders, and those involved only in subgroups of the larger church). In this stage, you should involve as many people as possible in the conversation. Make sure that teams include not only core members but those whose participation in church life ranges from high to low. The *Leadership Audit* questions may best be answered independently by staff and lay leaders, and by a human resources or personnel committee. However, focus groups and intentional interviews with core and marginal members of the church will frequently be necessary.

Remember to look behind what people say to what they really reveal in their living. In the eyes of the spiritually yearning public, *it is the unintentional word that reveals the truth!*

Congregational Identity Questions

Data Recovery

1. What are the basic statistics of your congregation:
Membership?
Average worship attendance?
Median age of members?
Median age of worship participants?
Primary cultural or ethnic orientation?
Average membership net loss or gain each year, for the past ten years?
Average worship participation net loss or gain each year, for the past ten years?

2. What percentage of your annual congregational meeting agenda specifically and intentionally defines, refines, and celebrates "the basic umbrella of congregational life" (core values, bedrock beliefs, motivating vision, and key mission)?

3. How often do weekly worship services specifically and intentionally define, refine, and celebrate "the basic umbrella of congregational life"? List specific tactics used to communicate and surround in prayer the values, beliefs, vision, and mission of the congregation.

Ministry Review

4. What is it about your corporate experience of Jesus Christ that your community (or communities) cannot live without? (This is not a creed. This is a description of your own congregational experience of God, which has been so transforming and decisive in changing the course of your living that unless you tell others about it their own lives will be impoverished.)

5. What are the basic, essential values that the congregation affirms, upholds, and seeks to demonstrate in both intentional and spontaneous ways—within and beyond the church?

6. What church-related experiences (important or trivial) have clearly shocked individual participants in the church in the last five years?

7. What are the bedrock, essential beliefs that the congregation affirms, proclaims, and spontaneously returns to during times of

confusion or stress? Clearly and briefly state congregational consensus regarding belief in:

God	Sacrament	Sin
Christian Life	Christ	Church
Grace	Christian Ministry	Spirit
Scripture	Destiny	Social Change

8. Identify several key "faith stories" that are cherished by congregational participants and that illustrate profound ways in which participants have found strength to overcome confusion, crisis, or stress.

9. What is the motivating vision that constantly, profoundly stirs the emotions of the congregation? (This is not a program summary, but a song, symbol, image, or story that uniformly excites the people when it is recognized. The vision is the corporate, heartfelt, emotional, motivating reason that the congregation will do anything to continue to exist.)

10. How is "the basic umbrella of congregational life" regularly articulated and celebrated by the congregation?

11. How is "the basic umbrella of congregational life" regularly communicated to the public?

12. How is "the basic umbrella of congregational life" regularly tested for credibility by the congregation among the publics of the surrounding community?

Leadership Audit

13. Does your pastor affirm, model, and regularly articulate "the basic umbrella of congregational life" in professional and private life?

14. Do your lay leaders affirm, model, and regularly articulate "the basic umbrella of congregational life" in their working and private lives?

15. In what way is "the basic umbrella of congregational life" communicated in all membership training or leadership training initiatives?

16. How is "the basic umbrella of congregational life" used in the accountability processes of the church?

CONGREGATIONAL MISSION

Congregational mission relates to everything the congregation does for people other than themselves. There is a direct correspondence between the degree to which the congregation is engaged with people beyond themselves and the growth and health of the congregation.

Your goal is to discern:

● what is absolutely unique and vital in *your own mission as it arises from your* experience of Jesus Christ.

● the nature and degree of congregational involvement *with people beyond the church.*

● the nature and degree of *leadership engagement* with the unchurched.

The *Data Recovery* questions will require two or more teams familiar with demographic research and the full diversity of the congregation. The *Ministry Review* questions may best be answered in focus groups—or through a congregational survey. If a survey is used, be sure to extend it beyond the regular worshiping congregation to reach marginal members. The *Leadership Audit* questions are best answered independently by staff and lay leaders, plus perceptions from focus groups.

Remember to look beyond mere fund raising that pays others to do mission to discover the missions in which church people actually participate. In the eyes of the spiritually yearning public, *how people spend their free time is more revealing than how people spend their money!*

Congregational Mission Questions
(Questions Numbered from Previous Section)

Data Recovery

17. What is the logo, symbol, or image used by the congregation to graphically communicate its mission to the community? (You may wish to refer to external, visual symbols; letterhead; worship bulletins; and so forth.)

18. Does the demographic pattern of the community or neighborhood match the demographic pattern of your congregation? (You will need to obtain from national census or municipal surveys facts relating to age, culture, race, economic status, marital status, family status, language, home ownership, and so forth. You will also need to survey your own congregation and compare statistics.)

19. Do the demographic trends and projections for the community or neighborhood match the trends in growth or decline in your congregation?

20. What missions are sponsored by the congregation aside from the generic mission fund of the denomination, and how are they promoted and funded?

Local missions?

Regional missions?

National missions?

Global missions?

21. What percentage of the laity in the congregation volunteer for hands-on ministries, charitable activities, or social services?

22. Has the percentage of the total congregational budget that is devoted to mission increased, decreased, or stayed the same over the past ten years?

23. List partners in mission that cooperate in any way with the congregation:

Ecumenical:

Public Sector:

Parachurch:

Corporate Sector:

Ministry Review

24. If the church ceased to exist tomorrow, how many community services, ministries, or outreach initiatives would also cease to exist?

25. Does the congregation have a formal mission statement? What is it? How is it recognized by the congregation? How is it shared with the spiritually yearning, institutionally alienated public?

26. What is the single most important thought you wish to evoke in the minds of others by the mere mention of your church name?

Leadership Audit

27. What percentage of your pastor's energy is devoted to people inside the congregation, and what percentage is devoted to people outside the congregation and in the community? How does this compare with your pastor's own self-perception?

28. What percentage of your pastor's time is spent in personal counseling or advocacy, and what percentage is spent intentionally training laity to do their mission? How does this compare with your pastor's own self-perception?

29. What percentage of the laity in the congregation volunteer for hands-on ministries, charitable activities, or social services *for which they consider weekly worship through the year to be absolutely essential?*

30. What training do volunteers receive in faith-sharing and service expertise in the area of mission interest?

31. Does your congregational leadership have an intentional, implemented plan to listen to and pray for the spiritual yearnings of the unchurched public?

CONGREGATIONAL ORGANIZATION

Congregational organization is the structure through which the identity is articulated and the mission is released. There is no single blueprint for an effective organization, but there is direct correlation between the degree of readiness to take risks on creative ideas and the growth and health of the church.

Your goal is to discern:

• the ability of the structure to distinguish *between "control" and "stability."*

• the readiness of the congregation to build *respect and trust for leadership.*

• the commitment of leadership to a *feasible, positive, long-range plan.*

The *Data Recovery* questions will best be answered by a team of volunteers familiar with the nominations processes of the congregation and the leadership experiences of the congregation for at least ten years. The *Ministry Review* questions may best be answered by a combination of focus groups plus intentional interviews with marginal members by teams of two volunteers with wide credibility in the congregation. The *Leadership Audit* questions may best be answered independently by staff and focus groups, as well as by the human resources or personnel committee of the church. *Note that inability to answer questions can be as revealing of the hidden addictions of the church as the answers themselves.*

Remember that giving permission takes greater energy and demonstrates greater love than withholding permission. In the eyes of the spiritually yearning public, *multiplying opportunities for mission is more important than preserving a heritage!*

Congregational Organization Questions
(Questions Numbered from Previous Section)

Data Recovery

32. Provide a diagram for the organization of the congregation.
33. How many volunteer vacancies must be filled each year for the organization to function according to the local church constitution or tradition?
34. How many volunteer hours are spent each month attending administrative meetings?
35. What percentage of the membership is required to serve offices or work in committees (assuming one person to one office or committee)?
36. How is the nominations committee selected, and how many years has the average nominations committee member been a member of the congregation?
37. How long have current staff been with the congregation?

Ministry Review

38. How long does it take to approve and implement a creative idea that does not fit in the mandate of any standing committee?
39. Whose permission is required to implement a creative idea?

40. Is your congregation willing to lose a long-standing member in order to implement a creative idea?

41. What has been the biggest controversy that divided people within the congregation over the past five years? Has this controversy been resolved? How?

42. Do most ministries, activities, or missions arise from small groups, motivated individuals, or program committees?

43. Does your organization have a strong sense of humor? Can your organization accept and learn from failure?

44. Does your congregation have a long-range plan? What is it? How is its achievement measured? How long would it take the congregation to change that plan?

45. Without reference to the formal diagram of organization, how would you draw an organizational diagram that reflects your own experience with the church? This exercise may be done by individuals or as a project of a focus group.

Leadership Audit

46. Is your pastor a leader? (Rate the following perceptions *yes, somewhat,* or *no.*) Does your pastor . . .
. . . cause things to happen?
. . . really get people moving?
. . . see deep and see far?
. . . take risks and experiment with new ideas?
. . . build bridges between opposite views or diverse ideas?

47. How long do pastors usually stay with your congregation? Why do they stay, and why do they move? (You may wish to confidentially survey previous and present pastors.)

48. Are staffing changes dictated by finances or by changing ministry needs?

49. Do your paid staff feel appreciated? Do they consider themselves doing *tasks* or doing *ministries*? Does the staff grow or do workloads grow in response to growing ministries? How does the congregation express appreciation to staff?

50. Are staff salaries adequate? Are they competitive with equivalent positions in the community? Are pastor's salaries set by a denominational guideline, even when the congregation is not receiving a denominational financial subsidy?

51. Can all salaried staff contribute to the agenda of the official board?

52. What percentage of your budget is devoted to continuing education for ordained ministers and lay leaders? What percentage of your budget is devoted to training for lay ministries?

53. Are all members of the official board gifted, called, and equipped in administration? How does the congregation know this and plan for this?

54. Is your human resources or personnel committee regularly trained? Do they regularly and intentionally monitor performance of all staff? Do they equip and reward excellence?

55. Do you have a clearly defined grievance procedure? Does it include lay leadership as well as salaried staff? If so, what is it?

— 5 —

FUNCTION

EXPERIENCING GOD

T he thriving church seeks to help people experience the continuing, transforming power of God that touches their hearts and changes their lives. They remove all barriers that inhibit rapid immersion into spirituality. Correct information, institutional awareness, and membership recruitment are all secondary to the healing touch of God. Your goal is to discern:

- how newcomers are welcomed, not into the church, *but into an experience* of the Holy.
- how worshipers are involved, not in an education of the mind, *but into an* affair of the heart.
- how participants are immediately nurtured, not toward institutional support, *but toward mentoring relationships.*

Data Recovery questions can best be answered by volunteers who have both long-standing and recent experience in worship. However, be sure to include youth and relative newcomers, and do not limit teams to members of staff or worship committees. *Ministry Review* questions may be answered by focus groups, but expect to record a collage of perspectives. Look for themes and trends. *Leadership Audit* questions may be answered with a combined focus group that includes staff. You may wish to develop a questionnaire for use on three or four consecutive Sundays.

Remember, the spiritual yearning of the public is for authentic experiences of God, not membership in a philanthropic society marked by rituals. In the eyes of the spiritually yearning public, *freedom from addictions is more desirable than union with traditions.*

Experiencing God Questions
(Questions Numbered from Previous Section)

Data Recovery

56. What percentage of newcomers each year are personally invited and accompanied by church members?

57. Are newcomers greeted immediately, in every worship service, year round . . . by knowledgeable and enthusiastic people . . . who represent all ages . . . and all cultures in the congregation?

58. What do newcomers see when they first enter the church building? (List everything visible, on walls or tables, in the vestibule or narthex.)

59. Are all your regular worship services on Sunday morning? When, and how regularly, are multiple worship services celebrated?

60. How many adult baptisms have you celebrated each year, for the last five years?

61. How many children and youth are members of the church or have parents who are members of the church? What is the average attendance of children and youth in worship?

62. How many special religious terms not commonly used in everyday speech appear in an average worship bulletin in November?

63. What percentage of the year is the primary musical accompaniment to worship *not* the organ or piano? What instruments are used?

64. What are the three most popular radio stations in your community? What are the three most popular radio stations among church members?

65. What percentage of the year does worship include drama, dance, or film? How often and in how many different ways do you celebrate the sacraments?

66. How many hours following the worship service does it take for a layperson from the congregation to visit a newcomer?

67. What print or video information is immediately provided newcomers, other than information relating to membership, heritage, finances, or organization of the institutional church.

68. Do newcomers have genuine options:

... to be anonymous or to be conspicuous?

... to come and go, sit or stand, at any time, without embarrassment?

... to keep their children with them or entrust them to quality childcare?

69. Do people commonly worship with visible emotion (tears, smiles, laughter, and so forth)?

70. Do you assume that newcomers come to church because they want to belong or because they want to change?

71. Do you assume people who attend worship know the basics of the Bible? (For example, is everyone familiar with the Lord's Prayer, the Beatitudes, the Ten Commandments, and so forth?)

72. Do participants in worship primarily understand the offering to be financial support for the church, covenant with Christ, sign of spiritual discipline—or what else?

73. How would you describe the ministry purpose of each of the worship services in your church? For example, do you have services for healing, celebration, coaching through the ambiguities of life, cherishing eternal truths, or other purposes?

74. How are scriptures and topical themes chosen for worship? Who chooses them?

75. What are the marks of a successful worship service of the church? What evaluative comments are most often made during coffee hour?

Attendance	Size of choir	Numbers of lay readers or leaders
Size of offering	Volume of singing	Positive sermon comments
Number of youth	Quality of anthems	Laughter or good feelings
Theme of service	Special guests	Conversions
Room decorations	Sound quality	Spiritual outbursts

76. In what ways are children and youth encouraged to participate regularly in worship?

77. How many people regularly linger after the worship service is over, and what do they talk about?

Leadership Audit

78. Are your ushers trained to counsel or personally support people during worship?

79. How many specially trained lay counselors stand ready for spontaneous ministry before, during, and immediately after worship services?

80. What are the marks of a successful worship service for the pastor and lay leaders of the church? What evaluative comments are most often expressed to leaders during coffee hour?

Attendance	Size of choir	Numbers of lay readers or leaders
Size of offering	Volume of singing	Positive sermon comments
Number of youth	Quality of anthems	Laughter or good feelings
Theme of service	Special guests	Conversions
Room decorations	Sound quality	Spiritual outbursts

81. Does worship receive consistent and quality planning and preparation 52 weeks of the year? Or does worship planning receive less energy at certain times of the year?

82. What degree of discomfort is there with surprises, interruptions, or unexpected changes in worship for participants and leaders? (Select low, medium, or high. You may wish to test perceptions with staff and focus groups.)

83. How many members of the worship committee became members of the church within the last 3 years?

84. How many specially trained and equipped worship leaders direct each service?

85. How many musical groups within the congregation participate in worship through the year? What musical styles do they have?

86. Does the primary musical planner or leader have expertise beyond the organ? Is he or she encouraged by the congregation to explore multiple styles of music and instrumental accompaniment?

87. How many congregational participants have opportunities to share faith or preach through the year?

88. Do the staff (including pastor, church secretary, custodian,

and music leader) intentionally affirm and celebrate the transformations experienced by participants in the worship service(s)?

89. How many trained lay visiting-teams are deployed immediately following the worship service to contact newcomers? How many visiting-team members are new to the church in the last 3 years? How many have been members for more than 7 years?

GROWING IN GOD

The thriving church perceives membership as a covenant to go deeper in faith, to discern the true origins and purposes behind the changes they are experiencing in life. Church membership moves people into processes of intimacy, mutual support, and personal growth. Acquisition of basic religious information by children is secondary to the discovery of God, self, and the worth of others by adults.

Your goal is to discern:

- to what degree and by what means *adults* in your church go deep in faith.
- how many *options for children and youth* faith development exist in your church.
- how prepared your church leaders are to *share personal faith* with seekers and *coach* adults maturing in faith.

Data Recovery questions will require consultation with various program leaders of the church. *Ministry Review* questions can best be answered in focus groups, although some data may need to be available to focus groups in advance. Keep in mind that it is both the data itself and the *perceptions* of the congregation that are important. *Leadership Audit* questions may be answered by the human resources or personnel committee, official board, and staff. However, responses should be reality checked with the congregation through random surveys and interviews with marginal members.

Remember that for spiritually yearning youth and adults, opportunity and guidance to go deeper into spirituality is valued far more than mere friendliness. *Trading first names is nothing compared to sharing our very souls.*

Growing in God Questions
(Questions Numbered from Previous Section)

Data Recovery

90. What is the average distance church members must travel to attend church? to go to work?

91. What percentage of the newcomers become active (that is, attend worship at least twice per month, join the church, use financial envelopes, participate in groups, or receive pastoral care) within the first 6 months?

92. What percentage of members are involved in small groups within the church that meet regularly? (A small group has approximately 12 people, gathered around a common topic of interest, and some identifiable leader. Group life includes intentional components of Bible reading, prayer, sharing, and activity.)

93. What percentage of members are engaged in midweek faith development activities? within the church? beyond the church with other religious and spirituality groups?

94. How many midweek, church-related programs, led by church people, does your congregation support? What are they?

95. What percentage of the groups within the church (small, large, and of any kind) are more than 2 years old? (Thriving churches aim to begin 1 new group for every 50 newcomers; 10-20 percent of all groups are less than 2 years old.)

96. What percentage of the adult members of the church attend a regular Sunday school class (Bible study, topical discussion, study books, and so forth)?

Ministry Review

97. Do people perceive *membership* to mean the right to have a vote or a covenant to go deeper in spirituality?

98. To what degree do people talk about Christ, their experience with Christ, or new developments in personal growth during postservice coffee hours and informal church gatherings?

99. Is the nursery equivalent in quality to the best-designed, best-equipped, and best-staffed daycare center in your community? If not, what is lacking?

100. Are quality childcare options provided for every group, meeting, or event sponsored by the church?

101. How many options does your congregation offer for Sunday school curriculums or alternate educational tracks? for children? for youth? What are they?

102. Do the groups of the church have an intentional strategy to multiply? What is it? (Thriving churches aim to transform, refocus, or multiply every group at least once every two years.)

103. Does your church offer athletic opportunities or team sports in a Christian context for youth and adults? What are they?

104. Does your church offer musical opportunities or musical organizations in a Christian context for youth and adults? What are they?

105. Does your church offer opportunities in arts and crafts, guided by church members, as a spirituality cell group? What are they?

106. Does the congregation have a telecare ministry?

107. What percentage of the congregation's volunteer energy is given to each of the following: pastoral care? social action? evangelism?

Leadership Audit

108. Does the congregation employ an ongoing, intentional Spiritual Gifts Inventory in a process that enables participants to know how God has gifted them for ministry?

109. Does the congregation offer regular opportunities for personality trait discernment using such processes as the Myers-Briggs Inventory, Enniograms, or others?

110. Are specific laity trained by the congregation to counsel individuals in spiritual gifts and personality types?

111. Do group leaders receive regularly updated training in Bible, prayer, interpersonal relationships, and conflict resolution?

112. Do people often turn to a lay leader in a time of crisis, rather than to the salaried minister?

113. Are the staff (including church secretary, custodian, and music leadership) perceived to be attentive to the personal needs and issues of others during the pursuit of their work? A confidential survey may invite individuals to evaluate the gifts of each staff person:

1	2	3	4	5
Indifferent			Extremely Sensitive	

114. What percentage of salaried staff energy is given to each of the following: pastoral care? social action? evangelism?

115. Does the pastor regularly participate in a small spirituality cell group within the church? beyond the church?

116. Do the elders or lay leaders participate in small spirituality cell groups within the church? beyond the church?

117. Rank the following roles for the pastor (high, medium, or low):

Role	Skill Level	Energy Level	Congregational Expectation
mentor			
coach			
faith-sharer			
trainer			
spiritual guide			
group leader			
manager			
administrator			
preacher			
liturgist			
advocate			
counselor			

(You may wish to ask the pastor and a focus group to independently do this exercise and compare the results.)

118. Rank the following roles for the lay leaders of the congregation (high, medium, or low):

Role	Skill Level	Energy Level	Congregational Expectation
minister			
missionary			
faith-sharer			
shepherd			
entrepreneur			
team member			
administrator			
fund raiser			

Role	Skill Level	Energy Level	Congregational Expectation
program planner			
worship participant			
heritage protector			
supervisor			

(You may wish to ask the pastor and a focus group to independently do this exercise and compare the results.)

119. Do the pastor and lay leaders speak courageously of their own life struggles and spiritual victories? within the congregation? beyond the congregation?

120. Do the pastor and lay leaders exercise spiritual disciplines and continuing education strategies that are clearly seen and encouraged by the congregation?

LISTENING TO GOD

The thriving church seeks to move people from spiritual maturity to ministry. The fullness of spirituality is not achieved until an individual: celebrates new life, through the exercise of gifts, at the direction of Christ, and for the benefit of others. Thriving churches provide multiple, diverse ways of listening for God's call. They are prepared to risk creative ideas and original projects. Recruitment for institutional management is secondary to motivating individuals for faith sharing and service.

Your goal is to discern:

● the *real measure of Christian maturity* assumed by your church.

● the *degree of readiness for creativity* in your congregation.

● the *number of intentionally designed options* the church provides people to discover their own calling by Christ.

This subsystem is less easily quantifiable. Therefore, the *Data Recovery* questions are fewer and can best be answered by volunteers who are well acquainted with both the programmatic and individual spiritual disciplines within the congregation. Such volunteers may not be on the official board but should be widely recognized to have rich prayer lives and disciplined spirituality. *Ministry Review* questions can only partially be answered by focus groups. Some form of survey or intentional interview process with marginal members will be crucial. This may be combined with research that answers the *Leadership Audit* questions as well. Staff and lay leaders will wish to answer these last questions independently and then compare their responses with the perceptions of the congregation.

Remember, most people in the twenty-first century find meaning in life through purposeful activity, not through the performance of roles in a bureaucracy. In the eyes of the spiritually yearning public, *serving an office is an unacceptable alternative for the fulfillment of personal destiny.*

Listening to God Questions
(Questions Numbered from Previous Section)

Data Recovery

121. What percentage of the membership pursues a regular discipline of prayer and Bible reading during the week: men? women? teens? children?

122. How many options does the congregation provide for guided meditation, prayer, or introspection? List them in detail, and identify the key leader for each option.

123. Name three crazy ideas that were implemented by the congregation in the last five years.

124. What personal devotional resources are intentionally promoted by the congregation?

Ministry Review

125. What is the measure of Christian maturity in your church: experience in church management or awareness of personal callings in Christ? (Quick Insight: When you ask people about their involvement in the church, do they list the committees they have served or describe their journey of faith?)

126. Is it more important to your congregation to do the right thing or to do things the right way? (Quick Insight: When you ask fringe people why they are frustrated with the church, do they

complain about the process of decision making or about actual church decisions?)

127. What is the process or mechanism for the congregation to learn from failure and experiment again?

128. Does the congregation recruit volunteers for the mission of the institution—or enable gifted people to discern whatever it is Christ calls them to do?

129. Does the congregation have a free, safe environment that can accept disagreement on ideological or doctrinal subjects without personal risk of judgment or ostracism? Test your perceptions with inactive members and former participants.

130. Is the congregation afraid to take public stands on controversial issues for fear it will drive away potential newcomers? drive away veteran members? or reduce financial contributions?

131. Is the congregation afraid to publicly recognize ambiguity in controversial issues for fear it will drive away power groups that insist they have the right answers? drive away the pastor who believes she or he has the right answers? appear wishy-washy in the eyes of the community?

132. How does the congregation help participants build continuity between faith, lifestyle, and career?

Leadership Audit

133. Do congregational leaders believe that they are doing exactly what it is that Jesus Christ calls them to do?

134. How does the congregation regularly communicate their belief that every person is gifted by God?

135. When leaders are pushed to the bottom line, what takes priority in congregational life? (Place a mark on the continuum that best illustrates your congregational pattern.)

consensus	- - -	diversity
keeping veterans	- - -	welcoming newcomers
tradition	- - -	experimentation

136. Do lay leaders have an annual visioning and prayer retreat?

137. Do lay leaders intentionally seek out and listen to fringe people in the congregation? and in the community? How?

138. Do all staff (including church secretary, custodian, and music leaders) assist people to identify the ministries to which they are called by Christ?

139. Does the pastor believe that every Christian is called into ministry?

140. Are the pastor and gifted lay leaders trained to guide people in spiritual listening?

141. Does the pastor accept that people may disagree with her or him on ideological and doctrinal subjects?

142. Does the pastor accept the legitimacy of different expressions of faith, different lifestyles, or different political opinions?

143. How much time does the pastor spend counseling people to resolve personal problems, and how much time is spent mentoring people to discover personal opportunities?

SERVING GOD

The thriving church equips people for excellence. They prioritize energy to train individuals to do, with the highest quality of performance and integrity possible, whatever it is Christ calls them to do. They never just accept the best volunteers offer; they assist volunteers to achieve their highest potential of service.

Your goal is to discern:

• the degree of *control or permission* that the congregation exercises over potential ministries of the church.

• the number of ministries and services *already being done* by participants in the church and the *effectiveness of support* given by the congregation for each.

• the *readiness of the staff* to be trainers, rather than doers, of ministry.

The thriving church system gradually shifts emphasis from program development to leadership development. Therefore, *Data Recovery* questions may best be answered by people familiar with leadership training in the church. Focus groups that answer *Ministry Review* questions help reality test the perceptions and expectations of the congregation regarding leadership. *Leadership Audit* questions may be answered by the official board or congregational surveys in order to identify needed skills.

Remember, the most difficult transition for the staff and board is to surrender control of the mission agenda of the congregation, and the most difficult transition of the congregation is to insist on quality in lay ministries. These two stresses are just two sides of the same coin! In the eyes of the spiritually yearning public, *the credible Christian is not an office holder with the right credentials but a confident volunteer doing quality service.*

Serving God Questions
(Questions Numbered from Previous Section)

Data Recovery

144. Does the congregation have a year-round plan to enlist the appropriate expertise to train gifted and called laity? What is it?

145. List opportunities beyond the local church to which laity are regularly sent for continuing education or training:

Ecumenical   Parachurch   Public Sector

146. What percentage of the total budget is committed to continuing education for laity?

147. What percentage of the total budget is committed to continuing education for all staff?

148. Does the congregation train gifted and called people to relate effectively and sensitively to sectors of the public of different cultures, languages, and races?

149. Does the congregation train laity to model interracial cooperation in their ministries?

150. Are there options to receive training in other languages? What are they?

151. List all services or ministries that congregational participants are currently doing. Identify how the congregation is specifically equipping and celebrating each service or ministry.

Ministry Review

152. Does the congregation prescribe the mission that people should pursue, or do they equip the mission the people are motivated to do?

153. Is the congregation seriously committed to excellence, or do they simply accept whatever people offer?

154. Does the congregation understand that the primary purpose of staff is not to do ministry but to train others to do ministry with excellence?

155. Are lay leaders easily approached by both people at the center of church life and on the fringes of church life?

156. How does the congregation recognize, commission, and prayerfully support emerging lay leadership?

157. How readily do congregational participants share faith with family, neighbors, and work associates?

158. List the social service programs of the congregation, and identify how the faith that motivates the service is simultaneously shared in the midst of the good work.

Service   *Method of Faith Sharing*

159. List the evangelism programs of the congregation, and identify how practical help simultaneously benefits the people who hear the Good News.

Evangelism Strategy   *Accompanying Service*

Leadership Audit

160. Is there an intentional plan to train persons elected to offices in the congregation? What is it?

161. What regular opportunities are provided to upgrade the skills of small group leaders?

162. Is the board gifted and equipped to be midwives for creative ideas, rather than supervisors of salaried experts? How does the congregation ensure this to be true?

163. Does the pastor understand that the primary purpose of

staff is not to do ministry but to train and coach others to do ministry with excellence?

164. Is the pastor gifted and equipped to be a coach for lay ministry initiatives?

165. Rank the following roles for the pastor (high, medium, or low):

Role	Skill	Energy	Congregational Expectation
Small Group Leader			
Midwife			
Short-Term Counselor			
Large Group Leader			
Committee Chairperson			
Long-Term Counselor			

(You may wish to ask the pastor and a focus group to independently do this exercise and compare the results.)

166. Do all staff (including church secretary, custodian, and music leaders) intentionally devote energy to training and coaching gifted and called laity in work related to that staff person's areas of expertise?

167. Does a human resources (or personnel) committee meet regularly?

168. Is every person on the human resources committee gifted and trained for that task? Are they committed to maintain a year-round spiritual gifts discernment process? Do they have a year-round plan to monitor and upgrade all ministries?

169. Does the congregation extend the responsibility of the human resources committee over volunteer leadership, as well as salaried leadership?

SHARING GOD

The thriving church bonds a deepening, personal spirituality with multiple outreach ministries. No faith sharing happens without practical service to others, and no social service happens without sharing the transforming power of Christ. The congregation does not pay experts to do ministry; they equip themselves to do ministry. Ultimately, the goal of helping other people is secondary. Their goal is to invite others to participate in the same cycle of change, growth, discernment, training, and ministry that they experience in Christ through the thriving church. They know that meaningful living is not achieved in the receiving of bread—but in the giving of bread.

Your goal is to discern:

● the *real connection between spirituality and social service* made by participants in the congregation.

● the *real diversity of faith sharing and service that actually exists* among participants in the congregation.

● the *strategies the church employs to listen* to the yearnings of the public *and to invite* them into the life cycle of the thriving church.

Data Recovery questions will require both access to church records and official board minutes, plus personal experience with the congregation for over five years. You may wish to survey the congregation or take a random sampling of several worship services. *Ministry Review* questions are divided here into internal and external questions. The answers will not come from focus groups but from research teams prepared to interview, observe, or listen in intentional strategies. Some tactics are suggested along with the questions. *Leadership Audit* questions will also require intentionally deployed research teams to interview individual leaders and congregational participants. As always, remember to include marginal members and fringe participants of the church.

Remember, clear articulation of faith and concrete service to others are just two sides of the same coin. In the eyes of the spiritually yearning public, *why you do something is even more important than what you do!*

Sharing God Questions
(Questions Numbered from the Previous Section)

Data Recovery

170. List the ministries that are associated with your congregation. How many are led by active congregational participants? How long has each ministry been active?

171. Is regular participation in worship clearly essential to the people who are doing ministries? (Research the worship attendance record in October, February, May, and July for a selected group of church members recognized to be active in specific services or ministries. This should be done with permission, and you may rely on church records or conversations with those concerned.)

172. How many newcomers came to church in the last year as a result of interaction with equipped laity doing ministry?

173. How many newcomers came to church for the first time accompanied by a layperson whom they met in connection with that person's service or ministry?

Ministry Review (Internal Analysis)

174. Is the heritage of the congregation seen as a resource for new ministry or as a limitation to new ministry? Provide specific examples from the past five years.

175. Do members (individuals or families) of the church pray regularly for others? If so, how? If not, why not? (Note: Any definition or practice of prayer is fine. The goal is to discern if individual members of the church have a regular, intentional occasion to be in connection with God through the week.)

176. Do the laity of the church see their primary role as raising money to pay some other expert to do ministry, whom lay leaders subsequently supervise? Or do they see their primary role as doing ministry?

177. Does congregational worship regularly recognize, elaborate on, and pray for local, regional, national, and global missions? How often are leaders from these missions present in worship services?

178. Do laity have the motivation to move beyond talk to action? Do laity have the confidence to move beyond action to faith sharing? (Interview and observe as many participants in worship as possible. Teams may wish to develop a series of key questions with which to interview. Be sure to include a diversity of age, culture, and church experience).

Ministry Review (External Analysis)

179. What are the needs of the community and the spiritual yearnings of the public? Place an asterisk (*) beside those needs and yearnings which do not appear to be met by any current pro-

gram or group. (Do not assume that you already know. Do not rely on the newspapers or TV talk shows. Try using the above strategies, or politely talk to neighbors, work colleagues, and family members.)

180. Does the congregation have a strategy to go beyond friendliness to aggressively include newcomers among the friendship circles and within the activities of the congregation? What is it? Who leads it?

181. Does the congregation have a strategy to go beyond welcoming to intentionally interact with the public? What is it? Who leads it?

182. What do members of the public, who are not connected with your church in any way, say about you? (Try the following strategies: spend intentional time in public places listening to conversations; politely introduce yourself to strangers and ask them their opinion of the church; interview various real estate agents regarding their conversations with clients who seek to learn about a community.)

183. Does the public perceive the congregation to be more interested in recruiting steady financial contributors to the institution or in assisting others to experience life transformation? (In addition to the above strategies, try interviewing visitors to the church who signed a register but did not return and newcomers to the church who have become active.)

Leadership Audit

184. Consider the salaries and activities of staff, the time taken in meetings, and the overall activity of the congregation: Does the congregation invest more energy in the property, building, and management or in ministries?

185. Do lay people doing ministries have authority to implement new ideas and recruit help?

186. Do people doing ministries have a vision of both personal transformation and social change? (Interview and observe staff, selected lay leaders, and selected worship participants. Findings should be confidential, and reporting should be anonymous.)

187. Does leadership in ministry require participation on standing committees? Does leadership in ministry imply writing or presenting regular reports?

188. Do the elders or lay leaders have a year-round strategy to spend intentional time listening to the spiritual, emotional, and physical needs of the public? What is it?

189. Do the staff (church secretary, custodian, and music leaders) understand their roles to include sharing personal faith in addition to information or other practical services? Were they hired with this understanding in the job description?

190. Is the pastor ready to let others take responsibility for the design and implementation of ministry?

191. Are the pastor and lay leaders prepared to support ministries that do not go beyond the basic beliefs, values, vision, and standards of behavior of the congregation but that do not reflect their tastes or personal inclinations? Give examples.

— 6 —
FORM

PROPERTY

The thriving church property proclaims the thriving church vision in every possible way. The thriving church locates, designs, and utilizes property to make participation in the life cycle of change, growth, discernment, training, and ministry as easy and as effective as possible. Their property is visible, accessible, and hospitable to strangers. Property is never identified with heritage. It is always identified with ministry.

Your goal is to discern:

- how church property *proclaims your vision.*
- the degree to which property location and design *help or hinder* your ministries.
- the *changes that need to be made* to property for the church to grow.

Most of the questions here are *Data Recovery* questions. Three volunteer teams can collect information related to the exterior and site plan, interior and floor plan, and housing for staff (if applicable). *Ministry Review* questions should be answered by focus groups, not the property management committee. They primarily test for attitudes and openness for change. *Leadership Audit* questions should also be answered through focus groups, rather than committee, since they are intended to test issues of heritage protection and control.

Remember, property is like clay. It should be constantly remolded to address the changing needs of the public and facilitate the changing ministries of the church. In the eyes of the spiritually yearning public, *property is a window into the soul of the church.*

Property Questions
(Questions Numbered from Previous Section)

Data Recovery: Site and Exterior Facility

192. Describe the primary exterior symbol that identifies the vision of the congregation for the public.

193. Describe the primary sign that identifies the congregation on the church property. (Include location, size, color, graphics, message, lighted or unlighted, and so forth.)

194. Where are the other signs in the neighborhood or area located? Describe their condition (including size, color, graphics, message, and so forth). Are they visible from a vehicle traveling the speed limit and from a distance sufficient for a driver to adjust direction toward the church? Are they well maintained and updated?

195. How much land is owned by the congregation at the site of the church building? Is there room to expand the building without basement if needed?

196. How many properties does the congregation own or lease? Does the congregation own the primary church building and land?

197. Describe the location of the primary church building. Is it located on a major street or road? If not, at what distance from a major thoroughfare is the church located? Is there other land owned by the congregation in another location? What is its use?

198. Can vehicles discharge and pick up passengers directly at a church door that has no steps?

199. Is parking adequate? Do you use 80 percent or more of available parking on church-owned land for Sundays in November? How much on-street parking is available within a 3-minute walk of the church? Are handicapped spaces clearly marked and located nearest to the door? Are visitors' parking spaces clearly marked, sufficiently numerous, and positioned closest to the entrance to the church?

200. In the opinion of guests and newcomers, are the exterior grounds and building well maintained?

201. Is there a designated, well-maintained outdoor athletic area on the property?

202. Is the building secure? Are keys numbered and assigned?

Will doors automatically close and lock? Are parking areas and doorways well lighted?

203. Is the entire building accessible by ramp or elevator?

204. Could the building itself be moved and relocated if necessary? If not, what is the real market value of the building, and what is the potential to sell the building if necessary?

Data Recovery: Facility Interior

205. What is the primary interior symbol that identifies the vision of the congregation?

206. Describe the vestibule (or narthex) beyond the entry doors of the church, including contents, decorations, symbols, and so forth.

207. Are interior directions clearly marked for washrooms, coatrooms, offices, nursery, and meeting rooms?

208. Are all rooms, including washrooms, accessible to wheelchairs?

209. Describe the nursery and furnishings. Is the nursery located near the sanctuary and accessible without stairways? Is the quality of the nursery comparable to the highest-quality neighborhood daycare? (That means it should be naturally lighted; warm; bright; safe; with clean air and clean carpets; and equipped with toys that are unbroken, clean, and well sorted.) Are there separate, designated areas for infants and toddlers? Are wall coverings brightly colored? Is access easily monitored by adults supervising the nursery? What percentage of the nursery is used during Sundays in November?

210. Is there a large room for refreshments immediately adjacent the sanctuary that does not require access by elevator or stairways? If not, where is it located, and how do people get there? What percentage of a full worshiping congregation can comfortably share fellowship standing in this room?

211. Describe the sanctuary and furnishings, and draw a diagram of the room: What percentage of sanctuary seating is used during Sundays in November? Are there fixed pews or movable chairs? Does the chancel area allow room for drama, projection screens, dance, and so forth? Is the chancel area accessible for the physically challenged? Will the electrical supply sustain extra audio amplification or video equipment? Is the lighting for both

day and night sufficiently bright? Can lighting be finely adjusted? Is there a quality flow of air? Can the sound system be used by people with soft voices and heard by people with hearing impairments—in all parts of the room? Are there at least two cordless microphones available? Are musical instruments well maintained and properly stored? Are all parts of the sanctuary accessible? Can people enter late or leave early without calling attention to themselves? What percentage of the sanctuary space is used during Sundays in November?

212. Describe the Christian education rooms and furnishings: Are the rooms and furnishings equal in quality to the public education space in your community? Is audio and video equipment readily available and easy to set up? Are classrooms adequately stocked with quality supplies and well organized? Do children and adults have sufficient chairs? Are rooms adequately heated or cooled, with adequate flow of clean air? Are floor and wall coverings clean and colorful? Are rooms reasonably soundproofed to avoid distractions? Are classrooms computerized? How many? Are they networked? With what software? What percentage of Sunday school space is used during Sundays in November?

213. Describe the office space: Are there separate offices for each staff person? Are all doors to pastoral leadership offices within sight of the church secretary? Can confidential conversations be guaranteed? Can the church secretary see, or at least know, when anyone enters or leaves the building? In the secretary's office, is there adequate space for machinery, storage, and an extra chair? Are offices computerized? How many? Are they networked? What software is used? Does the office area have a designated fax line?

214. Are interior offices, classrooms, nursery, and storage rooms secure and safe? Are keys numbered and assigned? Can anyone ever be accidentally locked into a room? Are fire escape procedures clearly visible and easily accomplished? Are musical instruments and equipment locked in secure areas when not in use?

Data Recovery: Housing

215. Describe the housing of the pastor. Does the church own a house for the pastor or provide a housing allowance? Where is it

located in relation to the primary church building? Is there a formal office in the house? Is the office networked to the church computer? Does the church assume that part of the house is an extension of program space? If owned by the church: In the opinion of the pastors who lived in the house over the past 5 years, is the house comfortable, private, and secure for all members of the family?

Ministry Review

216. Is your congregation willing to make changes to the church property, building, and organization for the sake of new ministry? Provide specific examples from the past five years.

217. Do the architecture, symbolism, and site and floor plans of the facility communicate accurately the essential values, beliefs, vision, and mission of the congregation?

218. Can property be readily changed to facilitate emerging mission? (Provide examples of mission-driven renovations within the last ten years.)

219. Is the property understood by the congregation or the community as a heritage property?

Leadership Audit

220. What authority is required to make major changes to property? Or to make minor changes to property? How does the congregation decide what is major or minor?

221. Are trustees elected for limited terms of office?

222. Are property managers perceived to be—and understand themselves to be—facilitators of mission?

223. Are property managers committed to maintain a facility that is recognizable by the public as a quality environment that is safe, versatile, and equipped with up-to-date technology?

FUNDING

The thriving church always links its financial expectations to its opportunities in ministry. They never raise money for the purpose of preserving a heritage. They always raise money to benefit other people: to help people experience positive change and growth in their lives; to help people discern their destiny in

Christ; to help people be trained and to exercise quality ministry. The thriving church encourages financial generosity in a year-round strategy. They offer multiple options, and multiple methods, for giving. Your goal is to discern:

- how your church *values money.*
- how your church *communicates financial expectations* to participants.
- what *options, methods, and patterns* of giving are available to participants.
- how your church *connects money and ministry.*

Once again, most of the questions here are *Data Recovery* questions. A volunteer team can collect information related to fund raising and budget planning. This team should include the church treasurer and members of the finance committee. *Ministry Review* questions should be answered by focus groups, not the finance committee. They primarily test for attitudes and openness for change. *Leadership Audit* questions should also be answered through focus groups, rather than committee, since they are intended to test issues of control over program and personnel. Remember, institutions represent the disappearing middle management of twenty-first-century social service. They must earn their credibility. Credibility is gained by translating the maximum portion of every dollar into direct, personal, and clearly visible benefits in the world. In the eyes of the spiritually yearning public, *results count more than liturgies, and motivation is vastly more important than information.*

Funding Questions
(Questions Numbered from Previous Section)

Data Recovery

224. List all congregational indebtedness. When and why were these debts incurred? Are these capital debts or operating deficits? What percentage of the budget services these debts? To whom are these debts owed, and on what terms? Is total indebtedness growing or shrinking?

225. List all resources, reserves, endowments, investments, or savings. Who manages these resources, and on what terms? Does the congregation receive denominational grants or subsidies? On what terms?

226. Does the congregation have a year-round fund raising strategy? What is it? Does it include an every-member canvass? Does it involve all participants in church life?

227. Describe your pledge strategy: Are pledges intentionally geared to percent of income? Are people encouraged to tithe? How many choices are people given to pledge? What are they? How are people provided with quality background information in making a pledge?

228. How many choices do people have to make their regular financial contributions? List them.

229. What are the peak giving times of the year? What is the lifestyle reason for this fact? What is the spiritual reason for this fact? What is the congregation doing to maximize giving at these times?

230. What are the poorest giving times of the year? What is the lifestyle reason for this fact? What is the spiritual reason for this fact? What is the congregation doing to change this pattern?

231. What percentage of the budget is devoted to the following categories? (*The percentages provided after each category represent targets for church growth.*)

Staff salaries (40%)
Debt service (25%)
Equipping and doing ministries and mission (25%)
Maintenance and governance (5%)
Advertising (4%)
Stewardship (1%)

232. What percentage of the budget is devoted to continuing education to equip ministry?

233. Recast the budget using the thriving church stages, indicating total amounts dedicated to:

Experiencing God
Growing in God
Listening to God
Serving God
Sharing God

(Note: This exercise will provide two key challenges, (1) it will break the budget out of its program committee form and reveal the funding strengths and weaknesses for each stage; (2) it will force salaries to be divided according to time prioritized at each stage and reveal leadership strengths and weaknesses at each stage.)

234. Chart the total amount given for ministries affecting people outside and beyond your local congregation each year, for the last five years.

Ministry Review

235. Does the congregation generally give from a sense of thanksgiving and celebration, or do they give from a sense of obligation and duty? (Helpful clues: When people talk about giving, do they tend to speak of what they *should* do or what they *want* to do? Also, is the conclusion of the annual pledging campaign *reported* to the congregation or *celebrated* by the congregation in worship?)

236. Does the congregation seek to raise funds for the mission of the denomination or institution, or does the congregation assist gifted and equipped individuals and groups to raise funds for the missions to which they are called? (Helpful clues: When people talk about mission, do they tend to refer to a *program* or to *people?* Also, do people pledge to a unified budget or a single mission fund, or to specific missions and ministries?)

237. For what basic reason do people give to your church? Mark the place on the continuum that locates their motivations:

```
Mission - - - - - - - - - - - -  Maintenance
Grow something better  - - -  Preserve something good
Open new doors - - - - - - - -  Keep the doors open
```

238. Does the congregation habitually trim program to fit budget? Or does the congregation habitually do extra fund raising to expand program?

239. How are church participants kept informed about mission-funding opportunities and ministry needs?

240. Are multiple worship services given equal funding?

Leadership Audit

241. How does the congregation perceive the finance committee? Mark the place on the continuum which best locates their perceptions:

Missionaries	- - -	Managers
Entrepreneurs	- - -	Accountants
Voices of encouragement	- - -	Voices of restraint

How do members of the finance committee perceive themselves?

242. Are the members of the finance committee gifted in administration and intentionally trained each year?

243. Are congregational leaders forthright or embarrassed to ask for money? Does the congregation perceive their leaders to be pushy about money or unconcerned about money?

244. Is the pastor's house or housing allowance adequate to provide a quality, stress-free environment for the pastor and family?

245. List all salaries (full- or part-time) and honoraria paid by the church for leadership or special services.

246. Is the pastor's salary above the minimum denominational guideline? Why or why not?

247. Are pastoral staff salaries increased to offset the loss of personal honoraria for weddings and funerals that are turned over to the congregation?

248. Does the congregation provide Christmas bonuses, other signs of appreciation, or other rewards for performance?

COMMUNICATION

The thriving church is in constant communication with both participants and public. So much is happening, so much creative energy is being released, and so much good news is emerging that frequent updates are necessary. This helps avoid confusion, misunderstanding, and potential conflict. It also opens multiple avenues of introduction into the congregation. The thriving church must communicate often—because it is never quite the same from one moment to the next! Your goal is to discern:

- how the congregation communicates *with the public.*
- how the congregation communicates *among church participants.*
- how well staff and lay leaders *facilitate communication.*

Each goal above can be addressed by a different team.

Data Recovery questions require knowledge of both formal and informal communication networks in the church. *Ministry Review* questions return focus groups to reflect on the "basic umbrella of congregational life" in the context of communication to the public. Some questions help focus groups explore issues of control through clarity about grievance procedures. *Leadership Audit* questions may best be answered by a team of staff and human resources (personnel) committee members. Note, however, that the answers to some questions require interviews with core and marginal members of the church.

Remember, the great challenges for quality communication in the twenty-first century are *urgency, accessibility,* and *accuracy.* All groups and individuals must have power to promote and interpret their own work, and it is vital that such communications be clear and correct. In the eyes of the spiritually yearning public, *"I need to know it at precisely the point that I need it. I need to learn it from the source. And I need to hear it now."*

Communication Questions
(Questions Numbered from Previous Section)

Data Recovery

249. Make three columns on a blank sheet of paper:

1. Ministry   2. Purpose   3. Target

In column 1 list all the groups, programs, ministries or services of the church. In column 2 state in a few words the key purpose of the ministry. In column 3 identify the segment of the population most likely to be touched by the ministry.

250. Which of the following media does the church, or any ministry of the church, use regularly. Identify as many examples as possible.

____ Radio
____ Newspapers
____ Direct mail
____ Door-to-door visitation
____ Computer networks
____ Billboard, bus, park bench advertising
____ Telephone
____ Posters in stores, public places
____ Cable television
____ Alternate newsletters
____ Special interest networks
____ Other?

251. What message is communicated on the signs guiding people to the church building? Can these messages be easily changed or updated? Are signs lighted at night and plainly visible?

252. How does the congregation advertise in the community for: worship services? special events? ministries and missions? small and large group opportunities?

253. Do you have a print newsletter? How often is it prepared? Who prepares it? How is information gathered for it? How is it delivered, and to whom? Is there an audio version?

254. Do you have a video newsletter? How often is it prepared? Who prepares it? Where is it filmed? How is information selected for it? How is it delivered, and to whom?

255. Do participants in worship receive printed information before, during, or after the service? What percentage of this information is represented by the following:
Timetables for meetings and events
Financial information
Personal concerns and celebrations
Mission opportunities
Liturgical information
Other?

256. Is there a designated telephone line attached to an answering machine with an enthusiastic message that is updated every week? How is that telephone number made known?

257. Do you have a telecare ministry? How often is it updated?

258. Do you have a telephone information-sharing system that reaches every participant in the congregation within one week?

259. Are photographs of new members, persons with special celebrations, and others prominently displayed?

260. Do members carry gifts (for example, pencils, matchbooks, or notepads) with key information about the church that they can leave with people following spontaneous conversations?

Ministry Review

261. State in 35 words or less the core message your church wants to communicate to the public. Who among the public most urgently yearns to receive that message? How do you know?

262. Is the congregation prepared to experiment with any creative new idea to communicate to *specific demographic groups* in the language or cultural forms of that group? (Please provide examples.)

263. How does the church make sure that all communications are accurate and appropriate to the core message the church wants to communicate?

264. How does the congregation take advantage of Christmas Eve, Thanksgiving, Halloween, and Mother's Day to communicate the message of the church to the public?

265. How does the congregation take advantage of Christmas Eve, Thanksgiving, Halloween, and Mother's Day to inform newcomers, visitors, and participants about all the ministry options of the church?

266. Is every ministry or mission supported by the congregation visibly and colorfully portrayed in the vestibule or fellowship room?

267. When complaints refer vaguely to what "we think" or what "people say," is there a system to concretely verify allegations and rumors?

268. Is there a clearly defined, published, equitable grievance procedure that can be accessed by any person (staff or volunteer, church insider or community member)?

269. Are there clearly defined, highly visible ways for the church to celebrate individual or group milestones and achievements—or to express appreciation for leadership?

Leadership Audit

270. How are the editors, producers, or leaders of the above communication networks selected and trained?

271. Are ushers, greeters, counselors, lay leaders, and staff identifiable with name tags or other visual symbols—and equipped to answer questions?

272. Are staff and lay leaders regularly available to answer questions or dialogue with individuals or special interest groups? When and where? How do people know when and where?

273. In the opinion of visitors and newcomers, is the church secretary a good communicator? Is the church secretary full- or part-time? Does the secretary have a reputation for warmth and friendliness? Does the secretary have a reputation for confidentiality? Does the secretary have a reputation for accuracy?

274. Are lay leaders and staff widely trusted to maintain confidentiality regarding personal and family issues?

275. Can lay leaders and staff clearly identify confidentiality with protection of people, rather than protection of power?

276. Is there a gifted, called, and equipped lay visitation team that rapidly responds to newcomers? With what material are they equipped? (Please provide examples.)

277. Is there a gifted, called, and equipped lay visitation team that visits any member who has missed worship three consecutive Sundays?

278. Are there gifted, called, and equipped laity who mentor individuals or families subsequent to baptism or initial membership?

279. Are congregational leaders linked by electronic mail within the church?

280. Are congregational leaders linked by the Internet to leaders of other congregations, denominational judicatories, and parachurch organizations?

—— 7 ——
INTERPRETATION OF THE
CONGREGATIONAL MISSION
ASSESSMENT

The completion of the Congregational Mission Assessment provides congregational leaders with detailed insight into all eleven subsystems of congregational life. Some of the information will be in the form of concrete, quantifiable data. Other information will be in the form of a collage of perspectives from various focus groups, surveys, or interviews with marginal members and the general public. Further information will be both quantitative data and qualitative perspectives from—and about—congregational leadership. The following strategies will help the congregation interpret this large body of information and discern ways to apply what they learn for church transformation.

1. *Take time!* This information will not be digested, interpreted, and translated into transformational tactics in a single meeting or weekend retreat. Leaders will need to brood over the information to discern themes and trends.

2. *Broaden the conversation!* This information is best understood through dialogue that includes as many church participants as possible. Just as the research process sought to include marginal members and the full demographic diversity of the community, so also the interpretation needs to include these same people.

3. *Consider the information as a whole!* Resist the temptation to segment the information by assigning pieces to existing standing committees or program groups. This tends to impose existing programmatic assumptions on the information and dilutes its power to expose systemic weaknesses. If every committee or group addresses the entire assessment, hidden addictions that cross programmatic boundaries are more easily detected.

4. *Assign an interpretation team!* The interpretation of this information should not be simply left with the clergy or the commonly elected officers of the church. Although clergy and veteran

church leaders should be included in the team, the congregation should also invite nonclergy staff, relative newcomers, youth, and others who may not normally serve on the official board. Volunteers with professional experience in community surveys and strategic planning are especially valuable.

5. *Invite the insights from church leaders beyond your congregation!* These comments can provide an objectivity that helps clarify further the hidden addictions of the congregation. Choose a congregational partner that shares a similar demographic profile and that shares your own passion for systemic change. Do not be limited by geography, denomination, or judicatory boundaries. In fact, the perspectives of congregational partners beyond these artificial limitations may be the most valuable.

6. *Invite the interpretation of a professional church consultant!* There are increasing numbers of experienced "interventionists," both denominational and independent, whose broad experience in church consultation will help interpret this information. Understand that these consultants are not "experts" who will provide the definitive interpretation of the data. Instead, they are partners in a transformational journey whose insight can supplement your learning in unique ways.

As the congregation takes time to interpret the accumulated information in these ways, strengths, weaknesses, and hidden addictions will emerge with great clarity. What is learned will set the agenda for strategic planning and systemic change.

In my earlier book *Kicking Habits: Welcome Relief for Addicted Churches,* I first described the pentagon models for declining and thriving churches. The declining church system model appears on the page facing this one.

In the declining church system, congregational life is all about *belonging* to an ecclesiastical institution. People are enrolled into an organizational "machine," informed with necessary institutional information, nominated into bureaucracy, supervised by senior church members, and kept securely within a protective infrastructure. These congregations will find the Congregational Mission Assessment challenging to complete. Many of the questions will seem odd, and a few may even seem insulting. They will be tempted to complete the assessment by assigning the project to a handful of matriarchs and patriarchs, or other controllers of church life. They will be frustrated by the amount of work the

DECLINING CHURCH
"ALL ABOUT BELONGING"

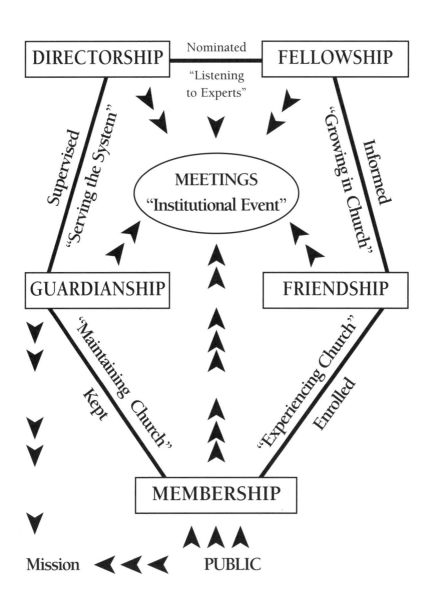

Congregational Mission Assessment requires, eager for quick programmatic answers that will rescue their ailing church system. A review of *Kicking Habits* will refresh your memory regarding the problems of the declining church system. Generally speaking, these congregations tend to create worshiping congregations with demographic homogeneity, for whom worship is the single Christian education moment in the week. They are preoccupied with children and youth education, and they give low priority to adult spiritual disciplines. They emphasize administration and involve as many people as possible in the bureaucratic life of the church. Outreach will be limited, programmatic, and guided by committees that implement hierarchical agendas. They are also very friendly. Once a person is a church insider, the congregation will do all in its power to care for that person's personal needs and keep him or her satisfied with congregational life.

When congregations within the declining church system do the Congregational Mission Assessment, the assessment will often reveal certain broad strengths:

1. *They are welcoming.* Almost every dying church in North America is a friendly congregation. They may await newcomers at the doors of the church, but when newcomers do arrive they are greeted with genuine warmth. They will do everything possible to make the property accessible, the liturgy understandable, the organization predictable, and the refreshments delicious.

2. *They love children.* Almost every dying church in North America loves kids—in a "grandparent" kind of way. That is to say, they love the innocent smiles, cute behavior, witty spontaneity, and exuberant energy of youth. They assume that these children and youth will eventually dedicate that energy to maintaining the heritage of their church. Therefore, the church will give budget and energy to the Sunday school, youth groups, and membership training classes.

3. *They enjoy intergenerational worship.* Almost every dying church in North America seeks to involve children and youth in worship. This involvement will often be limited to certain portions of the worship service and to specific times during the ecclesiastical year. It will not alter the general style of music or the routine format of the service.

4. *They are very good at fund raising.* Almost every dying church in North America is skilled at raising money. They are eager to

learn about new stewardship strategies. While they tend to be uneasy with annual, every-member pledging, they are adept at short-term financial campaigns and special occasion fund raising. The finance committee is often better trained and more highly skilled than any other committee in the church.

5. *They maintain property with excellence.* Almost every dying church in North America keeps the building site and church facility looking good. The site is clean and painted. The facility is safe, accessible, and usable. Furnishings meet the minimum expectations of quality of the oldest members of the church. Technology may be out of date, but it does slowly evolve to address changing program needs—especially if these needs relate to children or seniors.

Given these strengths, it is no surprise that the Congregational Mission Assessment often reveals that the clergy leadership that is prized most highly is leadership that is friendly and warm, magnetically attractive to youth, adept at integrating children into traditional worship forms, skilled in stewardship and administration, and respectful of property. Interestingly, the minimum standards for clergy housing will almost always be significantly lower than the standards for the church site and facility.

Just as the Congregational Mission Assessment will reveal certain broad strengths for churches dedicated to systems of belonging, so also the assessment will usually reveal broad weaknesses.

1. *Ambiguous identity.* There is often very little clarity or consensus about "the basic umbrella of congregational life." Core values all tend to be passive and relational, bedrock beliefs tend to be creedal formulas, and there is no motivating vision or key mission.

2. *Low mission emphases.* Survival tends to be uppermost in the minds of church leaders. They contribute to little beyond the generic mission funds of the denomination, and few people are involved in hands-on ways with outreach that is specifically motivated by their Christian faith and church experience.

3. *Unwieldy organizations.* The bureaucracies tend to be very large, requiring large numbers of volunteers to serve offices or fewer volunteers to serve multiple offices. As a result, burnout and nomination crises are common. Risk taking is difficult. Creativity is rare.

4. *Informational worship.* Worship services tend to be dry,

briefly illuminated by the children's story or other intergenerational event. They are wordy and presentational, and seek to convey ecclesiastical information about the Christian year and the local calendar.

5. *Demographic homogeneity.* The congregation tends to reflect the race, language, culture, education, and economic background of the oldest church veterans, rather than the diversity of the surrounding community. Despite programmatic emphasis on friendliness and inclusiveness, the congregation is systemically exclusive.

6. *Little adult spiritual discipline.* Expectations for adult membership is usually limited to financial support, occasional attendance, and periodic office holding. Few adults are involved in regular Bible study, intercessory prayer, meditation processes, selective reading, or small groups.

7. *Clergy dependency.* The congregation relies upon professional, credentialed clergy to do the ministries of the church—with the heaviest expectations for internal pastoral care among church insiders. Supervision and accountability for clergy are often controversial issues.

8. *Little lay training.* Quality volunteer leadership is not a priority for these churches. There is little or no lay leadership training budget, and the congregation relies upon redundant middle management, prescriptive job descriptions, and committee mandates to implement mission agendas.

9. *Minimal team mission.* There is little or no provision to partner volunteers for hands-on ministries, and therefore little opportunity for mutual mentoring or mutual support. Ongoing coaching for volunteers doing missions is rare. Creative ministries tend to rise and fall with distressing regularity.

10. *Poor communications.* These churches tend to rely upon infrequent print newsletters, announcements in worship services, informal "grapevine" gossip, and committee attendance to communicate news within the congregation. Today these are the least effective methods of communication amid dual-career families and busy lifestyles.

Generally speaking, the Congregational Mission Assessment tends to reveal a pattern in which churches welcome newcomers effectively and incorporate them into the institution but fail to help individuals grow spiritually and discover personal callings into active ministries.

The discovery of trends, themes, or threads of connection is the most significant (and the most stressful) benefit of the Congregational Mission Assessment. This involves discernment of hidden corporate addictions in congregational life. These addictions are the habitual, self-defeating behavior patterns that the congregation chronically denies but to which they will always return in times of confusion or stress. These habitually self-defeating behavior patterns will sabotage the best strategic and long range plans. Time and again a congregation will seek to transform itself by appointing a skillful, knowledgeable, motivated strategic planning committee. They will identify programmatic strengths and weaknesses, and develop a long range plan to address them. Nevertheless, a year or two after the committee gives its report, the congregation complains that nothing has changed! Why? Because hidden corporate addictions have sabotaged the ability of the church to implement the recommendations of the committee.

EXPERIENCING CONGREGATIONAL MISSION ASSESSMENT

The hidden addictions revealed by the Congregational Mission Assessment will vary from congregation to congregation. This is why the various methods of broadening interpretation of the assessment, identified earlier, are so important. However, some examples of addictive behavior can be described based on past experience.

Those who have read my earlier book *Kicking Habits: Welcome Relief for Addicted Churches* will recall "St. Friendly-on-the-Hill Church" as an example of the declining church system. They watched core congregational members drift to the margins of congregational life and ultimately leave the congregation to participate in "New Hope-in-the-Heart Church." However, their story did not end there. They had the courage to approach the leaders of that thriving congregation to discover their secret. Initially, of course, they were seeking a "secret ingredient" that could simply be added to their present system to revitalize it. They were looking for a program, curriculum, music alternative, youth ministry, or some other trick or tip, the mere introduction of which would rebuild their congregation. In the end, the folks of St. Friendly's were challenged to think systemically, rather than programmatically. The task of church transformation became more complicated, and more comprehensive, than they ever imagined.

St. Friendly Church completed the full Congregational Mission Assessment. This alone was not easy. The congregation found many of the questions to be odd and did not even answer some of them. They were impatient for programmatic, institutional results, and they resented the amount of time and energy systemic analysis required. They constantly wanted to assign veteran matriarchs and patriarchs sole responsibility to answer questions. These reactions in themselves were revealing of hidden addictions. Many of the questions they avoided answering were later discovered to be the most significant, challenging, and unsettling questions that needed to be asked. Their desire for instant programmatic gratification hinted at the inability of adult volunteers to seriously embrace spiritual disciplines for personal growth, a situation that would later be revealed in the assessment. Their tendency to avoid responsibility, by letting a few burned out leaders and clergy bear the burden of the assessment, anticipated the revelation of their clergy dependency and lack of volunteer training.

Despite all this, St. Friendly Church persevered. They actually began to enjoy the focus groups and the discussions of differing perspectives. As the collage of information grew, they wondered how anyone would make sense of it all, but they also appreciated opportunities to discuss matters of values, beliefs, and vision that had never been possible amid the bureaucratic business of church life.

They found it unsettling that certain assumptions about congregational identity that they thought unshakable were now cast in doubt. Traditional programs they had long fought to maintain were revealed to have very unclear purposes. Most unsettling of all, traditional expectancies of staff and volunteers needed to be readjusted in surprising ways.

They also found sudden illumination. They began to understand why they suffered chronic operating deficits, why youth dropped out after joining the church, why their previous minister was placed on disability, why they could not recruit Sunday school teachers and youth group leaders, why coffee hour was more fun than worship, why most newcomers failed to stick with the church, why controversy erupted over seeming trivialities, and why the median age of church members continued to climb. More than this, they began to understand that these problems were not unrelated to each other but were all symptoms of deeper corporate addictions. What follows is the addictive pattern they traced through all eleven subsystems of congregational life.

Congregational identity was a good deal more ambiguous than congregational leaders thought. The core values tended to be relational and passive. St. Friendly valued warmth, caring, families, children, friendships, respect, inclusiveness, nurture, inner peace, and tradition. Values for creativity, personal growth, action, and change did not readily emerge, and those newcomers who prioritized such values rarely stuck with the church. Moreover, bedrock beliefs tended to be ritualized formulas oriented to abstractions about God, scripture, and the sacraments. Little was expressed about Christian duty or calling, Christian ministry or life, and personal destiny. The congregation had no strong sense of key mission beyond institutional survival and some rather vague ambitions for the "betterment of humanity." Given these values and beliefs, it was no surprise to discover that the congregation raised money for generic denominational mission funds while at the same time the congregation rarely aggressively pursued any particular, local, controversial justice issue. After all, they wanted desperately to be liked and to preserve those warm relationships. If they got involved in local, hands-on mission, there would be potential for conflict.

Meanwhile, less that 15 percent of the people of St. Friendly were involved in any intentional small growth group. Of those who were involved in growth groups, most of them were teenagers or senior citizens, and few of them were male. Less than 5 percent of St. Friendly adults were engaged in any intentional, faith development discipline. At the same time, over 25 percent of the membership were formally recruited to serve offices, join committees, and manage congregational life. Lay leadership burnout was very high, and several committees existed on paper only. The church resisted answering Congregational Mission Assessment questions related to calling because they found the concept "confusing." They just did not know what it meant.

Creative, risky ideas at St. Friendly-on-the-Hill had been few over the past ten years. There had been a move to place a basketball hoop on an outside wall of the church facing the parking lot. However, after weeks of debate and several ad hoc committees, the congregation decided sports might invite unstable youth to vandalize the property. Instead, they erected a large, brightly lit sign that read "NO LOITERING." As a creative fund raising idea, the official board persuaded the minister to shave his head if the fund raising target was reached. It was, and he did. When he pointed out that it would be a far more powerful witness if the target was reached and all the members of the official board shaved *their* heads, he was cheerfully (but firmly) chastised by the personnel committee.

St. Friendly-on-the-Hill Church offered two worship services on Sunday mornings. These were identical services, with no specific missional purpose, using traditional liturgies and music. The only difference between the services was the time. Neither congregation reflected the demographic diversity of the community. Worship bulletins were wordy and included numerous announcements about the local church and community calendar. A survey of the two worshiping congregations revealed that less than one-third of the participants prayed regularly through the week, and for most of these, prayer meant only table grace. True to their core values, most people prized the children's story, and few people remembered the sermon. There was little emotion shown during worship, but animated conversation happened during the coffee hour.

Although research revealed that well over 50 percent of the adults attending St. Friendly were involved in charitable work or service clubs beyond the church, less that 1 percent indicated that worship had any bearing on their community volunteerism. Less than 5 percent of the newcomers to the church came expressly invited by, or accompanied by, laity they had encountered in the community. Sections 1 and 2 of the assessment (Congregational Identity and Mission) revealed the congregation did not have a clear understanding of personal calling to ministry, and few people could answer the key question "What is it about my experience with Jesus this community cannot live without?" Sections 6, 7, and 8 (Listening to God, Serving God, and Sharing God) revealed that the congregation did not train laity to share their faith. It was no surprise to discover in sections 4 (Experiencing God) and 11 (Communication) that the congregation had no volunteer teams to visit newcomers after their first experience with worship. Less than 30 percent of the newcomers to the church continued to relate to the church after six months, and less than 10 percent eventually became members.

The addictive pattern continued to unfold in each subsystem of congregational life at St. Friendly. Low priority for personal growth led to little interest in adult small groups, Bible study, or Sunday school. Confusion about calling and Christian life led to little involvement in prayer, meditation, or other listening disciplines. More than this, the congregation did not bother to include lay training in the budget, but clergy dependency did lead them to increase clergy continuing education in the budget. No interest was displayed in a quest for quality, but middle management with the official board steadily increased. The congregation did good work in the community, but members could not articulate their faith motivation to do it.

Tracing these addictive behavior patterns, congregational leaders at St. Friendly began to understand the systemic reasons why membership had plateaued, households under pastoral care had decreased by 40 percent in ten years, and the median age of participants was 63. They also began to understand the direct connection between adult spiritual discipline and stewardship, and for the first time, they understood the reasons for their chronic operating deficit. The deficit had nothing to do with lack of available money, or even with the lack of a clever stewardship program. It had everything to do with the core values and beliefs of the church, as well as the lack of commitment to adult spiritual growth. They began to understand that for St. Friendly-on-the-Hill:

- relationship to each other was crucial, but relationship to Christ was not.
- spiritual contentment was crucial, but spiritual growth was optional.
- professionalism for staff was crucial, but excellence in volunteerism was not.
- social service was nonthreatening to church outsiders, and evangelism was scary to church insiders.

The forms of congregational life (property, finance, and communications) were an outgrowth of the foundations and functions of congregational life. The problems at St. Friendly related to the property, finances, and communications systems of congregational life could never be effectively solved unless the hidden addictions that ran through congregational assumptions and ministries were addressed.

In the end, the final report and recommendations based on the Congregational Mission Assessment were both exciting and threatening to St. Friendly-on-the-Hill Church. The challenge to find clarity and consensus around "the basic umbrella of congregational life" was daunting. Some of the traditional matriarchs and patriarchs worried that their authority to control the church with their personal perspectives, lifestyles, and opinions, might be undermined. More threatening still was the need for adult faith development and spiritual discipline. Some adults were quite content with their lives as they were, while other adults assumed they would never have anything profound to offer God no matter how much they grew. A large faction in the congregation was fully prepared to ignore what had been learned from the Congregational Mission Assessment, and initiate the same old programmatic changes that had been tried before. Such is the power of corporate addictions!

On the other hand, other leaders of St. Friendly-on-the-Hill Church had begun to see a genuine alternative in Christian living. They had frankly enjoyed the focus groups and research process. Church life had become more understandable and exciting than ever before. They were particularly impressed that, following the Congregational Mission Assessment process, the congregation had avoided an annual operating deficit for the first time in 25 years! Lastly, their hearts ached for Bob and Sally Public and the two-thirds of church newcomers who had failed to find their spiritual hunger filled in St. Friendly-on-the-Hill Church and had gone elsewhere. They began to recover a compassion for the lost.

As churches like this slowly transform themselves for the twenty-first century, the Congregational Mission Assessment will help them evaluate their progress and track down the nagging, self-defeating habits that continue to pursue them into the future. Here are some examples:

Example 1

Revisiting the "basic umbrella of congregational life" to regularly define, refine, and celebrate values, beliefs, vision, and mission becomes the primary purpose of annual congregational meetings. One congregation replaced all references to "family" in the definition of core values with an emphasis on "persons." They recognized that if the congregation was to truly mirror the demographic diversity of the community, then acceptance of single, unwed, separated, and divorced persons was crucial. Many of these persons also experienced various forms of alienation from children and parents.

Still later, this same congregation believed the Spirit led them to revise their understanding of scriptural authority and their core value for "abundant life." They agonized over the growing polarization in the community between "pro-life" and "pro-choice" factions around the abortion issue, and they recognized that disciplined, deeply spiritual people within the congregation were arriving at different conclusions about this ambiguous issue. Rather than force anyone out of the church (intentionally or unintentionally), they associated strong values for "respect," "safety," and "spirituality" with their celebration of "abundant life." This allowed even antagonists to find a healthy place within the church despite strong ideological disagreement.

The Congregational Mission Assessment helped this particular congregation understand the practical impact of these refinements to their "basic umbrella of congregational life." Mentoring strategies for newcomers, the options for multitrack worship, the character of small group life, and training objectives for lay leadership were all modified. Not only were *functional* changes introduced, but *formal* changes to property and communications were also introduced. The congregation renovated property to transform formerly cold classroom space into additional warm parlor space to build intimate environments that protected the personal space of adults. They also made consultation rooms soundproof to protect confidential conversations. The advertising strategy was enhanced to communicate their acceptance of ideological diversity so that the public was well aware of their new identity.

Example 2

In a second example, another congregation celebrated a vision to be a "holistic health center" to the community, sheltering ministries for physical, emotional, relational, and spiritual well-being under one roof. An assessment of all eleven subsystems of congregational life helped them define the missional focus of each worship service offered by the church. It also helped them prioritize renovation of facilities to include outdoor garden courtyards for Tai Chi and indoor exercise rooms with state-of-the-art equipment. A previous staffing plan calling for additional youth ministers was redesigned to acquire staff expertise in meditation, stress management, and interpersonal mediation that would cross generational boundaries.

More importantly, the disciplined use of an assessment of all eleven subsystems did more than simply affirm programmatic strengths and identify programmatic weaknesses. It helped uncover the corporate addiction that had caused adult spirituality cell group growth to plateau at 40 percent. The congregation could not seem to enable more than 40 percent of the participating adults to connect with partnered spiritual disciplines. They discovered that hidden addictions for control had slowly multiplied a prescriptive bureaucracy of church governance that was no longer fully "permission-giving" to entrepreneurial missions of the laity. In response, they streamlined governance, introduced more intentional training for administrators and managers to improve overall quality, and rewrote all committee mandates and job descriptions proscriptively rather than prescriptively.

Example 3

A final example reveals the benefits of the Congregational Mission Assessment for small churches. One pastoral charge that included four small, rural congregations discovered that the process helped them break down years of community rivalry to develop a united, enthusiastic consensus for all four congregations. This clarity and consensus enabled them to share financial and leadership resources more effectively to the mutual benefit of each small congregation. The process of the assessment guided them to the full realization that the Internet and the automobile had forever changed their "rural church" assumptions about isolation, and for the first time they understood the impact of the demographic and psychographic diversity in their communities on their own sense of Christian calling.

Research into all five *functional* subsystems of church life helped these congregations understand that the youth would never be the future of their congregations. After all, most of the youth moved to the city for jobs. They reoriented Christian education to bring adults into profound spiritual disciplines. Because the pastor was burning out trying to guide worship and Christian development in four distinct communities, they created a large continuing education budget for laity and intentionally deployed gifted and called lay leaders to do work previously associated with the clergy.

In the end, the Congregational Mission Assessment helped the congregations make several radical changes to property and leadership. First, they were able to surrender their addiction to heritage. Three of the four congregations amalgamated and relocated into a new facility central to all three communities. The combined congregation was larger than the sum total of the worship attendance of the former three congregations. Diverting memorial fund money away from stained glass windows to modern technology, they were able to match the technology in worship with the technology actually used in contemporary living. The fourth congregation in the charge was farther away, but it continued in intentional unity with the charge for enhanced resource and leadership sharing. Since this Canadian congregation was near a First Nations reserve (similar to Native American Reservations in the United States), the entire charge found a new opportunity for intentional ministry.

The second radical change empowered by the Congregational Mission Assessment involved team ministry. In the end, a congregation of another denomination became inspired to participate in the amalgamation and relocation project. The "basic umbrella of congregational life" was further refined with their participation, and the congregations were all enabled to overcome their addiction to denominational dependency. Not only did these distinct denominational units come to share a facility, but between them they multiplied the worship options for all four communities in the region. In the end, clergy leadership became a shared ecumenical ministry.

The above examples trace a process of congregational transformation that took time, persistence, and partnerships to accomplish. However, many congregations approach church transformation the way that St. Friendly-on-the-Hill did. They want it to happen quickly and easily, through the hard work of only a few core leaders. They are looking for a few keys, a creative tip, a clever program, a dynamic new curriculum, and a charismatic addition to the staff. Doing research into eleven subsystems of congregational life and answering 280 key questions seem impossible. Indeed, their leaders even get angry when presented with the challenge. "How dare you!" they exclaim. "How dare you ask us to devote so much time and energy to the transformation of our congregation!" They are like alcoholics who become irate when told that just switching from hard liquor to wine, or just abstention for a few weeks, will not liberate them from addiction. Instead, freedom will require strong medicine, hard work, mutual support, a new personal prioritization of energy . . . and a long time. The very size of the demand implies a judgment on their present condition.

Change in the Old and New Testaments is rarely evolutionary. It is almost always apocalyptic. The essence of apocalyptic change is not that it happens quickly, but that it changes the very identity of individuals and nations. The Israelites spent forty years getting to the Promised Land, and when they arrived, they were an entirely different people than when they first departed. Over forty years, God systematically rebuilt the people of Israel. Systemic change for the church is just as apocalyptic. It requires significant, intentional time and energy; and in the end, the congregation will be decisively different. This means that the Congregational Mission Assessment process will ultimately bring the church to a decisive crossroad. They can allow themselves to be different—or they can return to their comfortable addictions. They can cross the Jordan River into the Promised Land—or they can return to Egypt. Sadly, some congregations will come all that way through the desert, see the potential for the future clearly, and turn back. Joyfully, other congregations will come all that way through the desert, weep for those who may have been lost on the way, and cross over into a new world.

The Congregational Mission Assessment is not designed to happen quickly and easily with the hard work of only a few core leaders. The Assessment is designed this way because this is the only way to accomplish systemic change! If you do not want to take time, do not have the energy or commitment to be persistent, or have a need to control or be controlled, the Congregational Mission Assessment is not for you. On the other hand, if you are zealous for enduring change that will maximize the ministry of Jesus Christ through your congregation to transform individuals and communities in the twenty-first century, then the intensive assessment of all eleven subsystems of congregational life is for you. By all means, customize it, contextualize it, and adjust for your unique situation. *DO IT* . . . and see what God can do!

— PART III —

FREEING THE FAITHFUL!

THE BASIC BOUNDARIES OF CONGREGATIONAL LIFE

— 8 —
THE BASIC BOUNDARIES OF CONGREGATIONAL LIFE

Church transformation can begin at any point, and at any place, in the system of congregational life. One begins where it is easiest to begin. That is, begin where permission is easiest to obtain. Energy wasted in combat trying to force change against strong resistance lowers morale, alienates leadership, and makes all subsequent change more difficult. Systemic change moves from celebration to celebration, rather than from victory to victory. The celebration of one successful experiment motivates the congregation to take greater subsequent risks.

It is necessary that the core congregational leaders share a passion to prioritize the Gospel above all else and a readiness to experiment with new (and even crazy!) ideas. In short, they must feel in their hearts the inspiration of Paul's mission to the Gentiles: "I have become all things, to all people, that I might by all means, rescue some" (1 Corinthians 9:22, author's translation). It is this passion to help others experience the transforming power of God in their lives and to help others walk in daily relationship with Jesus that motivates church transformation. Unchurched "outsiders" can tell if this passion is true and authentic in two ways.

First, the participants in the congregation are themselves experiencing the ongoing transforming power of God. They talk about it readily, constantly, and enthusiastically.

Second, the adults in the congregation are involved in intentional spiritual disciplines. This will include not only weekly worship but small groups and personal or family disciplines at home or work.

Creative missions and ministries will emerge from this continuous experience of positive change and disciplined growth. It is important to understand, however, that these activities will not in themselves convince the unchurched public of the authenticity of the congregation's spiritual passion. In the twenty-first century, actions no longer speak louder than words! Participants must be able to articulate or share their experience of God that motivates all their good deeds, and they must demonstrate through spiritual disciplines their readiness to walk daily with Jesus. "Good deeds" in the twenty-first century world may be motivated by any kind of absurdity or manipulation. You must reveal your motivation and link good works to a spiritual lifestyle.

It is not necessary that the core congregational leaders develop a full and detailed strategic plan for the future. Indeed, it is better if their strategic plan is always unsettlingly incomplete. In the organic, cellular churches that Bill Easum and I have described as "Spiritual Redwoods," the mission agenda emerges *from below* or, in other words, from the spiritual growth of the people themselves. The congregational leaders never know exactly where they will end up, and they never know precisely where the Holy Spirit is leading them. Twenty-first century planning implies innovation from start to finish.

Church transformation is a matter of systemic change, not mere programmatic change. The whole system of congregational life and mission, the ebb and flow of both spontaneous and intentional activity, must ultimately be changed. Unlike the initiation of a new program, systemic change will not be accomplished by a bureaucratic decision of the central board and several months of hard work. It will only be accomplished by a consensus of the participants that is clear and enthusiastic, and it will emerge in waves of change over two to seven years. Systemic change is both revolutionary and evolutionary. It is revolutionary in that it demands an entirely new way of thinking and behaving that dramatically contrasts with past thinking and behavior. It is evolutionary in that change in one subsystem of congregational life leads to another subsystem and then to another subsystem and so on and on. Therefore, church transformation can begin at any point, and at any place, in the system of congregational life. One begins where it is easiest to begin.

The pentagon model of the thriving church, which I first introduced in *Kicking Habits: Welcome Relief for Addicted Churches,* identifies five of the eleven subsystems of congregational life. These *functional* subsystems are: experiencing God, growing in God, listening to God, serving God, and sharing God. Behind these five subsystems are *foundational* systems of identity, mission, and organization, which Bill Easum and I discussed in greater depth in our book *Growing Spiritual Redwoods.* Finally, three *formal* subsystems provide tactical vehicles for mission: property, funding, and communication. Analysis of these eleven subsystems is facilitated by the Congregational Mission Assessment included in this book.

ELEVEN SUBSYSTEMS

Foundation

Identity
Mission
Organization

Function

Experiencing God
Growing in God
Listening to God
Serving God
Sharing God

Form

Property
Funding
Communication

A congregation can begin transformation in any of these subsystems, but as progress is made in any one subsystem, pressure for change in the other subsystems will mount. There will come a time when change in one subsystem plateaus, pending change in another subsystem. The most common entries into church transformation are:

THRIVING CHURCH
"ALL ABOUT CHANGING"

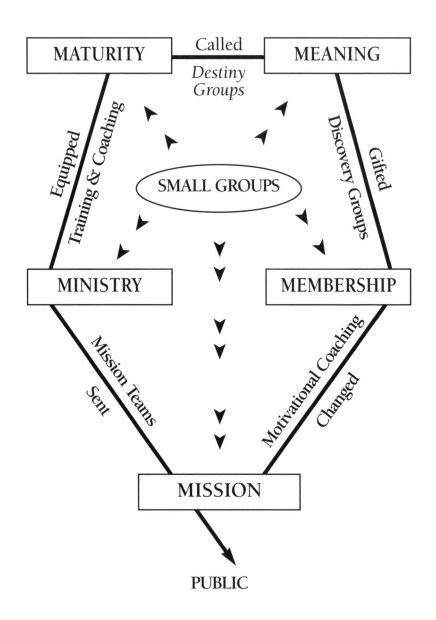

- the spiritual discipline of listening to the public.
- the spiritual discipline of visioning.
- the formation of spirituality cell groups.
- the process of spiritual gifts discernment.
- the creation of a proscriptive organizational model.
- the spiritual discipline and growth of a cadre of key lay leaders and clergy.
- the initiation of the first of a series of multitrack worship services.
- and the renovation or acquisition of property (especially the worship center).

Each of these assumes an intentional reorientation of leadership energy and an intentional strategy to train and equip leadership with new skills. Part of the intentional leadership development will be skills development prior to the above initiatives. Another part of the intentional leadership development will be commitment to the Risk-Learn Cycle in which leaders are allowed to fail, laugh at themselves, learn from their mistakes, and try again.

THE RISK-LEARN CYCLE

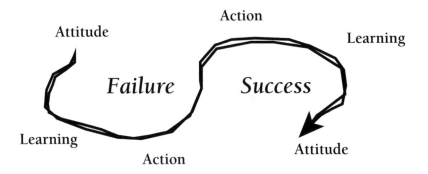

Whatever the entry point into church transformation, it is vital to clearly identify the basic boundaries of congregational life beyond which core leaders will not take risks. These are the proscriptive boundaries beyond which the church will not go. Look at the list of eleven subsystems for congregational life. Change can begin anywhere; it will eventually plateau and bring pressure to bear on the other subsystems; and ultimately systemic change itself will plateau until the congregation gains clarity about the core values, bedrock beliefs, motivating vision, and key mission— which together form the boundaries beyond which the creativity of the congregation cannot go.

For example, one congregation initiated systemic change by placing a cadre of lay leadership and clergy in a discipline of prayer, study, and intense conversation over breakfast, every Saturday morning for 12 weeks. Their spiritual growth was reflected in the revisions to the agenda of the official board. They began their agenda with the key question "Where does Jesus lead us into the twenty-first century?" and then itemized decisions to be made regarding the heating of the building, the stewardship program, restructuring the board, choice of Sunday school curriculum, and so forth. However, the congregation could not ultimately make decisions regarding these items. Factions emerged, opinions were heatedly exchanged, and research could not be interpreted or integrated into a strategic plan for the future. Why? The congregation had no enthusiastic clarity about the basic boundaries of values, beliefs, vision, and mission that marked the boundaries of congregational life. Without such clarity, decision making by congregational leaders will be remarkably timid, and change will slow or stop altogether. The congregation will find refuge in the status quo.

Another congregation initiated systemic change by starting an alternate, contemporary worship service. Their spiritual growth was reflected in the distinct missional purpose of the worship service for healing and in the informal and participatory style of the worship. Change in the subsystem of experiencing God eventually pushed them to change the subsystem of growing in God by developing adult spiritual cell groups. This was stressful because the congregation reoriented lay participation away from committees to affinity groups. Systemic change ultimately plateaued, however, when the enthusiasm for alternative worship pushed the congregation to consider changes to the subsystem of property. The congregation could not make breakthrough decisions for technology (electronic keyboards and video screens) or for renovations (flexible seating, expanded refreshment centers). All of these decisions demanded clarity about the core values, bedrock beliefs, motivating vision, and key mission that were the consensus of the church beyond which creativity could not go.

The lesson from experiences such as these is that, although systemic change may begin anywhere in the system, it will eventually pressure the congregation to forthrightly address the foundational subsystems of identity, mission, and organization. Some congregations might be able to start systemic change by discerning the basic boundaries of congregational life at the very beginning. However, many congregations will find the process too abstract. They may not understand why it is important and may be restless to bring practical change to other subsystems of the church. Many congregations address discernment of the basic boundaries of congregational life only after they have begun systemic change. Only as systemic change brings waves of stress to all the subsystems of congregational life, or as systemic change itself plateaus, does the congregation understand through its experience the importance of such foundational clarity.

In Christendom churches of the twentieth century, the basic boundaries of congregational life and mission were often poorly articulated—and yet very powerful. Indeed, much of the power of these boundaries lay in the fact that they were rarely raised to consciousness, or they were defined in a manner so complex that only a chosen few could ever understand them. This allowed controllers to quickly block any creative initiative in church life. Such initiatives could be criticized for:

● "not being part of our ethos."
● "not following proper procedure."
● "not being true to our heritage or identity."

These boundaries were protected by a fog of obscurity. Controllers could deny the existence of such boundaries—and even make exaggerated claims for the "openness" of the congregation—and still clamp down whenever a new idea alarmed them. The basic boundaries of congregational life in Christendom churches included:

- the personal tastes, lifestyles, opinions, and perspectives of the patriarchs and matriarchs.
- the uniform polity of a distant denomination or evangelical heritage imposed from beyond the local congregation.
- the habitual behavior patterns that pragmatically evolved through the uneasy interaction of the above.

Hidden within all of these boundaries of congregational life were the corporate addictions that dominated church life more powerfully than any periodic strategic plan or mission statement. No matter how open, friendly, or creative the congregation claimed to be, the reality was that congregations were remarkably homogeneous in membership, rarely initiated any radically new ideas, and desperately feared failure. Leaders were always timid to introduce change, and change always moved incredibly slowly.

Among twenty-first-century churches in a pre-Christian era, the basic boundaries of congregational life are clearly articulated, regularly reviewed, and routinely celebrated. They are neither hidden nor are they unnecessarily complex. They are immediately apparent to the most casual observer or the most novice seeker, and they are immediately accessible to every participant in the church. No expert is required to guide people through a labyrinth of denominational process and polity. No authority is required to pass judgment on the worthiness of an idea for implementation. Clarity about the basic boundaries of congregational life removes the power of "controllers" and frees the congregation for experimentation.

It is important to either gain clarity about the basic boundaries of congregational life at the very beginning of church transformation or seek clarity immediately when energy for systemic change plateaus in congregational development. Whatever entry point you choose for systemic change, it will not be long before stress emerges. Anxieties will increase, and someone will ask the question "Can you really do this?" Control will become a major issue, and the potential for congregational conflict will increase. People in the twenty-first century are far, far less patient than in the days of Christendom. Unless the blockage to systemic change is quickly removed, they will become frustrated and find ways to fulfill themselves beyond the life of the congregation.

Christendom churches would resolve these tensions in two ways. First, they would turn to authorities to give or withhold permission. The matriarch or patriarch, the clergy, or the denominational office would be asked to give a definitive opinion, and the congregation would be expected to accept it. Second, Christendom churches would turn to conflict management experts. Consultants would guide the congregation through a process of communication and compromise to achieve harmonious resolution. Unfortunately, with the death of Christendom, the above options no longer work. The clergy and the denomination are no longer given the same respect, and mere compromise denies the integrity of true diversity. The ultimate goal of church transformation is not to manage conflict but to birth the Spiritual Redwood! Whether or not harmony is restored, unless birth takes place, congregational life begins to decline and disintegrate.

Churches of the emerging pre-Christian era of the twenty-first century have learned to define, refine, and celebrate their basic boundaries for congregational life. They rarely turn to authorities for definitive opinions because the boundaries are accessible to all and understandable by all. They rarely need conflict management experts because the boundaries within which they live allow enormous diversity. These boundaries are the:

- Core Values of congregational life.
- Bedrock Beliefs of congregational life.
- Motivating Vision for congregational life.
- Key Mission for congregational life.

Once these boundaries are clear, the congregation is free to experiment with creative ministries and build a true diversity of mission.

The congregation *intentionally* defines, refines, and celebrates these boundaries. Communication of these boundaries will be prioritized as the *first* item in training new lay leadership, contracting with new staff, or covenanting with new church members. These boundaries will be regularly articulated in worship, visible in the vestibule, and central to the marketing strategy of the church. Individual participants do not need to ask permission to do things. They are empowered to ask of themselves: "Does this creative idea go beyond the boundaries of core values, bedrock beliefs, motivating vision, or key mission?" If the answer is NO, they are free to do whatever they wish, no matter how crazy the idea might be, immediately.

There are three specific reasons why clarity for these basic boundaries becomes crucial for the twenty-first-century church.

1. *The basic boundaries of congregational life are the foundation for the streamlined, proscriptive organization.* The accountability for church leadership is directly tied to these boundaries. In addition to the quest for quality and the need to train leaders for excellence, the congregation must always be able to ask—and answer—the question: "Has any leader or entrepreneur in this church gone beyond the basic boundaries of congregational life?"

2. *The basic boundaries of congregational life are the foundation for all long-range, strategic planning.* Only when these boundaries are clear can the congregation know where they want to go, why they need to go there, and how they can accomplish their journey. They can be wildly imaginative and take incredible risks because they know the limits of creativity.

3. *The basic boundaries of congregational life are the foundation for all spontaneity of word and deed.* In the twenty-first century, it is not the planned program or the rehearsed word that reveals the truth about your spirituality, but it is the spontaneous deed or the unrehearsed word that will reveal the truth. The spiritual authenticity of a church will be revealed by the conversations in the kitchen, not by the rhetoric of the sermon.

Christendom churches, which live in a fog about basic boundaries—and which allow the personal tastes of controllers, the distant polity of a denomination, or the addictive behavior patterns of a heritage to form the hidden boundaries for creativity—encourage "foghorns" to rule the future of the church. These "foghorns" are the most aggressive, noisy, controlling individuals in the church, and they dictate the paths of participation. The result is homogeneity of participation, slow change, and reinforcement of the status quo. Pre-Christian churches, which live in a climate of clarity about values, beliefs, vision, and mission, encourage initiative and diversity. In a sense, as the fog is blown away, each ship is free to navigate on its own without fear of shipwreck.

Both *Kicking Habits* and *Growing Spiritual Redwoods* discuss extensively the nature and significance of this systemic change. Stated simply, the formula for growing Spiritual Redwoods is:

CORE VALUES

+

BEDROCK BELIEFS

+

MOTIVATING VISION

+

KEY MISSION

———————————

DIVERSE
RAPIDLY DEPLOYED
MINISTRIES

The reason most Christendom churches do not have any powerful mission purpose is that their congregational identity is nebulous. Core values have been reduced to personal tastes; bedrock beliefs have been lost in a fog of rhetoric and denominational polity; motivating vision has become a desire to survive and perpetuate a heritage; and key mission has become a bureaucratic summary of their organizational structure. Thriving churches are so clear about their values, beliefs, vision, and mission that they can write their mission statement on the side of a bus, the roof of a barn, or the back of a park bench. That single, pithy, powerful mission statement will say everything you need to know about the church, and it will capture the imagination of the public.

The basic boundaries of congregational life are like an umbrella that is held above the heads of the participants. The umbrella defines their space amid the overall rainstorm of modern culture. Many diverse people will need to huddle together and take shelter under that same umbrella. The bigger the umbrella, the more people can be included underneath it.

Congregational leaders hold this umbrella high for all to see and experience. Some may come and go from the shelter of the umbrella. Others will stand continually within its boundaries. All will be welcome. Underneath the umbrella people can work and play, act or serve, in any way they wish. They can work together to celebrate and enlarge the umbrella. If people go beyond the umbrella, they are still good people, but they do not share the same umbrella anymore.

The primary task of congregational leadership in the twenty-first century will be to lift high this "basic umbrella of congregational life." Leading clergy and laity need not be the originators of the basic boundaries, but they must be the chief articulators of the basic boundaries. The congregation as a whole will regularly define, refine, and celebrate the boundaries in their annual meetings. The leadership lifts the umbrella for all to see in the daily life of the congregation. As people take initiative for growth and mission, and as diversity and change emerge as dominant features of congregational life, leading clergy and laity can motivate, train, and coach their ministries. They need not waste energy making peace with the conflicting opinions and lifestyles of church "controllers," interpreting or enforcing denominational demands, or preserving an institutional heritage. They give energy to lifting high the "basic umbrella of congregational life," in which anything can happen—and happen instantly.

The following processes are designed to help congregations gain clarity about their basic boundaries. Each process prepares the congregation for the next process, and the subsequent process also helps test the conclusions of the first process. I recommend that you begin with the identification of Core Values. This will equip you for the second process to discern Bedrock Beliefs, since the values discerned will shape your future behavior and passionate conversation about beliefs. The energetic conversation about beliefs will also test your conclusions about the core values that the congregation really shares. Clarity about values and beliefs will prepare you for the discussion of Motivating Vision, which in turn will challenge and refine your understanding of Bedrock Beliefs. Ultimately, consensus around values, beliefs, and vision will allow the church to clearly perceive its dynamic Key Mission for the future.

It will probably be helpful right now to turn to the final section of the process (titled "The End of the Process . . . the Beginning of a Journey") and read it carefully. Please keep in mind the following:

1. *Participants need to clearly understand the reason for the exercise and the goal of the process.* You may wish to explain the introduction to this resource and employ the umbrella symbol as a visual image and guide.

2. *Involve as many people as possible in the process.* Consensus should intentionally seek to include marginal members and fringe participants of the church, plus listening disciplines among the general public.

3. *Have fun.* Build the process around informal table fellowship. Develop a corporate sense of humor that helps people laugh at themselves and each other. This will help people become as honest and candid as possible.

4. *Maximize communication.* Sometimes the processes can be

quite stressful and leave congregational gatherings or focus groups with lingering dissonance. The best way to help people work through their feelings is to multiply opportunities for informal, one-to-one conversations.

5. *Be patient with redundancy.* Original insights and ideas are vital, but confirmation of these ideas among others is even more important. No one should be embarrassed by simply agreeing with what another has said, just as no one should be judged for articulating a different opinion.

6. *Identify what sticks out.* On the one hand, look for trends and continuities. These will help move the process toward consensus. On the other hand, look for anomalies and ideas that do not seem to fit anywhere. These will challenge and refine the growing consensus, and may even lead to new strands of continuity.

7. *The discernment process is always messy.* It never follows a distinct blueprint and is rarely neat and tidy. Feelings that will only be resolved by conversation overflow from large gatherings and small groups. There will always be a degree of dissonance or unease. This is good. It motivates people to think and talk beyond the formal process itself. It requires planners to adapt the process to changing circumstance.

In the end, clarity regarding values, beliefs, vision, and mission will enable the congregation to build unity and enthusiasm for their church. The mission statement they develop will be pointed, distinct, and powerful. It will proclaim to the public exactly where they are going, and it will shape every ministry, program, or initiative of the church. The mission statement will capture the imaginations of the public, and the spiritual authenticity of the church will encourage their participation.

— 9 —
PREPARATION

The discernment process described in the following pages requires preparation. Always keep in mind that this is a consensus-building process intended to lay a foundation for creative action and long-range planning. It is not intended to be a conflict resolution process, since it will tend to increase stress in the congregation. Each stage in the process pushes the congregation members to become more honest and more vulnerable with each other. More than this, it will push the congregation to risk everything solely for the sake of the Gospel. If there are sharp conflicts between the pastor and the congregation, or among factions of the congregation, first seek to resolve those conflicts before following this discernment process. In the end, the discernment process should help the congregation experience deeper unity and greater joy, and it should motivate the congregation to become more adventurous in ministry than ever before. They will have discerned the boundaries beyond which no leader or ministry of the church can go, but within which any leader or ministry can take initiative at once.

The entire process may be introduced to the congregation in a variety of ways. It is vital, however, that core lay leaders and the pastor (or pastoral team) all support the process enthusiastically. At various points in the process the worship and committee life of the church will need to be intentionally customized to support the process, and they must be ready to adapt their customary habits and the congregational calendar. More than this, they must be prepared to experience increasing stress for a time. The growing honesty and vulnerability will touch upon their leadership and reveal some of the "growing edges" that they will need to address in the future. It is often helpful for the pastor (or pastoral team) and key lay leaders to form an informal, mutual support group for prayer and encouragement. This is not an administrative team. It is simply a vehicle to articulate anxieties and receive encouragement.

The process does require a planning team. The team does not need to be large (perhaps 5-8 members), and it should not seek to be representational of all the various subgroups and committees of the church. Sometimes the team may be composed strictly of volunteers, but it is usually best if at least some of the team are expressly invited to participate by the pastor or core lay leaders of the church. Planning team members should not be simply selected from the official board, and they are often found in the less-formal caring networks of the congregation or on the fringes of congregational life. Although the pastor or other staff members may meet with the planning team in the capacity of advisers or coaches, it is usually best if they do not lead the team or participate as full members. Planning team members should all have certain characteristics.

• *Credibility.* These are persons who are held in high regard by multiple groups of the church (age, gender, race, language, and educational background). They are perceived to be bridge builders of the church.

• *Spirituality.* These are persons who pursue disciplines of prayer, meditation, Bible study, and/or theological reflection. They are perceived to be informal coaches whose advice on spiritual matters is often sought by others.

• *Confidentiality.* These are persons who have good listening skills. People often spontaneously share with them personal concerns or joys.

Individual planning team members also have specific skills in public speaking, workshop leadership, publicity, or group process and leadership training. However, many specific tasks may be given by the planning team to others. As the process unfolds, the planning team will find that coordination and implementation are only a part of the real ministry. They will be called upon to constantly interpret, explain, and even defend the importance of the process itself for the future of the church.

Before the process begins, the planning team will need to devote several weeks (and perhaps months) to communicate the details and goals of the process to the congregation. It is vital that the congregation know who the members of the team are and that the team enjoy the enthusiastic support of the pastor, staff, and core lay leaders of the church. There is bound to be a measure of stress surrounding the process, because the outcomes cannot be predicted in advance. However, the planning team needs to initiate communication vehicles that will continue throughout the process and can interpret each stage and avoid misunderstandings. The process will be surrounded by prayer and become a focus of attention in every worship service. It is often helpful to choose a theme song for the process and create an identifiable logo that can draw attention to any printed communication.

The discernment process involves various kinds of gatherings and groups. The planning team may wish to explain to the congregation in advance the nature of these gatherings and groups so that people have some idea what to expect. This will also make it easier to recruit and train various group leaders that will be needed.

CONGREGATIONAL GATHERINGS

Congregational gatherings enable the greatest congregational diversity possible to synthesize data. Each stage in the process begins and ends with a congregational gathering. These are not business meetings. There will be no business agenda, no committee reports, no parliamentary procedure, and no voting. These gatherings are informal gatherings of the congregation to initiate a consensus-building process that will continue through small groups and teams—or that will conclude a consensus-building process by synthesizing the work of small groups and teams. Such congregational gatherings resemble rather large parties. They often begin with a meal, and desserts and refreshments are always readily available. Music may begin and end the gathering and occasionally interrupt the conversation.

Because these gatherings resemble parties rather than meetings, they tend to be messy. That is, the process of the gathering may sometimes go in unexpected directions, and there will inevitably be loose ends when it is over. Evaluation of the success of a congregational gathering also resembles the evaluation of a party rather than a meeting. Even amid all the surprises and loose ends of a party, a party is generally a success if it has:

- been enjoyable, safe, and fun.
- involved a diversity of people.
- helped participants bond and share more clearly their common identity.
- celebrated that common identity joyously.
- motivated participants to look forward to other opportunities for sharing.

Congregational gatherings (like the best parties) may at times become very serious or poignant. There may also be times of stress or disagreement among participants. The poignancy of the gathering, or the stress of disagreement, may linger after the gathering, and it will be important to maximize opportunities for person-to-person conversation in the life of the church to follow up on these moments. In the end, however, a successful congregational gathering will send people home with a conviction that the experience was a good time.

There is no simple rule for the minimum number of people who should be present in the congregational gatherings in order to pursue the consensus-building process. Remember that there will be other small groups and gatherings in the process, so that those who miss a large gathering will not be left behind. The process intentionally builds a measure of redundancy into it, and this helps others keep involved despite their busy lives. One rule of thumb in planning a congregational gathering is to aim at a minimum attendance of one-third of the regular worshiping congregation(s) as counted on a typical week in November. However, keep in mind that the involvement of as many marginal members and infrequent worship attenders as possible is also important. The content of conversation will vary in congregational gatherings, but there are some common features for which the planning team can generally prepare:

1. *Setting:* Participants should sit in table groups of 5-10 people. Some form of name tag should be worn by everyone. Although families may wish to sit together, use the name tags to mix the seating. Avoid cliques sitting at tables, and try to mix marginal members among core participants. Refreshments should

be always available, and participants should feel free to help themselves at any time. The walls of the room need to accept taped newsprint for display.

2. *Tools: Two overhead projectors* will be invaluable. Use oversize screens or the walls. Each projector should be equipped with several *blank transparencies and colored markers* and be staffed by someone who can help synthesize table group reporting. *Multiple sheets of newsprint* should be available for each table group, plus good, dark *marking pens and masking tape.* One *microphone* will almost certainly be needed for the leader. Ideally an additional cordless microphone could be passed to each table group during reporting. *Taped music* might be played softly during the experience (secular or sacred, energetic or meditative), and overhead projections for well-known songs can be used occasionally during the gathering time. The ideal would be to have a musician to help lead singing. *Printed summaries* with the results of past stages in the process—or the results of small group discussion—should be placed in quantity on every table.

3. *Worship:* Begin the gathering with prayer and song. If the gathering is held on a Sunday, the regular worship might be customized and abbreviated for the process. Children should be included in the worship experience.

4. *Childcare:* During the gathering, children under 10 years old probably need an alternative time and space. It is helpful if one member of the planning team bears key responsibility to organize childcare. One component of this alternative time might be drawing or coloring on a theme related to the congregational gathering. The children's pictures might be shared during the gathering to inspire the adults.

5. *Leadership:* The planning team provides leadership for the gathering. Aside from the tasks of preparation and welcoming, one or more persons will need to introduce and facilitate the general process of the gathering. Others need to be flexibly available to coach table groups or answer emerging questions.

6. *Introduction:* Each gathering should be introduced and the process explained. This should not be a long introduction, but it should stress:

a. the importance of the process for the future of the church;
b. a summary of the key learnings so far;

   c. a clear statement of the focus and goals of the current gathering;

   d. introduction of the support team for the gathering; and

   e. a review of the anticipated process.

You may wish to invite questions for clarification or simply refer questions to the other team members who are available in the room.

   7. *Process:* Most congregational gatherings follow a similar pattern and are based on an imaginative simulation exercise. The basic pattern will be:

   a. story

   b. table group conversation

   c. reporting to the large group

Music and singing may occasionally break the pattern. There is no formal break and participants are encouraged to get up for refreshments whenever they wish. Each table group will choose their own recorder and reporter. The facilitator of the process does need to expedite the process as sensitively and rapidly as possible. Staff for the overhead projectors can participate in table groups but will need to synthesize ideas as the reporting occurs.

   8. *Closure:* It is important to finish on time, for this will encourage future participation in the process. However, before the gathering ends, stress the following:

   a. thanks for participation;

   b. promise that printed summaries will be speedily and widely shared;

   c. future opportunities for person-to-person conversation; and

   d. prayers of thanksgiving and intercession.

Depending on the nature of the group, you may wish to consider inviting the children to rejoin you for this time of closure.

FOCUS GROUPS

Focus groups enable core church participants to discern their values, beliefs, and vision. Focus groups usually attract the core participants of the church who are regularly involved in worship. Many of the focus group participants will have participated in the congregational gathering or will have intentionally sought to know the results of the gathering. They will see the focus group as a primary way they can build upon the work of the congregational gathering or as a way that they can get on board with what is happening.

1. *Goal:* Active congregational participants often do not know, or have not shared with others, the core values, essential beliefs, or motivating vision that lie at the heart of their church involvement. Your goal is to help them articulate what really motivates their Christian lives and shapes their church commitment so they can share this with others in a way that builds mutual understanding and consensus.

2. *Strategy:* This is a very informal strategy of intentionally guided conversation. Each group will gather for just one evening in a private home. Make introductions, serve refreshments, and then share responses to the questions identified below. While a record of responses will be kept, no names will be associated with them.

There should be no more than 10-12 people in a group. Participants should feel free to sign up following a church service with the hosts of their choice. In order to avoid the perpetuation of cliques, the planning team may wish to publicize the names of all the focus group leaders, offer choices regarding time or place, but assign leaders to groups later. Group leaders can be encouraged to specifically invite persons who have been irregular or inactive in church participation to join a group. Focus group leaders may include members of the planning team, and they should all be selected using the same criteria of credibility, spirituality, and confidentiality.

The group leaders are host or hostess to the gathering and function as group facilitators. Their responsibilities, other than hospitality, include:

a. get the conversation going.
b. help the group focus on the process at hand and avoid sidetracks (guidance is provided for each stage).
c. help the conversation move on to the next question.
d. encourage people who are shy or quiet to speak.

e. record the responses to the questions.
f. share the summary of responses with the planning team.

3. *Process:* The focus group leader should arrange to begin and end with prayer. Introduce the evening by:

a. explaining the importance of the process for the future of the church.
b. sharing the printed results from the previous congregational gathering.
c. explaining the process for the current group.

Sometimes there may be a degree of emotion (negative or positive) during the group experience, and this should not be feared. The leader should offer support and encouragement to the group and remind or reassure participants of confidentiality. Only the summary of responses will be forwarded to the planning team. The broader discussion will not be shared, nor will any comments be identified with individual participants.

4. *Timeline:* The focus group meets on only one evening, for a minimum of two hours (for example, 7:00 P.M.–9:00 P.M. or 8:00 P.M.–10:00 P.M.). Once the group meeting is complete, participants have no obligation for further involvement in the process, except what they choose to do. Some focus groups may need to be scheduled or located in nursing homes or other institutions in order to facilitate the participation of members of the church who cannot easily participate.

5. *Reporting:* The host or hostess should arrange to keep a record of the group responses. Very soon after the focus group meets, while responses are still fresh in the host's memory, a summary of the results should be given to the planning team. Simply identify the question and list the responses. No further collation or interpretation is necessary. The planning team may wish to summarize responses on newsprint for display in the church vestibule or newsletter to stimulate further conversation in the church. All responses will be gathered for the concluding congregational gathering of each stage.

INTERVIEW TEAMS

Interview teams interview inactive and marginal members of the church to discern their perceptions of congregational life. Since focus groups tend to attract core participants in church life, rather than marginal members or fringe participants, the consensus-building process must intentionally reach out to include them. Some may involve themselves in the congregational gatherings by responding to invitations in church newsletters, mailings, or telephone invitations. However, it is crucial to listen to the perspectives from the margins for two reasons. First, these perspectives will broaden the basic boundaries of church life and help build a unity and enthusiasm that will draw these people closer to congregational life. Second, these perspectives will reality test the growing consensus of the congregation and challenge them to true authenticity.

1. *Goal:* Most people who drift to the margins of congregational life do so because the church is somehow not meeting their personal, spiritual needs. Your goal is to listen to their perceptions and experiences of congregational life in order to discover how their views affirm or contradict the values, beliefs, and vision identified by core participants.

2. *Strategy:* This is a rather formal strategy in which a team of two persons makes appointments to visit inactive or marginal members in their homes, for a very limited time, solely to listen to their views. A list of potential contacts can usually be developed by the church office. The number of interviews will vary from church to church. The goal is not to speak to every marginal member or fringe participant (an impossible task in such a short time), but to gain a core sampling of opinion or perspective. Although it is possible to gain responses to these questions in a telephone interview, it is far better to have a face-to-face conversation. Communication is better and more revealing. Strongly urge your contacts to have a personal conversation with you.

Telephone to make appointments. Explain that the church is engaged in a process of planning for the future and that the church believes that their views are important. You would like to ask them some key questions, which will require about 15–30 minutes of their time. Be clear from the beginning that this visit is not concerned with fund raising, nominations, or volunteer recruitment, but solely to gain their views on matters related to the future of the church.

When you arrive for the appointment, state the time you intend to leave. Do try to be flexible if the person visited wishes you to stay for tea or a longer conversation. However, even in a longer conversation, keep the focus on the questions you are asking. Assure the person visited that their responses will be completely anonymous and no name will be connected with the views they express.

In a few cases, inactive or marginal members may express some grievance or anger toward the church. Urge them to contact the minister or an elder to share their concern, but be clear that your role is not conflict resolution. You are not there to defend the church, mediate a conflict, or provide counseling. You are there to listen.

3. Timeline: The interview task should be completed about a week prior to the concluding congregational gathering for each stage. This allows time for the planning team to synthesize information for that gathering.

4. Reporting: Each team should share a summary of responses with the planning team as soon as possible following an interview. The information will be fresh in their minds. They should feel free to add interpretations and comments. Do not indicate the names of the persons interviewed.

SURVEY TEAMS

Survey teams survey the opinions and perceptions of those who use church facilities. In order to further reality test and broaden the consensus that is emerging in the process, it is valuable to listen to the views of the general public. There are two strategies to do this. The first strategy is to deploy *survey teams* who can do a basic marketing survey of those who use church facilities. Many churches rent or loan space to community groups. These people know where the church is but do not know, or perhaps do not care, about the church itself. It is helpful to know who they are and why they feel as they do. The second strategy involves listening-prayer triads, which will be described shortly.

1. Goal: Many community people who use the church facilities are not involved in the congregational life and mission. Your goal is to discern what would motivate them to participate in a Christian congregation and what their perceptions of this congregation honestly are.

2. *Strategy:* This is a simple market survey strategy that you may have experienced in supermarkets and shopping malls. Your group will form teams of 2 people, rotating their presence to cover each weekday evening. Form as many teams of 2 as needed to lighten the workload and cover rental uses. Station yourselves with pen and clipboard at the major entrances to the building. As people come and go, politely ask them to step aside for just a few moments. Explain that you are conducting a survey for the church and that you have the permission from the organizers of the particular groups renting space from the church. Invite their immediate, candid responses to the following questions. Assure them that their comments are given entirely anonymous.

a. In what church or religious organization do you currently participate?
b. Based on what you have seen or heard in the community, how would you describe the congregation that owns this building? (Please be candid. Your comments may be positive or negative.)
c. What do you think is the *most important* thing a Christian church should be or do?

Write their responses on your clipboard. Thank them for their time. Do not hand out any literature. If they have any questions about the church, invite them to phone the church office. Do not become sidetracked in conversations.

3. *Timeline:* Before teams begin, obtain permission for such survey work from the organizers of the groups that rent space in the building. Divide weekday evenings among the teams. Teams should be in place at least 15 minutes before evening programs and remain about 30 minutes after evening programs. Because these surveys are fairly general in nature, the work may continue through the first two stages of the discernment process. However, the survey process should be completed in time for the *vision* discernment process in stage 3.

4. Reporting: Collect the response summaries from the teams. Simply identify the question, and list the responses. No further collation or interpretation is required. The planning team will feed the information into the discernment process as it is gathered.

LISTENING-PRAYER TRIADS

This involves listening to the public and observing public behavior to discern key issues and needs. The second way the congregation can both reality test and broaden the emerging consensus is through intentional listening strategies among the general public. This particular technique will build on the results of the survey teams during stages 1 and 2 and be deployed in the *vision* process of stage 3. Many people in the community have no contact with, or even interest in, the church. Nevertheless, many of them are yearning for some form of spiritual fulfillment, and all of them have needs that deserve to be addressed. God loves them, and is already at work among them. The question is: How can the church participate with Jesus in ministry to the world?

1. Goal: People in North America have an interest in spiritual matters, and they are preoccupied with many pressing issues and needs. The church is often ignorant or unclear about their yearning. Your goal is to listen to conversations and observe behavior in order to discern the questions, issues, or needs that weigh upon the hearts and minds of the people "out there." The call of Jesus can be heard in the midst of these yearnings, and your mission agenda will be better informed.

2. Strategy: This simple strategy is a discipline of listening and intercessory prayer. Deploy as many teams of three persons as possible. Volunteers can choose their own partners, but the steering committee may wish to ensure a demographic diversity to the group (young and old, male and female, and so on).

Each triad determines its own process, but the basic strategy is as follows:

a. Covenant together to devote a single block of time each week for a discipline of listening and prayer (for example, a specific evening in the week).

b. Meet at the home of a triad member. Spend 15–20 minutes reading a portion of scripture from the Acts of the Apostles, and pray for God to guide you that evening.

c. Go to any public place (arena, donut shop, mall, restaurant, or other place). Spend about an hour or more intentionally eavesdropping on conversations and observing behavior. (In some places you may wish to obtain permission from store management.)

d. Say nothing to anyone! Keep conversation among the triad to a minimum. Focus on what is said and done around you. If you wish to keep notes, do so unobtrusively.

e. Return to the home of a triad member. Talk about what you saw and heard. Try to read between the lines to discern deeper motives and needs.

f. Intentionally pray aloud together for the complete strangers you have encountered. Ask God to open your hearts to understand them better. Ask God to bless them and help them. Try to be as specific as possible about their needs.

3. *Timeline:* There is no reason why this process should be limited to stage 3 of the discernment process, but it needs to be completed in time for the congregational gathering that completes the visioning process of stage 3. The information gathered can be shared in worship, focus groups, and the larger group process. Each triad should covenant to maintain this discipline for at least 6 weeks (one block of time each week). You will probably need to spend about 3 hours on each weekly experience.

4. *Reporting:* Each triad should keep a journal of their experiences and thoughts. Itemize in the journal your insights into the questions, concerns, or needs people are facing. Itemize in your journal the spiritual questions or religious ideas that are "out there" among the public. Key your journal onto computer disk as you go through the process.

Communicate what you learn to the minister, who can incorporate these insights into the prayers, sermons, or chancel dramas of the worship services. The planning team will summarize your triad insights for use in congregational gatherings.

These different strategies will be used in various ways in each of the discernment stages that follow. The planning team can prepare in advance by recruiting volunteers who have a special interest in these various group tasks.

I noted already that the stress level tends to increase as the discernment process unfolds. This is because the movement from sharing values to sharing beliefs to sharing visions leads the congregation progressively to greater honesty and vulnerability. Indeed, once the congregation enters stage 3 to wait for visions to emerge, control of church life has begun to leave the hands of the congregational leaders entirely and become open to the radical inbreaking of the Holy Spirit. This is stress indeed!

I can now point out how the deployment of the above strategies in this process also increase stress progressively in the life of the congregation:

• It is fairly easy to hold a congregational gathering with good food and good company.

• It is not too difficult to recruit focus group leaders and deploy focus groups to discuss special topics. After all, these tend to include core participants who already know and like each other.

• Recruiting volunteers for interview teams and incorporating their learnings in the process raises the stress level significantly. Perspectives about the church that are unpleasant or challenging may emerge! However, volunteers who can do this task well are usually found without too much difficulty.

• Developing the survey teams, however, increases the stress to church life yet another degree. The marketing survey itself is relatively easy, but the process of reality testing congregational self-perceptions against the true image of the church in the general public can be frightening to some. Just as many public opinion polls become controversial, so also the results of this survey can spark some heated debate.

• Finally, the listening-prayer triads can become the most difficult and stressful strategy in the whole process. Some people may deliberately confuse *listening* with *eavesdropping* and feel moral outrage. Others may find spoken prayer for complete strangers to be difficult. Still others may find the insights they gain into the needs of the public to be extraordinarily challenging. And many will feel stressed to discover that addressing the needs of the public may force them to change habits and traditions.

Fortunately, by the time the visioning process is begun, the congregation will have laid a good foundation for communication and faith through their emerging consensus about values and beliefs. Persevere with patience and prayer, and these strategies will become easier.

— 10 —

CORE VALUES

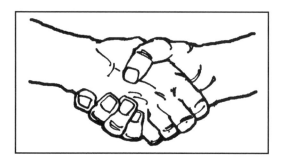

T he core values of congregational life are the preferences or choices that are consistently prioritized in the behavior of the participants. These choices may be deliberate and carefully considered, but they must also be spontaneous. They are apparent in the largest projects and in the smallest circumstances. They are often revealed most clearly in unplanned, unrehearsed experiences. Core values shape the normative behavior of congregational participants within, and beyond, the church. These core values make the behavior of congregational participants predictable, whether they are at home, at work, or at play.

Core values are not just ideals toward which congregational participants strive, but real preferences that congregational participants actually make in daily life. Core values are not just goals that congregational participants seek to achieve, but real choices that shape the lifestyles of congregational participants individually and collectively.

The discernment of core values may not be easy. First, the congregation must move beyond their understanding of how Jesus wants them to be, to discover how they actually are. Second, the congregation must move beyond how they imagine that they behave, to discover the truth about how they truly behave. And third, the congregation must move beyond how they market themselves to the public, to discover how the public truly perceives them to be. In other words, core values are not a matter of wishful thinking, imaginative self-interpretation, or projected self-image. Core values are a matter of consistent choices that shape the daily, monthly, and yearly behavior of the people in the congregation—both individually and collectively.

Once the core values of congregational life become clear, the congregation can begin to address issues of morale, method, relationship, and cooperation. Low morale, poor planning, broken relationships, and inability to cooperate in congregational projects all result from ambiguity about values. Decision making on matters of real importance becomes timid, slow, or even impossible—and the congregation preoccupies itself with ever more trivial matters. Lack of clarity about core values is revealed when meetings never seem to address matters of substance, last far too long, and habitually defer decisions to ad hoc committees or subsequent meetings. Other corporate addictions are then allowed to block congregational action and may even pose as "traditions," which in fact contradict congregational identity and frustrate potential congregational leadership. Here are some examples of what core values might be. You may want to make a similiar list on an overhead projection transparency.

Acceptance	Change	Community	Family
Equality	Joy	Excitement	Fun
Health	Love	Integrity	Mission
Morality	Respect	Knowledge	Growth
Stability	Freedom	Spirituality	Success
Beauty	Continuity	Children	Friends
Excellence	Peace	Quiet	Action
Humility	Witness	Helping	Future
Belonging	Past	Harmony	Now
Adventure	Ambition	Caring	Companionship
Courage	Dignity	Creativity	Compassion
Self-esteem	Honesty	Independence	Financial Security
Inner Peace	Laughter	Loyalty	Nurture
Passion	Reliability	Safety	Purposefulness
Serenity	Heritage	Security	Strength

The process to discern core values comprises four stages. The first stage involves one or more congregational gatherings. The second stage involves small groups, or focus groups, reflecting on transitional moments in the life of the church. The third stage involves testing the insights of the congregational gatherings through intentional conversations with marginal members of the church and the general public. The fourth stage builds final consensus within a congregational gathering.

Planners should anticipate two distinct flows of conversation in all four stages of the process:

1. *Analysis and Synthesis:* Part of the discernment process in every stage involves forced choice prioritization. These involve either/or decisions in which the core values are slowly narrowed or reduced to absolute essentials. Sometimes these forced choices are stressful to select, and the priorities are difficult to make. In focus groups or table groups, the negotiations can become heated. This stress is healthy. Sometimes it is helpful for participants to keep a record of precious values that have been set aside in the priorities list for later reference, or to keep a record of their feelings during the process.

The second part of the discernment process in every stage involves intentional inclusion of disparate values. These involve creative both/and decisions in which core values are blended with other core values to create a new, broader value. Often this is motivated by the recognition that unless a core value is enlarged, someone precious in our personal or community relationships will be excluded. As the list of core values becomes larger, or becomes redefined to be more inclusive, stress may emerge again as participants fear the core values of the church are becoming too diluted or vague. Sometimes it is helpful for people to share stories that illustrate a synthesis of ideas that has emerged only as a gut feeling of compassion for others.

This tension between analysis and synthesis will be present throughout the process, and it is important to address both sides of the tension. In the end, the key question is: What are the core values for which the most people will be willing to sacrifice everything?

2. *Reality and Desire:* Part of the discernment process in every stage involves uncovering the true values that may be hidden in the spontaneous behavior of the congregation and perhaps even denied by congregational participants. These tend to be "nega-

tive" values related to money, power, personal tastes, or other behavioral norms that have offended minorities in the congregation. Stress will emerge as some participants challenge the church to "face the truth about themselves" and refuse to claim values not clearly demonstrated in congregational life. It may be helpful to develop a second list of negative values about which participants are ashamed or negative behavioral patterns that participants know they must correct.

The second part of the discernment process, in every stage, involves identifying targets or goals that are highly prized. The congregation may not achieve these "positive values" all the time, but they intentionally strive to do so. Stress will emerge as participants reality check these values with marginal members and the general public. The real issue is not "which values do we believe better than others," but rather "which values are we ready to invest significant energy to achieve." In other words, the participants must measure their irrational enthusiasm for a value and identify their true passions.

This tension between reality and desire will be present throughout the process, and it is important to address both sides of the tension. In the end, the key question is: What are the core values to which this congregation passionately commits 100 percent of its energy?

STAGE 1: CONGREGATIONAL GATHERINGS

This first congregational gathering in the process is especially important, since it will set the tone for all future work. In preparing for the gathering, refer to the general guidelines found in the previous chapter. The introduction in this first gathering should include an overview of the entire discernment process and stress the importance of clarity about the "basic boundaries of congregational life" for future creativity and planning. The focus of this gathering is the discernment of core values.

1. Make handouts explaining the main themes of this section. This will help the leader introduce the topic.
2. Project on screens your list of possible core values. Give participants time to examine it and become familiar with what a core value might be. Participants should feel free to spontaneously add to the list. These additions can be written on transparency and projected by the second machine.

It may take a few moments of conversation for participants to fully grasp the concept of core values. Allow the table groups time to discuss it among themselves.

You are now ready to begin the learning and sharing process of the day. Read aloud or share in visual form the following story. Guide the table groups through each stage of the story. The time provided for discussion will vary from group to group. As you can imagine, you want to allow sufficient time for everyone in the table group to share, but you also need to move the process along quickly.

Imagine you are going on a journey across the continent. Like the early settlers of the West, you prepare yourselves to relocate to a new home. You do not know exactly where that new home will be, and you do not know exactly what challenges life in your new home will bring. All you know is that the journey will be long and arduous. Therefore, you pack all your belongings carefully in the wagon. Some things you are sure you will need, other things you think you might need, and still other things are packed because you cannot bear to leave them behind. At the start of the journey, you are not certain which is which.

Church growth is like a journey. You know you must change, but you do not know exactly how or where you will ultimately find yourselves. The baggage you load for the journey includes many values. Some are of greater importance, others of lesser importance. Some are clearly shared by everyone in the group. Others are not. Some are so important to an individual that, unless everyone shares that value, the individual cannot be part of the group. Others are so important to an individual that, unless the individual has the freedom to cherish that value in the group, that person cannot be part of the group. Only the journey itself can test which values are most important to all.

Step 1

Your small group of people will share a wagon. It will be a long journey, and you cannot take everything with you. Make as comprehensive a list as possible of all the values each person holds dear in your small group. You may use the list provided as a starting point. Add to it any value you wish. This is your inventory of all the values you hold. Some values may be precious to a few, others to many. Some values may be more important to some than to others. List them all. Don't try to prioritize them. Let's just get the big picture.

Step 2

Now imagine that you are loading the wagons to begin your journey. Remember, your group must share the wagon. You cannot take everything with you. Together choose the top ten values that you want to carry in your wagon on the journey. Set the others aside for the moment. We'll see how full the wagon is afterwards, and if we can load a few more values on, we will! Sometimes values in our inventory look so much alike that we can put them together creatively. Be sure, however, that they are still clearly understood! If so, load them!

Step 3

Good news! Even after loading the top ten values onto the wagon, we still have some room. Choose two more values that are precious to the entire group and add those to the wagon. Now you have twelve.

Step 4

Now imagine your wagons are crossing the desert on their journey west. The horses are exhausted. Water is running low. The wagon wheels are sinking into the sand. The horses are getting tired, and you can't push any harder. You need to lighten the load! From the top twelve values loaded onto your shared wagon, select the seven most important values you will keep to carry forward. Yes, it is permissible to combine two values into a larger value that includes the essence of both—but make sure that it is still clearly understandable by everyone in the group! Core values that become too vague will be like stale food that has lost its nutritional value: you can carry it a long way, but it will do you no good to eat it! And yes, it is permissible to change your mind and carry forward a value that was not originally among the top twelve. We'll send a rider back to pick it up.

Step 5

You have come to the mountains. They are very steep, and it is very cold. Snow is falling heavily. You must keep moving or be trapped in the snow. You must lighten the wagons one more time. It may mean that you will be forced to off-load precious food or clothing. This will mean discomfort. You will run the risk of leaving behind something that you might unexpectedly, desperately need in the future. Nevertheless, in order to keep going, you must. From the top seven values loaded on your shared wagon, now select the top five absolutely most important values you will carry to your final destination. This time you are too far on your journey to send a rider back for values left behind. You may not combine or add values. You must prioritize five from the seven.

Note: In some cases, the stress of the exercise may become too powerful for group participants at the point. If this is the case, skip to Step 7.

Step 6

It has been a long journey. You have crossed prairies full of mud and mountains full of snow. You are weary but determined to press forward to your destination. Slowly, your small group has bonded together, but it has not always been easy. Negotiation has sometimes been heated, and compromise has sometimes been painful. Nevertheless, your experiences of suffering and sensitivity to one another give you confidence. And yet here is one last unexpected obstacle! While crossing a glacier, a huge fissure has opened before you. It is miles and miles long and twenty feet wide. You cannot go around it (too far). You cannot build a bridge over it (no wood). And you certainly cannot stay where you are (too cold). There is only one thing to do. You must abandon the wagons altogether, throw ropes across the fissure, and ferry the members of your group over the chasm! Unfortunately, each member of the group can only carry what will fit on his or her back! From the top five absolutely most important values left on the wagon, choose the three values you simply cannot live without. You may not combine or add values. You must prioritize three from the five.

Step 7

Invite each small group to share their chosen values. List all twelve in rank order, indicating the top three, top five, and top seven. Write them on newsprint for all to see. The scribes at the projectors should copy the top three values from each group and project them for all to see. Let each table group take a few moments to discuss them among themselves. Are there common trends? Are their surprises? Share these insights as a large group. The facilitator needs to encourage people to be brief. If possible, provide a cordless microphone so that speakers do not have to move from their table. Their comments do not need to be written and projected.

Step 8

Let each table group take time to invite individuals to share the stress they experienced during the exercise. Are there hurt feelings? Are there deep regrets? Are there unexpected agreements or disagreements? Now share some of these with the large group. For example, how many people in the room made choices in which:

a. They sacrificed self for the sake of others? Which values?
b. They needed to stand fast for self-fulfillment? Which values?
c. They chose to compromise for the sake of the group? Which values?

Keep a record of the values identified in answer to the above questions on transparency as they accumulate, and project them for all to see.

Step 9

Let each table group compile a list of negative values that may have emerged in the discussion. These negative values are habitual behavior patterns, preferences, or choices that congregational participants deeply regret but to which they resort in times of stress or confusion. These negative values represent corporate addictions that will need to be intentionally resisted for positive core values to be fully transparent in the life of the congregation. Keep a record of these addictions as they emerge for all to see.

Step 10

Now return to the story. There is a happy ending yet to come.

Good news! Another wagon train followed your path. You have blazed a trail and shown them the way. They not only brought along all the values you had to leave behind at the start of your journey, but they also picked up all the values you were forced to discard along the way. You have learned what you really needed, and you have learned what you really didn't need. And you have learned from your mistakes! You now know better what you once thought was less important but realized later was all important! Knowing what you know now, and from among all possible values, each small group should rank in order of importance the top ten values they cherish above all. This new top ten list may include values from the original twelve or other values. It may also include values that have been combined (and are still clear), and even entirely new values that never appeared before.

Write these down, and collect the top ten lists of each table group for future use. This is how the top ten lists from each table group will be used: (1) Publicize them in the congregation through the worship bulletin or newsletter, post them on the walls of the sanctuary, invite comment and discussion, and pray about them intentionally in every worship service. (2) Prepare copies to hand out to the focus groups and interview teams coming in stages 2 and 3.

Top ten lists should be publicized with the congregation and shared with focus groups and interview teams as they emerge from the table groups of the congregational gathering. The redundancies within the lists should remain. This will allow each person to see and interpret emerging patterns. The planning team may wish to collate the lists in a more compact form for the final congregational gathering.

Step 11

Close the gathering with song and prayer. Pray especially for those who made sacrifices during the simulation exercise. Pray for the Holy Spirit to continue to inspire your thinking about core values. Remind participants that (1) opportunities to further discuss and refine core values are coming in the weeks ahead and (2) future congregational meetings will continue to define, refine, and celebrate core values.

Invite people to participate in coming focus groups. Thank them for their participation in this event.

STAGE 2: FOCUS GROUPS

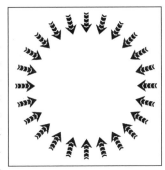

Develop as many focus groups as you wish. In preparing for focus groups, refer to the general guidelines in the previous chapter. Provide each focus group with a copy of the final top ten lists of core values that emerged from the congregational gathering. There will be a list from each table group.

Step 1

Let people introduce themselves. Pray together.

Step 2

Examine the top ten lists that emerged from the congregational gathering. Are patterns emerging? Do these patterns reveal anything about the general perspective, attitude, or lifestyle of the congregation? Do some values seem to stand out, or do some not seem to fit with the others? What does this mean?

Examine also the list of negative values or corporate addictions that has emerged from table groups along the way. Again, are patterns emerging? Do these patterns reveal specific contradictions in congregational life that block the full transparency of positive core values?

Step 3

Every congregation experiences times of great stress due to some transition or crisis. Make a list of stressful congregational times over the past ten years. These stressful times may be joyous or tragic, and they may have resulted in good feelings or bad feelings. In times of stress, people behave in certain natural or habitual ways, and these behavior patterns reveal what they truly value. From this list of stressful times, choose one for discussion. Remember that time together.

What caused the stress?

How did people react to the stress?

What resulted from the stressful time?

What core values are revealed by the behavior of the congregation?

Now answer these questions:

In times of stress, this congregation seems to naturally do certain things—and these natural reactions seem to reveal certain values.

This is what we always do:_____.

These are the real values such habits reveal:_____

_____.

Now compare these behavior patterns, and the values they reveal, to the top ten lists that emerged from the congregational gathering.

Are there positive values that should be added to the top ten lists?

Are there negative realities that contradict the values in the top ten lists?

Invite vigorous dialogue about what is confirmed or contradicted from the top ten lists from the congregational gathering.

Step 4

Finally, complete your focus group activity by developing a fresh top ten list of core values that you believe represents the collective priorities of the whole congregation. Synthesize your learnings from all the table group lists from the congregational gathering and from your discussion of congregational behavioral patterns in times of crisis. These are the positive values that you believe the congregation will give 100 percent of their energy to fulfill.

Your conversation may also have uncovered a list of negative values revealed by habitual behavior patterns about which you feel ashamed or embarrassed. These may contradict the positive values you enthusiastically support. Make a second list of these negative values.

This is how the information from the focus groups will be used: (1) Publicize the synthesized top ten list in the congregation through the worship bulletin or newsletter. Post them on the walls of the sanctuary, invite comment and discussion, and pray about them intentionally in every worship service. (2) Do the same for any secondary list of negative values that has emerged.

Step 5

Close your focus group with prayer. Pray for each other by name and for the future of the church. Pray especially for God's strength to break habitual behavior patterns that reinforce negative values and for the wisdom to pursue the top ten list of positive values wholeheartedly.

STAGE 3: INTERVIEW TEAMS

Make a list of people who are on the fringes of congregational life (inactive, rarely attend worship, do not participate in any small group of the church, or do not contribute regularly toward the church budget). By telephone, invite the participation of individuals from the list. Mail or deliver the final, prioritized top ten lists from stage 1, and invite people on the fringes of congregational life to:

a. circle those values that they perceive to be very true in their experience of the congregation;

b. cross out those values that they perceive to not be true at all from their own experience of the congregation;

c. place a question mark beside those values that have neither been confirmed nor contradicted in their experience of the congregation.

Then ask them to return the sheets to the church. Responses should be unsigned and anonymous. Compare these responses to the emerging pattern of values priorities.

Alternatively, make appointments with selected individuals from the list who have been associated with the church for at least ten years. Share with them the collected focus group responses, and invite them to comment on the extent to which they agree or disagree with those responses. Responses should be turned in without names in order to protect respondents' anonymity.

Now collate the feedback you have gathered. Indicate which values from the top ten lists were most often confirmed, which values were most often contradicted, and which values were neither confirmed nor contradicted.

This is how the information from the interview teams will be used: (1) Publicize the collated responses in the congregation through the worship bulletin or newsletter, post them on the walls of the sanctuary, invite comment and discussion, and pray about them intentionally in every worship service. All comments should be strictly anonymous. (2) The planning team will integrate this information with the "negative core values" (habitual behavior patterns or choices for which congregational participants express deep regret, but to which they seem to resort in times of stress or confusion). These will be shared again in the final congregational gathering.

STAGE 4: CONGREGATIONAL CONSENSUS

In preparation for this final gathering, the planning team needs to collate and synthesize the emerging information to facilitate its use by a large group in a limited time span. The raw data has been shared with the congregation throughout the process, including seeming redundancies and inconsistencies, in order to allow each congregational participant opportunity to reflect privately on emerging patterns and trends. Planning team members will have had a chance to participate in many spontaneous conversations about the material. Now, however, the planning team needs to synthesize the data. Organize the collage of information into a series of key thematic words, followed by a string of related words that seem to describe and refine the theme. Think of each key word as a comet with a tail. The key word is further defined and clarified by the words that follow it. The planning team will review the original top ten values from the table groups of the first congregational gathering, plus the refined lists from focus groups. They will also review the negative core values identified through the process, especially as perceived values have been tested by the interview teams. Distribute this synthesis a week prior to the final congregational gathering. The synthesis might look like this:

POSITIVE CORE VALUES

Identify *five* core values using any key words or groups of words you wish.

Spirituality, prayer, inner peace, godliness, spiritual journey, spiritual growth, music.

Nurturing, comfort, caring, flexibility, unity, support, responsibility, friendship.

Inclusivity, community, respect, acceptance, trust, equality.

Family, marriage, church family, children, youth, faith family, sense of belonging.

Communication, respect, acceptance, change, knowledge, prayer, honesty, clarity, healthy disagreement.

Commitment, mission, time, talent, money, global mission, goals, courage, risk, hope.

Leadership, courage, models for others, wisdom, growth, outreach.

Love, caring, trust, respect, joy, health.

Faith, spiritual growth, Bible, interactive study, education, personal growth.

Sense of humor, joy, risk, courage, humility, acceptance, flexibility.

Hospitality, sharing food, welcoming, togetherness, interpersonal relations, help.

Outreach, mission, witness, change, caring, goals.

Growth, overall health, wisdom, personal resources, life skills.

NEGATIVE CORE VALUES

Identify *three* negative values using any key words or groups of words you wish.

Control, competition, power cliques, intolerance, too few do too much.

Insensitivity, gossip, feeling left out, dwelling on shortcomings of others, too few doing pastoral care.

Scapegoating, blaming others, blaming leaders, taking sides, burnout.

Poor communication, gossip, unable to keep people involved, dropping out.

Self-centeredness, lack of global mission, lack of caring for people beyond church, fewer youth.

Call a congregational gathering for the sole purpose of identifying the core values of the congregation. By the time the gathering is held, most people in attendance should have been involved in, or knowledgeable of, one or more of the previous stages in the process. The purpose of the gathering is to discern and celebrate the core values of the congregation. Remind people that the basic boundaries of congregational life are never carved in stone. They will evolve as the congregation evolves. The primary role of future annual congregational meetings will be to further define, refine, and celebrate the evolving umbrella of congregational life.

You may wish to consider incorporating this congregational gathering in the context of Sunday morning worship. This surrounds the process in prayer, anchors the process in scripture, and allows music and song to reinforce the emerging list of core values. The worship service and gathering will likely be longer than a typical worship service, but many will prefer this to a separate meeting. Moreover, participation may well be more diverse and attendance improved. If you decide to combine this gathering with Sunday worship, consider the following: (1) Multiply music and song beyond the ordinary, and encourage as much participation as possible. (2) Form a panel of three participants in the total process (6-10 minutes). The panel might include a member of the planning team, a focus group leader, and an interview team member. Ask them to briefly reflect on:

- their feelings about the process (both positive and negative);
- surprises in the information that has been gathered (pleasant or unpleasant); and
- moments of insight into "why we do the things we do."

(3) Create a visual display (projected or graphic) of an umbrella, within or underneath which key words can be placed as core values are celebrated during this gathering. (Color coded raindrops labeled with key words can sometimes visually capture the emerging list of core values for the congregation. Gray storm clouds can sometimes visually capture the negative addictive behavior patterns that the congregation realizes they need to intentionally avoid.)

Step 1: Introduction

As an insert in the worship bulletin or as a handout to participants as they gather, share a summary of the process, identify the task for this gathering, and indicate how it will link with the overall discernment of the "basic umbrella of congregational life." The summary may look like this:

OUR CORE VALUES!

A *core value* is the preference or choice consistently reflected in the behavior of congregational participants in their daily lives.

How We Got to This Point!

The congregation wanted to gain clarity and unity around the core values, bedrock beliefs, and motivating vision, which together form their congregational identity. This foundation will enable the congregation to do future long-range planning with confidence.

1. We had a congregational gathering to identify the collage of values we prized most highly.
2. Focus groups further refined and prioritized these values.
3. Interview teams tested these values with marginal members and church dropouts.
4. The planning team synthesized the results you see today.

Our Task Today!

The worshiping congregation has divided into clusters. Each cluster has the same task. Each cluster has the same information. Each cluster is free to rearrange or redefine the "values" words or add to the list anything important that they feel is missing. Turn this page over to view the collected information.

1. *Identify the top 5 positive core values of the congregation.* Positive core values are the choices people give 100 percent of their energy to live up to in daily living.
2. *Identify the top 3 negative addictions of the congregation.* Negative core values are the self-defeating habits people fall back into in times of stress.

The planning team will collect, synthesize, and present the results of our cluster work during the worship that will follow. When your cluster is finished, please return to the sanctuary to pray for the work of the church.

Where Do We Go from Here?

The next step in our process will be to gain clarity and unity around our bedrock beliefs. We will follow a similar strategy of congregational gatherings and focus groups. Clarification of our motivating vision will take place later. Concrete strategic and long-range planning will follow.

   A primary role for all future congregational meetings will be to continue to define, refine, and celebrate our core values, bedrock beliefs, and motivating vision as our congregation grows, changes, and evolves.

Thank you for your continued companionship
on our spiritual journey into the future!

Step 2: Discernment

If the congregational gathering is separate from the worship service, divide the gathering into table groups. Review the synthesis of the planning team, as well as the top ten lists from the first congregational gathering and subsequent focus groups. Compare these with the feedback of interview teams and the negative values, or addictions, that have been noted along the way. Ask each group to discuss how these responses challenge their sincerity about the core values identified. In light of these comments, and using the top ten lists from the first gathering as a starting point, ask each table group to create a fresh list of the top five positive values and three negative addictions. If the gathering is connected with worship, divide the congregation into clusters of no more than twelve to a cluster. Because different rooms will likely be used, it is usually best to prearrange a leader for each cluster in order to clarify the task and guide the conversation. Review the synthesis of the planning team. There will likely be too little time to review the full collage of data. Let each cluster develop a fresh list of five core values and three negative addictions. The cluster may wish to add strings of descriptive words in order to more clearly define the key value.

Step 3: Consensus Building

If the congregational gathering is separate from the worship service, regather as a whole group and invite each table group to share the revised top ten lists. First, invite questions of clarification about the values named. Second, devote at least 10 minutes to silent prayer, asking God to help you synthesize these responses. Third, invite dialogue and discussion. Seek out trends and continuities. Identify values that do not seem to fit, and seek ways to include them. Finally, list the key words or themes that together represent the core values of the congregation. Aim for ten or twelve such key words, each of which may be further defined by related descriptions.

If the congregational gathering is connected with worship, regather in the sanctuary as each cluster completes its work. The key words can be added to a visual picture of an umbrella projected or displayed for all to see. A facilitator can cluster words together in emerging patterns. The participants in each cluster can return to their places in the sanctuary in prayer or singing as they await all clusters to return. Complete the worship service with prayers of intercession and signs of commitment.

Following the gathering, the planning team can further synthesize the results. A colorful, visual graphic should be created and displayed for the stages of discernment to follow. You do not need to prioritize the core values identified. These are the values that together are number 1 in the hearts of the gathered people.

Step 4: Looking Ahead

In subsequent days or weeks, remind congregational participants of the core values that have been identified. These will become one piece of a larger vehicle of accountability for all future leadership and creative ministry.

Clarity and consensus for core values now provide a foundation of trust and respect that will allow the congregation to discern and honestly share the bedrock beliefs that lie at the heart of the congregational life. The discernment of bedrock beliefs is usually more stressful that the previous process. Some may have difficulty identifying their bedrock beliefs and become troubled by their own lack of clarity. Others may have difficulty sharing their bedrock beliefs with others, for fear of being judged. The congregation will need to return to its core values to provide encouragement for the deeper sharing that is to come.

— 11 —

BEDROCK BELIEFS

The bedrock beliefs of congregational life are the principles or symbols of faith that matter most in the daily life of congregational participants. It is to these principles or symbols that participants immediately turn in times of crisis. Such principles are assumed in the weekly agenda planning of participants, shaping their use of time and energy. Such symbols are consistently identified and shared as revelatory of the fullness of Christian faith. Bedrock beliefs empower congregational participants to grasp each new day as holding positive potential to celebrate an eternal meaning.

Bedrock beliefs are not a catechism of Christian dogma, but the content of an enthusiasm. They do not detail every nuance of Christian faith, nor do they answer every spiritual question, nor do they demand a learned and judicious assent to a long list of philosophical propositions. Bedrock beliefs articulate in short form the rationale and purpose of congregational life and ministry. Bedrock beliefs are so important to the welfare of the world that congregational participants insist that they be heard—and are then prepared to engage in earnest dialogue about them.

Bedrock beliefs are not a systematic theology, but an insight into the profundity of Christian faith. They do not summarize a coherent worldview, nor do they attempt to make faith reasonable, nor do they demand additional study and research. Bedrock beliefs articulate in short form the point behind life and death. Bedrock beliefs celebrate paradox and mystery and invite animated conversation. Bedrock beliefs can be readily articulated and fervently celebrated by children, the mentally retarded, the sick, and the senile—as well as by adults, intellectuals, the healthy, and the doubtful.

The discernment of bedrock beliefs may not be easy. First, the congregation must move beyond their understanding of how Christians ought to think, to discover how they have experienced God themselves. Second, the congregation must move beyond what they think they believe to discover what matters above all else. Third, the congregation must move beyond personal preference to discover why a belief should matter to a complete stranger. In other words, bedrock beliefs are not a matter of correct thinking, reasoned opinion, or personal life philosophy. Bedrock beliefs are a matter of one's own experience of the Holy—and why that experience might keep people from suicide tomorrow morning.

Once bedrock beliefs have become clear, the congregation can begin to address issues of identity, message, direction, and strategic planning. Irregular worship attendance, chronic helplessness, boredom, and stagnant ministry all result from ambiguity about beliefs. Other corporate addictions once again block congregational action and may even pose as an openness to diversity that in fact contradicts congregational unity and freezes progressive creativity.

Some bedrock beliefs might easily be expressed in key words that refer to important doctrines of the church.

Creator	Savior	Holy Spirit	Holy Trinity
Sin	Grace	Redemption	Judgment
Sacraments	Holy Church	Resurrection	Ordered Ministry

A bedrock belief for Martin Luther, for example, was "justification by faith through grace." John Wesley might have said "sanctification."

The expression of bedrock beliefs should not be limited to traditional doctrinal language, however. Indeed, such language is often too abstract and does not reveal the depth of personal experience with God. Thematic key words that express bedrock beliefs might include:

God Is Love	Jesus	Friend	Oneness
Ecstasy	Unity	Universality	Growth
Forgiveness	Christian Duty	Compassion	Calling
Prayer	Worship	Mission	Mercy
Joy	Scriptural authority	Acceptance	Justice

A bedrock belief for Martin Luther King Jr., for example, would have been the "realizable dream of equality." Mother Teresa might have named "unconditional acceptance" as a bedrock belief.

Still other expressions of bedrock beliefs might be associated with images or symbols. Many people will not think in linear or verbal ways when expressing their deepest sources of spiritual strength. Instead, they will draw a picture.

Cross	Dove	Empty Tomb	Phoenix Rising
Sunrise	Flowers	Waterfalls	Shepherd and Sheep

The most common picture on the walls of the Roman catacombs, for example, is not the cross, nor even the fish, but drawings of the shepherd surrounded by sheep.

Finally, still other expressions of bedrock beliefs will be brief, pithy stories of life struggle and spiritual victory. Such moments of faith emerge from turning points in an individual's life. In such times of struggle, they make a spiritual discovery that informs and guides the rest of their lives.

Experiences of Healing	Release from Addiction
Unexpected Joy	Conviction of Sin and Awareness of Forgiveness
Personal Vindication	Mystical Unity
Rescue from Disaster	Victory over Adversity

Rosa Parks might have used the story of her struggle with municipal transit in Montgomery to illustrate her belief in vindication. Others might describe experiences of healing that formed their conviction about the irrational power of God, the mending of a broken relationship that motivated a lifelong enthusiasm for marriage enrichment ministries, or an inexplicable bonding with the created world that generated an overwhelming passion for environmental care.

However a bedrock belief is expressed, it will be embedded in the life experience of the individual. They will turn to it in times of stress or confusion. It will shape their choices, activities, and relationships. The collage of bedrock beliefs that forms the consensus of congregational life becomes the spiritual content or life-giving message of the gathered church participants. This is more than a list of truths that the people profess. This is the core meaning for congregational experience. It is the real bond that will hold newcomers in connection with the church. Disagreements about many propositional statements or creeds will not shake the congregation, so long as this more experiential bond cements relationships among the people. Worship will focus and refine the deeper ways in which people draw strength from God for daily living.

The process to discern bedrock beliefs is followed in four stages. The first stage involves one or more congregational gatherings. The second stage involves small groups (10 or fewer people), informally gathered in homes, who can go deeper into a conversation about faith. The third stage involves the same small groups, who build on their intimacy to talk about personal experiences with God. The fourth stage builds final consensus within a congregational meeting.

STAGE 1: CONGREGATIONAL GATHERINGS

Review the description of bedrock beliefs presented above, and project the sampling of possible bedrock beliefs on a screen. Invite people to add important beliefs that seem to be missing or seek clarification for the meaning of specific words. Now divide the large group into smaller groups of about five people. Provide each individual with copies of the Apostles' Creed, the Nicene Creed, or other affirmations of faith related to your denomination. Share with the gathering the following introduction to the process for today.

About 50 years ago, a shepherd boy who lived near Qumran in what is today southern Israel casually threw a stone into a cave . . . and heard the sound of pottery breaking. Subsequent examination of the cave revealed a lost library of ancient documents. These documents described the faith of a group of people identified as Essenes, who lived during the time of Jesus. Scholars have studied these Dead Sea Scrolls intensely, have learned much about the beliefs of this forgotten people, and have gained new insight into the roots of Christian belief as well.

However, the writers of these ancient documents never intended them for historical research. They intended them to be read by future generations of believers who would want to know the crucial, most important beliefs of this community in order to live their own lives of faithfulness. The writers of Qumran had fled the persecution of the Romans. The enemy was searching for their hiding place to destroy them. They had only limited time to write what was most important.

Imagine that your Christian community is even now hiding from persecutors in this house. Any moment the soldiers might find you. You desperately want to leave a record of the most crucial, most important beliefs that you cherish, as a record and guide for future generations. These are the beliefs that make all the difference for a full, joyous, and good life. You simply *must* pass the Good News to others! In the brief time you are allowed, *what treasure will you communicate to the future?*

Step 1

Working silently, take about 15 minutes to read the creeds or affirmations of faith carefully. Circle the key words or phrases that are most important to you personally. Cross out the words or phrases that are least important to you personally. Bracket the words or phrases that are puzzling to you.

Step 2

Word has just reached you that soldiers have begun searching house to house in this neighborhood. Brave brothers and sisters of your faith are even now risking their lives to divert their attention from your hiding place. They are giving their lives to allow you time to gain consensus about the most crucial, most important beliefs that simply *must* be preserved and communicated to the public in the future. Hopefully, their sacrifice will keep you safe, but you must bring your work to completion.

First, share within the table group the results of your individual work. Then, clarify or discuss those words or phrases in brackets, which were puzzling. Now make three lists:

a. Words or phrases unanimously considered most important;
b. Words or phrases unanimously considered least important; and
c. Words or phrases important to some, but not to others.

Step 3

The soldiers have not been diverted from their search of the neighborhood. They are being even more thorough as they move house to house. Originally, you had hoped that you would have sufficient storage space in the hidden cellar of the house to preserve a number of documents. This would have allowed you to preserve both historic texts and multiple commentaries that would interpret them. Now it is clear that the hiding place will have to be very small to escape detection. You must not only preserve the most crucial, most important beliefs of your faith community, you must articulate those beliefs to modern people with great clarity and a minimum of extra interpretation. You cannot preserve a library.

Recognize the fact that the traditional doctrinal language of creed or denominational affirmations often does not fully describe the beliefs that individuals or congregations find most precious. Perhaps the traditional words have nuances today that are unhelpful. Perhaps contemporary experience has reshaped beliefs in a profoundly different way. Perhaps a modern language restatement of traditional beliefs speaks to you more powerfully. Therefore, make a list of words or phrases in modern language that either adds to or restates more clearly the words or phrases considered most important by the table group.

Each group will now have a list of key words or phrases that is their consensus about the most important beliefs that need to be preserved for, and shared with, future generations. This list will be a combination of traditional and contemporary words and phrases. Let each group share the results of their work with the entire group. You may wish to project them on a screen or print them on large posters. Reporting should be brief. Once all groups have shared their work, invite people to react to the collage of faith that is appearing.

a. Are there any surprises?
b. Are there any trends or patterns?

c. Does anyone wish to speak passionately for something that seems to be missing?

Step 4

The soldiers are now just several houses away from you. You can hear their shouts and the noise of their search. Death or imprisonment may well be your fate if they find your hiding place. It has been decided that the summary of your most crucial, most important beliefs must be even more compact than ever. Perhaps a single sheet of paper will escape detection!

Return your focus to small table groups. Using the list developed by your table group, and learning from the lists generated by other groups, select as a table group the top ten (most important) beliefs, which are so precious that they must be preserved for, and shared with, future generations.

Step 5

The soldiers are surrounding your house. In moments they will burst through the door. The documents you have written may or may not be discovered and destroyed, but you must be sure that the treasure of faith is not lost. More than this, you must somehow carry the treasure of this faith with you. Whether in freedom or imprisonment, whether at work or at play, whether in life or in death, you must keep these beliefs closest to your hearts. You must be ready to teach them to your children, to share them with strangers, and, yes, even to give them to your persecutors as a means of transforming their lives. You must memorize these beliefs.

Still working in table groups, now reduce the number to the top seven (most important) beliefs.

Step 6

You have now been arrested. You stand before the public scrutiny of the magistrates and the media. In the midst of such stress, mere words fail you. You cannot even remember the seven beliefs you memorized earlier. As you are led before the public scrutiny of the world, uncertain what fate will befall you, you simply repeat over and over again the word or phrase that best conveys the core faith that gives you strength. *What is it that you repeat to yourself?*

Share your answer to the above question with the other participants in your table group.

Step 7

Let each table group share their top seven list with everyone. No further prioritization is required.

Let each table group also share the individual responses to the question posed in step 6. It would be best if these responses could be shared anonymously, without reference to the individual.

Collate the top seven lists, and gather separately the responses from step 7. Duplicate these summaries for every participant in the group gathering. Each person should keep these summaries for further reflection and prayer. They will be used later in the process.

This is how the two summaries or lists will be used: (1) Publicize them in the congregation through the worship bulletin or newsletter, post them on the walls of the sanctuary, invite comment and discussion, and pray about them intentionally in every worship service. (2) Prepare copies to hand out to the home discussion groups coming in stages 2 and 3. (3) Prepare copies to share once again in the final congregational gathering.

Stage 2: Home Discussion Groups (Part 1)

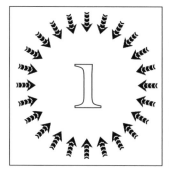

The congregational gathering developed lists of words or phrases (traditional and contemporary) that identified bedrock beliefs. However, the format of the gathering could not enable people to share their stories or describe the symbols or pictures, which, for many, is a better way to articulate their most precious beliefs. This will be accomplished in home discussion groups.

Develop as many home discussion groups as you wish. Groups should be time limited (for example, from 7:00 to 9:00 [P.M.] on a specific evening) and hosted informally with refreshments. Every effort should be made to include participants who were not among the larger congregational gathering in stage 1. It is better to allow people to sign up with a host or hostess as they choose, rather than to rely on previously organized committees or program groups. Each group should have a discussion leader to monitor time, enable people who are shy to speak, and record the results.

> In the previous congregational gathering, we imagined that we were in hiding from persecutors. In a brief time, we imagined that we desperately needed to identify that treasure of our faith that was most crucial, and most important, for future generations to know.
>
> Unlike the Essene community long ago, Christian communities have indeed survived persecution—and lived to grow and share in faith. Right now, your small group of Christians has inherited the treasure of belief that earlier Christians long ago preserved. Today is a quieter, more peaceful time. We can go deeper to define, refine, and celebrate what we believe.

Step 1

Share the collation of the top seven lists from the larger congregational gathering. Also share the list of individual responses to the question posed from step 6 of the previous stage. Every individual should have a copy. Read aloud the creeds or affirmations of faith that were used to begin the congregational gathering so that the traditional words are fresh in the minds of group participants.

Step 2

Discuss the two lists. Clarify words or phrases. Note especially any patterns or trends that emerge. Compare these lists to the creeds or affirmations of faith. Is something missing? Are there surprises? Are there contradictions?

Step 3

In the previous congregational gathering, we imagined the pressure of identifying the most crucial, most important beliefs for our faith community during a time of persecution. However, the truth is that Christian belief is most profound and powerful in times of crisis. We can think and think, read and read, discuss and discuss—but it is only when the chips are down and our life, health, or liberty is at stake that we *really* discover what we believe! Right now our energy will not be devoted to reading the statements of others describing belief, but rather to sharing our personal experiences of God in the midst of our own crises, transitions, and struggles.

Take 10 minutes for silent meditation. Recall to your memory a time of crisis, transition, or struggle in your own life. Remember what happened . . . the issues or challenges that you faced . . . your feelings . . . your actions . . . the outcome. . . . Now remember any way in which your faith in God helped you. Remember any Christian symbol, Bible verse, faithful song or hymn, or liturgy or prayer that comforted or inspired you. Remember any sense of the presence or activity of God in the midst of that experience and how that might have helped you.

Note: It is common for people to identify symbols, ideas, or verses of scripture that should have been inspiring as they look back on the crisis. However, that is not our goal. Make sure that you identify only those things about your Christian belief that you actually found helpful in the midst of the experience. When you remember a time of crisis, *what gave you strength?*

Invite participants in the group to share their crisis and the role Christian belief played to strengthen them. The leader of the group should set the example for honesty and begin. This process may require great trust by individuals in the group. The leader should assure everyone that the group is not asked to judge, interpret, or evaluate anyone's experience of God. Your goal is simply to listen. The leader should also remind everyone in the group that all personal stories will be kept confidential. The only record of your conversation to be shared beyond the group will be the ways in which people have actually experienced strength from God.

As the list grows, be sure to verify that it is accurate to the stories people have shared and that each individual is comfortable with the summary that is to be shared.

The list identifying "What gave you strength?" will be shared in the final congregational gathering.

Step 4

Make a list of those beliefs (words, themes, pictures, symbols, stories, and so on) affirmed by the group as so precious that they are invaluable for the well being of others. This is how the list from each group will be used: (1) Publicize them in the congregation through the worship bulletin or newsletter, post them on the walls of the sanctuary, invite comment and discussion, and pray about them intentionally in every worship service. (2) Copy the list for reference by the group in its next meeting. (3) Prepare copies for use in the final congregational gathering.

Devote the last 15 minutes of the gathering to prayers of thanksgiving and intercession. The leader should begin, and others should contribute to the prayer as they wish. Let the gathering conclude with the Lord's Prayer.

STAGE 3: HOME DISCUSSION GROUPS (PART 2)

The same groups of people meet a second time. This may be in a different home, with different hosts. It is best if the discussion leader is the same person. This second home gathering provides more time for each individual to tell his or her story or elaborate on the symbol or picture that best describes the core of that person's Christian experience. Moreover, it also allows group participants time to think about what has been said and identify the questions or comments that will deepen the conversation further.

Step 1

Invite participants in the group to refresh their collective memories by recalling key elements of the previous home group discussion. Share the interim list of precious beliefs generated by the first home gathering. Invite questions or comments for clarification only.

Step 2

Before further discussion about the beliefs that have been shared, complete the previous process by inviting any individuals who have not yet spoken to share what it is about their faith that gives them strength in times of stress or confusion.

Step 3

Now encourage general discussion about the bedrock beliefs that people have shared.

Step 4

Revise the list of those beliefs (words, themes, pictures, symbols, stories, and so on) affirmed by the group as so precious that they are invaluable for the well being of others. This is how the list from each group will be used: (1) Publicize them in the congregation through the worship bulletin or newsletter, post them on the walls of the sanctuary, invite comment and discussion, and pray about them intentionally in every worship service. (2) Prepare copies for use in the final congregational gathering.

Devote the last 15 minutes of the gathering to prayers of thanksgiving and intercession. The leader should begin, and others should contribute to the prayer as they wish. Let the gathering conclude with the Lord's Prayer.

STAGE 4: CONGREGATIONAL CONSENSUS

A week prior to the congregational gathering, distribute the results of the previous steps for private review. These include: (1) the top seven beliefs identified by table groups in stage 1 and (2) the responses to the question "What gave you strength?" given in stages 2 and 3. Extra copies should be provided as the congregation gathers. You may wish to provide summaries on newsprint visible to the eye or on overhead projections. There may be pictures or symbols to view, or songs that need to be sung. Call a congregational meeting for the sole purpose of identifying the bedrock beliefs of the congregation. By the time the meeting is held, most people in attendance should have been involved in one or more of the previous stages in the process. The purpose of the meeting is to discern and celebrate the bedrock beliefs of the congregation. Remind people that the basic boundaries of congregational life are never carved in stone. They will evolve as the congregation evolves. The primary role of future annual congregational meetings will be to further define, refine, and celebrate the evolving umbrella of congregational life.

If the final congregational gathering is held in connection with Sunday worship, you may wish to include the following elements.

1. A panel of three persons who can share their feelings about the process and identify key learnings, or who can articulate their own story of how their faith gives them strength.
2. Separate areas or rooms for the congregation to break into small clusters, with a facilitator for each cluster.
3. A visual aid for clusters to place key words or phrases regarding their faith for all to see.

If songs or hymns are a part of the collected information about bedrock beliefs, be sure to sing them.

Step 1

Divide the gathering into table groups or clusters. Share the information gathered from the previous stages. Each person should have a copy. Invite any questions for clarification only.

Step 2

Present the following story:

Your neighbors have come to your door one evening visibly upset. They have just had a long telephone conversation with their 25-year-old daughter, in which she has shared her profound unhappiness and hinted that she might be tempted to end her life. Her parents convinced her to seek professional counseling, but they feel that this may not be enough. Their daughter tearfully confessed: "I have no idea why I should bother to live another day." Your neighbors are your friends. They have never been a deeply religious family. They consider themselves to be Christian, although they never participated in a church and never took any particular interest in disciplined spirituality. As a result, they have no clear sense of God, and their daughter does not even know the words to the Lord's Prayer. Given their daughter's situation, they are wondering if they have failed her in some way, and they are wishing they had something encouraging to say to their daughter.

Your neighbors do know that you regularly attend church and that you have taken Christian faith rather more seriously. They have known your pastor to visit you in times of trouble and are aware that you generally speak positively of the value of faith for meaningful living. "Tell us what it is all about," they ask. "Give us some advice to pass on to our daughter. Why do you think it is worthwhile to live one more day?"

Remember: the attention span of most modern people is about 10 minutes. Whatever you say to impact their lives must be said in that time.

Your task in table groups is to discuss your response. Remember that you do not have a great deal of time, and that whatever you share about your faith will need to help both the distraught parents and the unhappy, distant daughter. What would you say?

Step 3

The time has come to distill the essence of all the reflections and thoughts of the process. In your table groups, take a blank half-page of paper. Write in bold letters at the top: "THIS WE BELIEVE." Now identify *seven* Christian beliefs that together in your group are absolutely the most important to you.

Step 4

If the congregational gathering is separate from Sunday worship, regather as a whole group and invite each table group to share the revised top seven lists. First, invite questions of clarification about the values named. Second, devote at least 10 minutes to silent prayer, asking God to help you synthesize these responses. Third, invite dialogue and discussion. Seek out trends and continuities. Identify beliefs that do not seem to fit, and seek ways to include them. Finally, list the top ten (or twelve! No need to be legalistic!) beliefs that clearly lie at the core of congregational life. You do not need to prioritize them. These are the beliefs that together are number 1 in the hearts of the gathered people.

If the congregational gathering is connected with Sunday worship, regather congregational clusters in the sanctuary. As the visual aid is gradually completed, participants can sing together or pray for the future of their congregation. The planning team can synthesize the results into ten or twelve key words or phrases following the service. Complete the worship service with signs of commitment and prayers of thanksgiving and intercession. To facilitate reflective conversation about the experience, you may wish to intentionally deploy lay leaders who can mingle with those having refreshments following the service.

Step 5: Looking Ahead

In subsequent days or weeks, remind congregational participants of the bedrock beliefs that have been identified. These will become one piece of a larger vehicle of accountability for all future leadership and creative ministry.

Clarity and consensus for bedrock beliefs now provide a deeper spirituality and a clearer awareness of the content and message of the church. Combining these bedrock beliefs with the core values that have provided a foundation of trust and respect, the congregation can now place itself in an environment of expectancy to receive vision from God and discern their true motivation for congregational life and mission. The discernment of motivating vision can be even more stressful than the previous two processes. Vision always comes in apocalyptic power. It not only changes the direction of church programs, but it transforms the identity of the congregation itself. The congregation will need to return to their core values to provide mutual support, and they will need to return to their bedrock beliefs to give them strength and wisdom to respond to the callings of God.

— 12 —
MOTIVATING VISION

Discernment of the motivating vision that drives the congregation toward mission may be the most difficult step in clarifying the basic umbrella of congregational life. There are several reasons:

First, vision is not constructed by the people, but it is revealed to the people by God. Therefore, the process requires the creation of a climate of waiting in which the core values and bedrock beliefs of the congregation are brought into creative interaction with scripture and the transformative experiences of individuals.

Second, vision is profoundly threatening. Core values and bedrock beliefs help define who you are, but authentic vision will change who you are—and carry you, your values, and your beliefs in unexpected and perhaps unsettling directions.

Third, vision can never be fully expressed in words. Unlike our previous work in core values and bedrock beliefs, this effort requires us to transcend mere words to express the raw enthusiasm or emotional power that leads us to take real risks.

A vision is *a song in the heart.* It is a metaphor or symbol, a rhythm or tune, a picture or experience, the mere presentation of which elicits spontaneous joy and excitement. Vision speaks to the heart, not the mind. It can never be fully contained in words, and one always feels rather breathless and frustrated trying to communicate it to another person. Yet at the same time, a vision is so compelling that one simply must share it with others—even with perfect strangers!

A vision makes you feel like nobility! It uplifts the human spirit and fills the heart with immense purpose and meaning. It fills a person with impatience, with a burning desire to do something immediately. The specific action required may be unclear. The support of others is helpful, but not essential. It is the vision itself that fills an individual with renewed self-esteem, and centers his or her life toward a single-minded destiny. It invests a small human life with universal significance and infinite worth.

A vision is *true north for the soul.* It is a permanent, intuitive compass direction for a human being. Every person inevitably strays from the path. Life is an endless experiment and course correction. The vision brings one back to the true path. One only needs to pause, refocus, concentrate on the vision; and new clarity for action emerges. The vision is like a magnet that draws the people, individually and collectively, unto itself.

A vision is the answer to the question "What is it about my experience with Jesus that this community cannot live without?" It is a clear grasp of that pivotal, heart-felt experience with Jesus that has so changed one's direction in life and activity of living— and has so filled one's life with joy and meaning—that unless one shares it with another, that other person's life will be impoverished. A vision fills one's life with generosity, which overflows in magnanimity toward the world. For Christians, authentic visions are always associated with the living Christ.

Authentic visions are only revealed to individuals. However, they only survive when they become team visions, and they only grow when they are shared spontaneously and enthusiastically with strangers. They are revealed in the depths of the heart and in the actual experience of life struggle and spiritual victory of an individual. That is why clarity about core values and bedrock beliefs provides a fruitful foundation for the revealing of vision. However, authentic visions cannot stop there. They must be shared with others, and in the process, the vision will be both refined and expanded to become a shared enthusiasm by more than one individual. Like ripples in a pond, the influence of the vision will continue to expand to the edges of the community or the world. Visions always risk rejection. People caught by a vision place themselves on a high learning curve, for the vision is always ahead of them. Every new friend who shares the vision teaches the others who previously shared the vision. The vision can never be contained. It must expand.

Once a vision ceases to be shared with complete strangers, and is contained within a community that merely cherishes it, it loses its power. A reverse spiritual movement begins. Just as vision emerges from the spiritual clarity of core values and bedrock beliefs, so now the artificial containment of vision eventually leads a congregation back into a fog of belief. They begin to lose touch with the principles, symbols, or stories that give them strength in times of stress or confusion. Belief becomes ritualized and intellectualized. Next, the congregation begins to fragment into competing political spheres of influence. Positive core values become vague, and negative addictions control group behavior. The gap widens between what church participants claim to value and how they actually behave in daily life. Church growth plateaus, and then church participation begins to steadily decline.

Biblical experiences illustrate the impact of authentic vision on the lives of individuals. The story of Jacob's ladder (Genesis 28) is one example. A vision is revealed to one individual, Jacob, and only in the agony of his spiritual yearning. Having stolen his brother Esau's birthright and now fleeing for his life, he discovers belatedly and painfully both his core values and bedrock beliefs. He once valued money, and now he discovers the true core value of brotherhood. He once believed only in himself, and only now does he remember the covenant of his father Abraham with God. In this environment of mixed despair and yearning, he unexpectedly receives the vision of the stairway to God—and the grace of a renewed promise from God. The vision will be shared and refined into a team vision with Rachel, Laban, and others. The same vision will be shared with his mortal enemy, Esau, and produce reconciliation. And the same vision will be shared with strangers over time as Jacob's name is changed to Israel and his people multiply. The image or picture of the ladder to heaven becomes a song in the heart that Miriam sings as Moses leads the people out of Egypt.

The story of Peter's vision on the rooftop (Acts 10) is another example. Again, a vision is revealed to one individual, Peter. Again, it is revealed only in the confusion and stress of the emerging Christian witness as it encounters the cultures of the Middle East. The inclusive blessing of the Holy Spirit, the growing conflict with religious authority, and the extraordinary news of the conversion of Saul all raise crucial questions about what is really valued in personal behavior and what is really important about faith. Into this environment of yearning comes the vision of the sheet coming down out of heaven laden with all the foods of creation, which God declares fit to be eaten. The vision is refined and shared by Peter's companions, then with the stranger Cornelius and his household. The vision defends the mission to the Gentiles initiated by Paul. In time, the vision is celebrated by mosaics, which archaeologists later discover adorning the private homes and worship centers of Christians, all of which contain the image of loaves and fishes surrounded by all the creatures of creation.

Here are some examples of phrases, symbols, or metaphors that might begin to describe *the song in the heart:*

The Waterfall of God's Grace. The congregation holds its congregational gatherings in the park surrounding Niagara Falls, and the church facility devotes an entire wall in the vestibule to a waterfall in which people can be baptized in any and every way.

The Phoenix Rising from Ashes. The congregation tears down its Gothic, urban building to create a high-rise with apartments for newly arrived immigrants. The sanctuary is on the first floor, and the central image is a modern tapestry depicting the phoenix rising from flames resembling the skyscrapers of the city and ashes made of the trash cans of the street.

The Summer in the Soul. This phrase is lifted from the third verse of the song "As Comes the Breath of Spring," a verse that epitomizes the congregation's experience with spiritual growth through small group ministries. It evokes lush, diverse, constant growth. This church is known as the "Summer in the Soul Church" and advertises as such in the entertainment section of the newspaper.

God's Northern Light. Located in a mining center in a remote northern region, among a transient, young population of people seeking their fortune, the congregation feels called to be a guiding light for foundational beliefs and values. Rather than display a sign on the property, they place huge colored spotlights to shine into the night sky. They are known on the night shift as a source for wise coaching through the ambiguities of daily living.

These phrases and images can, and will, be interpreted by church participants in hundreds of ways. Yet the song or the image unites their hearts in a single enthusiasm. It is the rhythm by which they walk and the motivation with which they work.

As in the previous processes, we surround the process with intentional prayer, Biblical reflection, and preaching and witness in regular worship services. The initial congregational gathering will help people understand the nature of authentic Biblical visions and build commitment to a *covenant of openness*. Stages 2, 3, and 4 may happen simultaneously. One involves individuals in personal spiritual disciplines and prayer triads. The other brings triads together in home discussion groups. As visions emerge to individuals, these are shared in worship services—without critique, only with celebration. Move to the final step when no more visions seem to be emerging in the worship services. The final congregational gathering will discover which vision seems to lay claim to the life of the church.

Congregational planners will need to feel free to customize the process to suit their own unique contexts. Much of the routine of congregational worship will need to be adjusted to create this spiritual environment to receive visions. The spirituality of waiting should not be fit into the routine liturgical life of the congregation, but the routine liturgical life of the congregation needs to be modified and molded to focus on the revelation of vision. The Biblical experience of receiving vision is being duplicated. A spirituality of waiting is being built on the foundations of clear values and beliefs, in which visions can come to individuals, individuals can share and refine their visions through conversations with other intimates, and the growing team vision can become the consensus of the church and ultimately empower congregational participants to share their vision with the community and world.

It is impossible to predict how long this process will take. However, since discernment of vision resembles birthing a baby, it may be helpful to remember that pregnancy and birth for human beings requires about nine months, careful discipline, and labor pains. The birthing process happens most effectively and joyfully if the environment is intentionally transformed into a birthing room and if all people—from the custodian and taxi driver to the doctors and midwives—see themselves as participants in the birthing process.

STAGE 1: COVENANT OF OPENNESS

This time the congregation does not need to gather in table groups, and they may prefer to gather in the sanctuary. Sing hymns or songs, and invite key lay leaders to pray for the revealing of visions and the future of the congregation. Be sure to project, print, or otherwise recognize the core values and bedrock beliefs of the church that have been discerned so far.

Share the description of a motivating vision from the beginning of this chapter. Now share the following challenge:

> Although it is not possible to create a vision, it is possible to create a climate that is most receptive to visions. Visions are being revealed by God constantly, but they may fail to connect with an individual human heart. We are too addicted to habitually destructive behavior patterns. We are too bound by our own desires. We are too caught up in idolatries of heritage preservation and mere survival.
>
> Given the fact that visions are apocalyptic, why should we even want one?? They are inevitably painful and utterly life transforming. They forever alter past, present, and future. A church gripped by a vision will never be the same again. A vision may be a joyous experience, but it is never a pleasant experience. A vision never eases the stress of congregational life; it always multiplies the stress of congregational life. Therefore, why should we want one?
>
> Indeed, many churches do not want one. They may talk about

church renewal, but they do not want church transformation. They may talk about welcoming newcomers, but they only want to receive certain kinds of people into membership. Churches that simply want to perpetuate a heritage, maintain an ethos, or survive as an institution cannot and will not receive a vision! They cannot endure its apocalyptic power.

Therefore, the first step in preparing a climate of receptivity for visions is that congregational leaders must be willing to place the whole heritage of the church on the block! The congregation must be willing to die. Nothing can be sacred—not property, not organization, not curriculum, not music, not worship, not tradition. Nothing can be sacred. The congregational leader and the congregation must be willing to surrender heritage, ethos, and institutional survival.

Why will congregational leaders and congregation do this? Because they want to walk with Jesus above all! They yearn for a wellspring of joy and meaning that will dominate every day of the week and every minute of the day. They yearn to really fulfill their lives on this planet. They yearn to be a part of a greater destiny that is a positive hope for the community and the world. They yearn to explore new possibilities, celebrate great victories, and visibly contribute to the health and wholeness of others. For this they will sacrifice everything.

Step 1

Distribute copies of the covenant of openness to every person in the gathering. Also project it on screen. Take time to silently read and reflect, and then invite discussion. The purpose of this discussion is not to brainstorm new ideas or to unleash creative imagination by listing activities the congregation might do. Remember, visions are not created. They are received. They will not emerge from the pandemonium of inventing new strategies and tactics that might somehow save the church, but out of the slower, deeper, more intense spiritual growth of individuals and their intentional, faithful conversations with one another.

The discussion will focus on the feelings of alarm and uncertainty or the questions for clarity and direction, which will form the reaction of the congregation to the challenge set before them. Of the three stages of discernment so far, this stage is by far the most stressful. The discernment of core values may have been enjoyable and illuminating. The discernment of bedrock beliefs pushed congregational participants to be more honest about faith with themselves and others than they may have ever had courage to be before. Now, however, the discernment of vision calls upon the congregation to let go of their control of the process entirely and to open themselves to the unexpected power of God. The previous stages were controllable and the outcomes still predictable. In this stage, emotions will run high and the outcome will be both exciting and threatening.

Covenant of Openness to Visions

We promise to help create a climate of openness to receive the visions God would reveal to us, from _____ to _____ (dates).

1. *We declare our readiness to "Let Go."* We are ready to risk our heritage, our tradition, and our survival in order to discern the new directions in which God would lead us.

2. *We declare our readiness to "Let God."* We are ready to be surprised or dismayed, challenged or judged, changed to new ways or confirmed in ancient ways in any way God addresses us.

3. *We declare our readiness to consider all options.* We are ready to consider any change or sacrifice, any opportunity or cost—even the amalgamation, relocation, or closure of our congregation, for the sake of our walk with Jesus.

4. *We declare our readiness to focus on priorities.* We are ready to entrust the relative trivialities of institutional management to a gifted few and to concentrate our energies on what is truly important about our future and our faith.

5. *We declare our readiness to share all ministries.* We are ready to free our clergy and equip our laity to share equal responsibility for ministry so that all may have time to deepen spirituality and listen for the callings of God.

6. *We declare our readiness to stretch our imaginations.* We are ready to listen to crazy ideas, consider the impossible, taste the distasteful, converse with strangers, and experiment with what is nontraditional so that God can help us to grow and change.

7. *We declare our readiness to laugh.* We are ready to tolerate odd personalities, go to extremes of diplomacy, and offer the maximum generosity. We are prepared to laugh at ourselves and laugh with each other. We are eager to try, fail, learn, and try again.

Once the discussion is finished, invite each participant to sign the covenant. This covenant should be continuously before the congregation in worship, meetings, small and large groups, individual conversations, and personal prayers. The greater the commitment to this covenant, the more successful the following strategies will be.

Step 2

Build a congregational consensus that frees Sunday morning worship from traditional formats (traditional liturgies, lectionary readings, classical or traditional hymns and songs, and standard orders of service) *for the time period specified in the above covenant only.* Agree to experiment with a variety of liturgical, musical, and dramatic forms. Five congregational commitments will be necessary:

1. Worship Team: Appoint a worship team that will temporarily replace the existing worship committee and may change the usual roles of the preacher and the organist. This team will have complete freedom to design worship in creative ways.

• The *message coordinator* may or may not be the pastor and may or may not be the speaker or liturgist for a particular worship service. This person helps focus the theme of worship and equip the person or persons who will be speaking.

• The *music coordinator* may or may not be the organist and may or may not be the musician for a particular worship service. This person helps select the music for worship and equip the person or persons who sing or perform.

• The *drama coach* may or may not actually participate in a particular worship service. This person prepares and directs dramatic presentations related to the worship theme and helps equip actors, dancers, and others involved in worship.

2. Biblical Focus: The congregation agrees that every worship service during this period will concentrate solely on the Gospel of Luke and the Acts of the Apostles. The worship team is free to explore these two books in any way they feel called.

3. Small Group and Prayer Triad Responsiveness: The congregation instructs the worship team to incorporate into every worship service any and all individual visions that emerge through the small group and prayer triad process.

4. *Attendance:* Congregational participants agree to attend every worship service during this time period, without exception, and to invite marginal or inactive members to worship. The congregation should advertise the nature of this temporary process for worship and remind participants that they may have strong reactions—positive or negative—to some components for worship and that these should be communicated to the worship team.

5. *Feedback Loop:* Following each worship service, or during the week following multiple worship services, a regular time must be established for all three members of the worship team to receive feedback and share discussion about the worship service. You may also wish to establish methods of written communication, surveys, and so on.

Generally speaking, a strategy of worship that creates a climate of openness for visions will reduce memorized liturgy, unison readings, and off-the-shelf worship resources. Try to minimize institutional information-sharing, reading words aloud, and managed movement. Spontaneity, individual creativity, and handcrafted worship resources must be emphasized.

First, fill the worship service with music and singing. Let music and singing include a wide variety of old and new songs, traditional and contemporary music. Even if some music is distasteful to some people, assure them that this is a temporary process designed to open our imaginations. During the feedback opportunities, watch for powerful metaphors in the lyrics or catchy tunes to a melody. Discern what images and musical phrases linger in the minds of participants after worship.

Second, fill the worship service with visual aids: visual art, photographs, symbols. Run a slide projector throughout the service, or meditate on pictures projected on a screen. Set up easels with paintings or tables with art objects around the room. Mix classical art and images of the neighborhood. Let them be traditional and avant garde, dramatic and mundane. During the feedback opportunities, watch for images or metaphors that capture the imagination.

Third, insert into the worship service opportunities for drama. Create skits that help tell the stories of the vision lectionary you have created. Dramatize some of the events observed by prayer triads through the week. Choreograph movement by dancers. Encourage worship participants to move, sing, speak, and participate in spontaneous ways.

Fourth, multiply opportunities for congregational participants to share their own faith, pray aloud, participate in sacraments, and articulate their concerns and celebrations. Encourage people to talk about their answer to the key question: What is it about my experience with Jesus that this community cannot live without?

STAGE 2: PERSONAL PRAYER DISCIPLINE

Involve as many congregational participants as possible in a spiritual discipline. The exact length of time for this discipline may vary, but it should be maintained throughout the following visioning stages. The scriptures of the discipline may be integrated into the corporate worship and preaching schedule of the congregation.

Bible Study (Option #1): The Great Visioning Texts of Scripture

Read the great visioning stories of the Bible listed below. Read stories aloud while eating breakfast or dinner. Talk about that portion of scripture with your spouse, family, or friends. Question it, wrestle with it, puzzle over it—but always apply it to your individual life and your congregational future. Keep a notebook to list any phrases, metaphors, images, or ideas that deeply move or inspire you.

I Am Your Shield: Abraham's Descendants (Genesis 15)
A Bridge Too Far: Jacob's Ladder to Infinity (Genesis 28:10-22)
Permanent Limp: Jacob Wrestles with God (Genesis 32:22-32)
The Dream Reader: Joseph and the Economics of Strategic Planning (Genesis 41)
Burning Mystery: Moses and the Ultimate Ambiguities of Risk (Exodus 3)
Where There's Smoke, There's Fire: Israel in the Wilderness (Exodus 13:17-22)

The Right Path: Israel's Guiding Light (Deuteronomy 5:22–6:9)

The Trusted, Gifted Few: Gideon Maximizes the Minority (Judges 6:36–7:8)

The Power of Two: Only Elijah Is Left (1 Kings 19:11-21)

Joy Is Strength: When People Get the Message (Nehemiah 8:5-12)

Scar Tissue: Isaiah's Break with the Establishment (Isaiah 6)

Bringing It to a Boil: Jeremiah's Break with the Establishment (Jeremiah 1)

Breathe on the Bones: Ezekiel's Dry Bones Live (Ezekiel 37:1-14)

Destiny Awaits: Habakkuk Strengthens the Faint Hearted (Habakkuk 2:1-3)

Starry Eyed: The Magi's Dangerous Trip (Matthew 2)

Cross Eyed: Jesus Dazzles the Imagination (Matthew 17:1-23)

Water on the Brain: Only the Sick Understand (Mark 6:30-56)

Yes Sir, That's My Baby!: The Essential Jesus (Luke 1:8-21, 26-45)

How to See the Obvious: Disciples on the Road to Emmaus (Luke 24:13-35)

For Whom Do You Weep?: It's the Reappearance that Changes Things (John 20:11-29)

Guided Missile: Stephen Sees Red (Acts 7:54-60)

How to Seize an Opportunity: Philip on the Road to Gaza (Acts 8:26-40)

How to Become Addiction-Free: Saul on the Road to Damascus (Acts 9)

Every Day's a Holiday, and Every Meal's a Feast: Peter and All the Food Fit to Eat (Acts 10)

Come on Down!: Lydia and the Birth of the First Urban Church (Acts 16)

Stormy Weather: Paul's Inclusive Vision of Safety (Acts 27:13-44)

The Gates Are Always Open: The New Jerusalem (Revelation 21)

The River: The Return of Eden (Revelation 22:1-7)

Bible Study (Option #2): The Birth of the Church

Read the story of the birth of the church and the mission to the Gentiles as described in the Gospel of Luke and the Acts of the Apostles. Simply read and reread the stories found in these scriptures. Read stories aloud while eating breakfast or dinner. Talk about that portion of scripture with your spouse, family, or friends. Question it, wrestle with it, puzzle over it—but always apply it to your individual life and your congregational future.

Prayer

Using your Bible study and conversation as a foundation, intentionally pray at least twice daily for the future of your congregation. Your prayers may be in any form, or of any length, that seems good to you. You may share them with others or pray by yourself. The important thing is to intentionally and regularly pray for the future of your congregation.

Write down any images, metaphors, symbols, or ideas that emerge from these readings and that deeply move or inspire you. Send them to the pastor or the church office anonymously; they will be gathered for future use. Your written inspirations will be used in the following ways: (1) Personal inspirations can be shared in the context of congregational worship. (2) Personal inspirations will be shared with the focus groups in a coming stage.

Multiply opportunities for informal conversation in large or small, planned or spontaneous gatherings of congregational participants. Be sure to include members and adherents, core participants, and marginal members. The planning team, staff, and lay leadership should intentionally facilitate conversation about shared visions.

STAGE 3: LISTENING-PRAYER TRIADS

At the same time that people engage in personal spiritual disciplines, form a variety of listening-prayer triads. Anyone is welcome to participate in a triad, but it is especially important to involve the core leaders who are currently in the center of congregational life. People should be encouraged to involve themselves in both small group and prayer triad strategies if possible.

These triads require no leader. People join with whomever they choose. They covenant together for a weekly discipline of listening and observing amid the public and for a daily discipline of prayer for all that they hear and see.

1. *Home Gathering:* The triad meets at a regular time each week in a participant's home. There they pray for guidance (for about 15 minutes) and then go to some public place. This will be any place where a large, diverse group of people frequently gathers (sports arenas, restaurants, shopping malls, and so on).

2. *Watching and Listening:* The triad spends time in a public place listening to conversations around them and observing the behavior of people. They may wish to take notes to refresh their memory later. The triad may remain together or mingle individually with people. What are people doing, and what does this reveal about needs and priorities? What are people talking about, and what does this reveal about their interests and concerns? The triad does not intentionally talk with others. They do not aggressively invade the privacy of others. They simply remain unobtrusive, listen to the conversations flowing about them, and watch behavior. This may take an hour or more.

3. *Home Prayer and Discussion:* The triad returns to a participant's home. There they discuss what they have seen and heard. They should try to read between the lines. What needs are revealed? What hopes and dreams, worries and fears are revealed? Next they spend at least 15 minutes in intercessory prayer for the individual strangers they have encountered. They should pray aloud, being as specific as possible.

4. *Daily Prayer:* The triad covenants to pray at a designated time each day specifically that the other participants in the triad will receive a vision for the future of the congregation. Each triad should list the key issues they perceive to be dominating the thoughts and behavior patterns of the public, and they should name any specific calling that moves them deeply or inspires them. Insights and inspirations will be used in the following ways: (1) Insights and inspirations can be shared in the context of congregational worship. (2) Insights and inspirations will be shared with the focus groups in a coming stage.

Continue to multiply opportunities for informal conversation about shared visions. The planning team may invite triads to share their experiences more formally in worship, meetings, or postworship refreshment times.

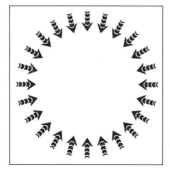

STAGE 4: FOCUS GROUPS

Once visions begin to emerge from individual spiritual disciplines and prayer triads, and are recognized and celebrated in worship, form a variety of focus groups. The purpose of these groups will be to discuss emerging visions and to build a team vision enthusiastically shared by the entire group.

Be clear in the formation of focus groups that: (1) The role of a focus group is not to judge the legitimacy or the quality of emerging visions. All emerging visions have value. Each has captured the imagination and heart of an individual. The goal of the focus group is to facilitate a full and complete sharing of visions so that patterns and trends can become visible and the group can refine and build a larger team vision that includes the enthusiasm of each participant. (2) The role of the focus group is not to do strategic planning. The group should not become trapped in detailed questions about tactics or implementation, nor should they be deterred from celebrating an emerging shared vision if no tactic or strategy of implementation is immediately apparent. The concern of the focus group is on the shared motivation of the congregation for all future tactics and strategic planning.

In general, the focus group is searching for the song in the heart that the entire congregation can enthusiastically sing together and that will provide the motivation for all subsequent tactics or activities. It is the song in the heart that is important at this time, not the particular dance steps with which people will subsequently follow the rhythm.

Involve as many congregational participants as possible in groups. Try hard to include fringe and marginal members as well as core participants. These groups should be no larger than 12 people, and each group should have a designated leader. Each group may design its process in any way it chooses. Some groups may meet together once. Other groups may wish to covenant to meet at a regular time for at least two or three meetings.

The role of the leader is very simple: to guide each group gathering through the process on which they have agreed and to create opportunities for every person to contribute. As individuals become excited about emerging visions, the leader focuses the group on celebration and affirmation, not evaluation and judgment. The leader helps the group look for common patterns or trends. The leader also refines and broadens emerging visions to form a larger team vision.

Leaders should report emerging visions to the worship planning team for inclusion in the worship services, and if needed, assist individuals in sharing their visions. Remember, a true vision can never be contained in mere words. Therefore, do not be afraid to use songs, symbols, pictures, stories, poetry, dance, or any other creative vehicle to communicate the emerging team vision. When visions are shared in worship, they will almost certainly not be limited to mere words. Yet the communication must clearly excite and motivate the congregation. Visions may seem audacious, impractical, and crazy—and yet these are the grand visions that motivate and excite the congregation to attempt the impossible.

Focus groups may or may not be lead by the pastor, but the pastor and all salaried staff (including custodians, secretaries, organists, and others) must all be involved in the focus groups. As focus groups return to the congregation with team visions, the pastor or other lay leaders should reflect on emerging patterns and trends during the sermon or faith-sharing times of the worship service—always seeking to build a larger, shared enthusiasm.

Step 1

Share verbally or in print the instructions regarding focus groups in this stage. Review the insights and inspirations that are emerging from personal prayer disciplines and listening-prayer triads. If other focus groups have begun sharing their emerging team visions, review these visions as well. Invite group participants to share any other vision that has begun to capture their imaginations yet does not quite fit with the visions revealed so far.

You may wish to use newsprint or overhead projections to keep track of emerging visions. This can also allow the group to cluster visions in emerging patterns.

Step 2

Each group will synthesize visions by asking the following questions:

    a. Can the visions that are emerging be linked together to form a pattern?

    b. How do these visions relate to our core values and bedrock beliefs?

    c. Which visions capture our imaginations and fill us with excitement?

    d. What poetic phrases, hymns, songs, or images are evoked by the synthesis that is emerging?

Note that the focus group is not seeking to articulate a definition, but to describe a passion. Words will never be enough. The shared enthusiasm that begins to build is less a matter of united understanding than a shared excitement and energy.

Sometimes an emerging vision is already building such shared enthusiasm that it is practically carrying you away. It may seem that focus groups are not necessary. However, it is good to slow down in order to refine and consider the vision that is emerging—and to make sure that it is not a hidden addiction to corporate behavior patterns that is simply being repeated. The focus group should double-check the vision using the criteria in the box on the next page.

As focus groups test visions for authenticity, they should share them over again in worship services. Hymns, songs, poetic phrases, and symbolic images will be especially important to build the unity of shared enthusiasm.

The goal of each focus group is to emerge with a synthesis—a single, larger, team vision that embraces each individual in the group. The team vision should not lessen the enthusiasm individuals have brought to the visioning process, but rather focus and enhance that enthusiasm through unity with others.

How Do We Know the Vision Is Authentic?

There is always the danger that hidden corporate addictions will reemerge, pretending to be authentic visions. Common hidden addictions include: the need for bureaucracy, mission by committee, burdening the youth with the future of the church, organ music, and dependency on clergy. Authentic Biblical visions can usually be identified in at least four ways.

1. Authentic Biblical visions are always too hot to handle. They challenge tradition, raise stress levels, and challenge even the most fearless leaders with daunting tasks.
2. Authentic Biblical visions elicit extraordinary courage and build self-esteem. Despite the challenge, individuals are affirmed, accepted, motivated, and equipped. God provides courage, and those who accept the challenge find a depth of fulfillment and joy that they have never known.
3. Authentic Biblical visions build team relationships. Although they are given to individuals, they lead to greater generosity and compassion. They generate community and reach out to embrace the alienated and the stranger.
4. Authentic Biblical visions are always linked to Jesus. The person and presence, the work and words of Jesus are inextricably bound to the vision. The experience of pursuing the vision is an experience of walking with the risen Lord.

STAGE 5: CONGREGATIONAL CONSENSUS

When new visions no longer emerge from the personal spiritual disciplines, prayer triads, and focus groups, it is probably time to call a congregational gathering. By this time, the many individual visions that have emerged have begun to fit into a larger pattern or patterns. Enthusiasm is beginning to build, but stress may also be growing.

Some people may simply not share enthusiasm for the emerging vision of the congregation. They may begin to fear that there is no place for them in this congregation's life. Other people may share enthusiasm for the emerging vision but find the vision too risky, audacious, or demanding on their personal lifestyle.

The consensus you have already gained about core values and bedrock beliefs will be very important to help create constructive dialogue. Before, during, and after the congregational gathering, multiply opportunities for congregational participants to converse informally and face-to-face in nonthreatening environments. The pastoral staff and the planning team should arrange for one-to-one counseling and prayer opportunities with people whose stress level is very high.

There is no blueprint for the process of the congregational gathering. Each congregation will need to find its own path to consensus. You may wish to form table groups, or you may wish to encourage one large discussion group. If you choose to incorporate the gathering with Sunday worship, you can surround the gathering with song, prayer, and scripture. On the other hand, if you choose to hold the congregational gathering apart from worship, you can allow the worship service to provide opportunities for deep meditation and prayer as a preparation for coming discussion.

Several guidelines for the congregational gathering may be helpful:

1. *Make it a party, not a meeting.* Membership is not an issue in this gathering. What matters is that these are the people who participate in the life of the congregation. Parliamentary procedure should be set aside in favor of common sense procedure:

- Be brief: say what you must and sit down.
- Be clear: make an understandable point.
- Be generous: allow every person to speak.

The atmosphere should be relaxed, festive, and optimistic. After all, God is doing great things in your midst!

2. *Provide helps for the shy and introverted.* In gatherings with high energy, shy and introverted people may have difficulty pushing forward to speak. Identify helpers in the room who can receive written or whispered comments and share them on behalf of others.

3. *Get the input of children and youth.* Provide, alongside the congregational gathering, a childcare option that has a purpose. Children can sing songs and relate to images, too. Their colorings

and drawings, comments and prayers can be shared with the adult gathering as it progresses. Similarly, you may wish to intentionally pause discussion to hear from teens or children who have not had a chance to speak.

4. *Surround the gathering with spontaneous music and prayer.* Before, after, and during the gathering, sing the songs that have emerged in the visioning process. An instrumentalist should always be ready. Make it clear that anyone can spontaneously ask for singing and prayer at any time during the party.

5. *Have overhead projectors and newsprint ready.* Make sure every tool is ready so that no time is wasted finding markers, pens, or tape. Keep a list of key ideas or images clearly visible at all times so that nothing gets lost or forgotten.

6. *Have ready materials for crafts or visual arts.* During the discussion and subsequent celebration, some individuals will be able to spontaneously express themselves in nonverbal ways.

7. *Invite artistic participants to intentionally synthesize the conversation.* If they are prepared in advance, musicians and visual artists can attend to the unfolding conversation in a way that will allow them to spontaneously bring it together in the worship celebration that follows.

8. *Ask a neighboring congregation—and any other congregation in the world with whom you are linked online and with whom you share a visioning process—to intentionally pray for your congregation at the exact time of your gathering.* Make sure that your own congregation knows that this prayer support is happening.

9. *Assign a designated personal support team.* Passions and emotions will emerge. The personal support team members need to stand apart from the whole gathering and look for those who might feel alienated, angry, or emotional during the discussion. They can intervene by inviting individuals to come away for a brief time for prayer, sharing, or silence to collect their thoughts.

The convener of the gathering may or may not be the pastor, but the pastor must be highly visible and supportive. The convener should have high and long-standing credibility with the congregation and be respected for his or her wisdom and spirituality. Since leadership for this gathering will be more art than science, other members of the staff or planning team should be constantly available to the convener to offer constructive advice.

Step 1

Review the key, powerfully motivating visions that have been identified by the focus groups, triads, and personal spiritual disciplines of the people. Then spend time in personal prayer and meditation.

Step 2

Now invite discussion and dialogue. If you are in table groups, each group may wish to work on its own and then share with the entire gathering. If you are a single group, individuals may wish to form triads for initial discussion. The discussion will likely be messy in that it will not be always orderly or calm. Passions will emerge. Laughter can temporarily bring conversation to a halt. There may be tears.

As table groups or individuals report or speak, keep track of the ideas using overhead projections. The leadership should encourage any speaker to not only share their thoughts, but intentionally link their thoughts with those of another group or individual. Leadership should:

- look for patterns that are emerging.
- summarize ideas that have been shared and suggest connections with the ideas of others.

The gathering will be marked by stages of interaction, rather than by the achievement of an agenda.

- Pay attention to the level of emotion among participants.
- Take breaks whenever discussion seems to wander.
- Enable those who are shy to speak.
- Allow time for people to speak, but notice when discussion begins to be repetitive.

When the discussion seems to become repetitive, and before participants become simply exhausted, the convener should test the consensus of the gathering. Decisively break for a moment of prayer, and then specifically ask volunteers to articulate the emerging team vision of the congregation as they experience it. It may be that planning team members will be able to take initiative and model this for others. It may be that this presentation will require some artistic or musical preparation, so that a longer break for refreshments will be helpful. When the people regather, let volunteers present the consensus as they experience it now.

It may be that a single presentation will gain immediate, joyous acceptance. On the other hand, further refinement and synthesis may be required. Do remind participants that this vision, like the core values and bedrock beliefs of the congregation, will not be carved in stone. It will always be defined, refined, and celebrated through future annual congregational meetings.

In the end, you may or may not want to take a vote on the vision that has finally won the hearts of the people. However, the vote should be nothing less than a shout of joyous acclamation!

Step 3: Celebration

Design future worship to celebrate the vision that has emerged. Use music, visual art, and dance to articulate the vision. Invite individuals to write brief, single paragraph reflections on the vision, and use this collection as a vehicle for daily devotions by congregational participants. Ask a graphic artist to illustrate these collected reflections, and give the resource to newcomers to the church. Return to the vision whenever there is a decisive or stressful moment in congregational life.

— 13 —
KEY MISSION

$\mathcal{C}$ongregational mission is the most important outcome of this process, and it will be the key to congregational growth, expansion of ministries, and successful stewardship in the future. Congregational mission is founded on the people's consensus around core values, bedrock beliefs, and motivating vision. The mission of the congregation is a clear, concise declaration of purpose that is aimed directly at the hearts of the unchurched public.

There are three common mistakes congregations make about mission statements. *First, a mission to survive is not mission.* The perpetuation of a heritage has no value in itself, and it is neither interesting nor helpful to the public. The survival of an institution—no matter how large, glorious, or expensive—is of no consequence for God. Biblical visions never lead people to survive. They lead people to grow.

Second, a mission statement is not a summary of program. It is not an abbreviated version of a congregational constitution or structure, nor is it a summary of committee mandates. Mission statements are all about *purpose,* and they make no assumptions whatever about tactics, structures, or leadership.

Third, a mission statement is not an essay. It does not interpret congregational identity or practice for public recognition. It does not offer a rationale or an explanation that justifies church membership. It is rarely longer than twenty words in length. Mission statements articulate in a nutshell where the congregation is going in the twenty-first century.

Powerful mission statements emerge from the clarity you have gained about the core values, essential beliefs, and motivating vision of the congregation. They have the following characteristics: *Powerful mission statements are clearly motivational.* They are exciting to people in both church and community, and they are regularly celebrated by the congregation to be truly the leading of Jesus. The mission energizes people. It is a source of pride. They readily speak of it among work associates, neighbors, relatives, and friends. Their personal identity is tied to this mission.

Powerful mission statements are clearly congregational. They involve and develop the totality of congregational life, not simply an aspect of that life. Everyone participating in the congregation is enthusiastic and wholehearted about that mission. It is their ultimate reason for participation in congregational life. Each person is on fire for that mission, and people participate in this congregation specifically because these people are working toward that purpose.

Powerful mission statements are clearly distinctive. They do not repeat old phrases or duplicate current work. They do not seek to do everything worthwhile, but they do seek to do one worthwhile thing with excellence and energy to ultimate fulfillment. They do not cast judgment on other possible visions and purposes, but take ownership of a particular vision and purpose. It is the stamp of identity in the midst of diversity.

Powerful mission statements are deserving of sacrifice. No matter how large the vision or how great the challenge, a powerful mission statement is always reasonable and achievable. People recognize that it is more than a dream—it is a possibility. It deserves immense personal sacrifice not only because it is worthy but also because it can be done.

Powerful mission statements are supported by perpetual prayer. Individuals, leaders, and the congregation as a whole continually pray for the success of the mission. Prayer is both planned and spontaneous. The mission is constantly lifted into consciousness, and it lies at the center of personal and corporate spirituality.

Your ultimate goal will be to articulate your mission in such a way that it can be easily printed on the side of a bus, on a park bench, on a matchbook cover, or on a banner trailing behind an airplane above a crowded beach. In that brief space, you need to communicate everything the public needs to know about your church that will motivate their support or involvement. Of course, these are exactly the places that your mission statement will be proclaimed.

STAGE 1: SYNTHESIS

The congregation will need to take time to review and celebrate the consensus that has been developed around core values, bedrock beliefs, and motivating vision. It may take time for the nuances and subtleties, implications and possibilities of this consensus to be absorbed by the minds and hearts of congregational participants.

Step 1

Articulate the congregational consensus around values, beliefs, and vision in worship services. Encourage pastoral staff and lay leadership to preach or speak about this consensus. Encourage children, youth, and adults to discuss this consensus in Sunday school or other formal group learning processes. Build the consensus into the daily devotional life of participants.

Involve lay leaders in a discipline of intercessory prayer for the community and the issues that they face. Invite every lay leader to articulate an answer to the question "What is it about our congregational experience with Jesus that this community cannot live without?" Responses should be anonymous and shared with the congregation through worship bulletins or newsletters.

Step 2

Assemble a team of people with strengths in synthesizing diverse information and in matching congregational gifts with spiritual and social needs. This team may well include volunteers with abilities in visual arts, music, creative writing, evangelism, advertising, and social advocacy. The team may be appointed in a variety of ways, but it should be commissioned in the corporate worship of the church.

This synthesis team should review the consensus that has been gained and should especially review the insights revealed to the listening-prayer triads in stage 3 of the visioning process. (These groups listened to the public and observed their behavior in order to perceive the issues and questions currently on the minds and hearts of the people.) This will help the team bring together the values, beliefs, and enthusiasm of the congregation in close connection with the personal and social needs of the public. The task of this team is to articulate the fullness of the congregational consensus in values, beliefs, and vision—in symbol and words—in a manner that can be easily communicated on the side of a bus or an advertisement on a subway car.

Step 3

Invite any individual or group to share with the synthesis team their own expression of the mission of the congregation. These expressions of mission may be in any form (images, drama, statement, or so on), but they must be brief and poignant. For example, written statements should be no more than 15-20 well chosen words.

This invitation can be extended to Sunday school classes, youth groups, cell groups, and any other collective of congregational participants. However, committees of the congregation should be cautious that the expression of mission they articulate should be larger then their program mandate and should embrace the whole of congregational life and work.

Step 4

Assemble a prayer team of people gifted and called for this ministry. They are to meet regularly during this time for the sole purpose of praying for the process of synthesis and the synthesis team.

Stage 2: Congregational Consensus

The synthesis team will focus the congregational consensus for values, beliefs, and vision into a simple, clear proclamation of congregational purpose. The result may resemble a symbol, logo, motto, or slogan that can be used in public dialogue, but it is more than this. It is the full identity of the congregation communicated to the general public. Everything one really needs to know about the congregation is expressed in these words or symbols. The mission statement of the congregation is readily communicated, easily remembered, and captures the imaginations and yearnings of the public. It will motivate their curiosity about the church and facilitate an immediate rapport between members of the church and perfect strangers.

Step 1

Share the mission statement in worship services over a period of several weeks. Invite congregational participants to share their reactions with the synthesis team in informal settings following worship services or in private homes. The mission statement and any accompanying graphic may be refined and modified in response to these reactions.

Step 2

Call a formal congregational meeting for the specific purpose of approving the mission statement and thanking all congregational leaders who have participated in this discernment process for the basic umbrella of congregational life.

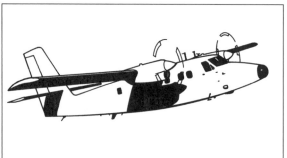

THE END OF A PROCESS —THE BEGINNING OF A JOURNEY

The process is now complete. After thanking all the leaders who have helped build this consensus—and after celebrating the values, beliefs, vision, and mission of the congregation—the church must now use this foundation to build ministry. You have identified the basic umbrella of congregational life, underneath which all congregational activities happen. These are the boundaries of congregational life beyond which the congregation will not go. This is the identity that marks the congregation in the community and the world.

Celebrate

Every worship service, organizational meeting, group gathering, and mission initiative should intentionally recall and pray for the basic umbrella of congregational life. It should not be possible to worship with the congregation or attend any congregational function without recognizing this basic umbrella of congregational life.

Communicate

The mission of the congregation should be proclaimed to the public in every way imaginable. It should appear in letterhead, outside signs, exterior symbols, and all advertising. This mission of the congregation should take precedence over any denominational, national, or cultural symbol.

The basic umbrella of congregational life should be clearly explained and communicated in all membership training, lay leadership training, and in the job descriptions and hiring processes for all staff (custodial, secretarial, or pastoral).

The basic umbrella of congregational life should be communicated to the denominational judicatories and shared with any congregational partners nearby or around the world who have been praying for the spiritual discernment of your congregation. Offer to coach other congregations in a similar process for their own spiritual renewal.

Define Accountability

The basic umbrella of congregational life is now the primary vehicle of accountability in the congregation. It is the boundary beyond which congregational work cannot go but within which any creative idea or mission initiative can be taken instantly and without gaining any bureaucratic permissions. The role of church leadership will be to hold this umbrella over the heads of the congregation, so that the essential consensus is immediately apparent to every person. Although church leaders need to discern whether or not some activity goes beyond the boundaries, the only role of leadership within the boundaries is to equip creative ministries for excellence. As long as creative ideas have not gone beyond the boundaries of core values, bedrock beliefs, motivating vision, and key mission, congregational leadership cannot say "No" to a creative idea.

The basic umbrella of congregational life:

• tests the adequacy and direction of any program or mission initiative.

• shapes and directs all leadership.

• demands a readiness to constantly upgrade programs and skills for excellence.

All job descriptions and committee mandates may now be rewritten to be proscriptive and permission-giving. They no longer need to prescribe everything an individual or group can and should do; they can simply acknowledge the basic umbrella and list anything that cannot be done. So long as an individual or group does not go beyond the boundaries, people in the congregation are free to do instantly and immediately whatever they feel called to do—even though their creative initiative may contradict the tastes, opinions, lifestyles, or perspectives of other members of the church.

Do It!

As the basic umbrella of congregational life begins to emerge clearly for the congregation, excitement will mount. You may find worship attendance and volunteerism increasing, and community attention will grow. At the same time, you may find some membership losses, and some key financial contributors may withhold their money. Although the process is designed to take time to gather the largest consensus possible, sometimes congregations may be tempted to wait too long!

The first temptation will be to wait until the congregational vision has absolute unanimity. Membership losses and financial threats unnerve people. Pain over the departure of long-time friends may not be immediately replaced by joy in welcoming newcomers. Resist the temptation. Visions are apocalyptic in nature. Complete unanimity for the basic umbrella of congregational life will be impossible. Unless you get going, enthusiasm will diminish and frustration and conflict will follow.

The second temptation will be to wait until a future strategic plan is absolutely clear in every detail. The permission-giving character of the basic umbrella of congregational life gives an ambiguity and mystery to the future that can increase anxiety. There may be a desire to have more meetings, do more research, rewrite church constitutions, clarify every mandate and job description, and generally extend the process interminably. Resist the temptation. Visions have nuances and facets that only become clear as the vision is lived and shared. Surprise and mystery, experimentation and creativity always accompany clarity about the basic umbrella of congregational life. Unless you get going, the expanding, team vision and enthusiasm for mission will be contained and stagnation will return.

There comes a time when you have to *DO IT!* The growth of enthusiasm and community participation will soon outweigh the grief of some losses. Remind the congregation and congregational leadership that visions lead people into the risk-learn cycle. Failure is an essential part of following a vision. Patience, persistence, and learning from failure are essential parts of fulfilling a vision.

Although strategic planning is important, it is no longer the cornerstone of church growth. The world is changing too quickly and the ministries called forth by Christ are emerging too quickly for strategic planning to reliably guide the church into the future. There must be room for instantaneous reaction and spontaneous initiative. This means that there must be a climate of laughter and trust for congregations to successfully grow in spirituality and ministries. People must be able to try, fail, laugh, and try again. Therefore, the cornerstone of church growth is, not strategic planning, but the basic umbrella of congregational life. This is the umbrella that can allow that kind of creativity to guide the church into the future.

Take a deep breath! Take your first steps out of Egypt! The

journey will be exciting and filled with challenge and surprise! Your core values will shape and deepen your relationships for ongoing mutual support. Your bedrock beliefs will give you strength to overcome hardships! And your motivating vision will stand before you as a pillar of smoke by day and a pillar of fire by night. Keep moving! Your key mission will show you the way. And you will find a Promised Land.

— 14 —

INTERPRETATION

DISCERNMENT OF THE BASIC UMBRELLA OF CONGREGATIONAL LIFE

The completion of the discernment process for the basic umbrella of congregational life provides congregational leaders (and congregational participants) with clarity and consensus about congregational identity. This congregational identity should be immediately transparent to every participant and quickly recognized by any newcomer to the church. Not only is it visible on the banners, projection screens, printed information, and resources for all ministries of the church, it is recognizable in the everyday behavior of congregational participants. The ministries may evolve, programs may come and go, and leadership will change over time; but this core identity of the congregation will endure.

I mentioned at the beginning of the process the three principal benefits of this clarity and consensus about congregational identity. (1) Clear congregational identity provides the basic boundaries for the permission-giving organization. It is the primary vehicle of accountability for all ministries and all entrepreneurial leadership. (2) Clear congregational identity creates the foundation for all reliable long-range planning. The congregation can be decisive about its future, and confident that even the most ambitious goals can be pursued with confidence to the end. (3) Clear congregational identity establishes a context for both planned programming and spontaneous action. The response time required for emerging opportunities for mission can be dramatically reduced.

In a sense, this clarity about the basic umbrella of congregational life informs and energizes all evangelism and community service that emerges from the church. Without it, effective interaction with the community would come to an end. With it, effective interaction with the community has no limit.

I also mentioned at the beginning of the process that many congregations actually resist such clarity and consensus. They prefer to live in a fog because controllers within the church can then arbitrarily limit risk taking and creative ministry, following their personal tastes, lifestyles, opinions, or perspectives. This unconscious (though sometimes deliberate) resistance to the process is often revealed in at least ten ways. The forms of resistance are themselves revealing about the corporate addictions of congregational life and should be observed closely.

TACTICAL OBSTACLES TO DISCERNMENT

1. Planning Team Expectations

"You mean there is more to leadership than management?" Most congregational planning teams are either appointed with an eye to balancing power groups or they are composed of volunteers who are particularly restless to change the church. Either way, the planning team tends to be a very diverse group with sharply different experiences of congregational life, strong personalities, or narrow agendas. Leaders usually join the team expecting that they will primarily be involved in coordination and promotion. The hidden expectation of the planning team is that they will have an opportunity to influence the emerging consensus of the congregation. The planning team often assumes this can be done by managing the congregational agenda in a different way for a short period of time and by shaping the results of the research to reflect goals already at least partially formed in the minds of team participants. In short, most team members assume they will lead a discernment process in the same way that most officers participate in an official board.

The reality of planning-team work, however, surprises members of the team. The congregation needs them to model the discernment process in their own lives and demonstrate the power of both-and consensus building. More than this, the coordination and promotion roles of the planning team soon become secondary to the need to interpret the discernment process over and over again to the congregation in ways that motivate ever greater participation. In short, planning-team members often join the team expecting to be managers and controllers. Instead, they discover their primary roles are to model for others what it means to relinquish power and motivate creativity.

The real work of the planning team is spiritual growth. They demonstrate it, struggle with it, model it, reveal it, and encourage others to do it. They find themselves in a discernment process that cannot be easily managed but that, even for themselves, is at the mercy of God. Beyond the relatively simple tasks of designing and implementing the process, they find themselves constantly interpreting, encouraging, and authenticating the process for others.

They grow *relationally*. Their interaction with the entire congregation increases, taking them beyond their usual friendship circles. They become ever more sensitive to the subtle, significant nuances of congregational attitude and behavior. They discover unexpected commonalities with former agenda foes and unexpected differences with former agenda allies. Most importantly, they come to appreciate the fringes of the church and the unchurched public as much as they do the core church participants, and they find themselves constantly interpreting the one to the other.

They grow *personally*. Their own partially formed expectations for the process are often simultaneously affirmed and shattered as the collage of research and perspective grows. They discover gifts and talents for listening, coaching, prayer, and persuasion that they never new they possessed. The restless are forced to develop patience; the quiet are pushed to be articulate; the aggressive are required to listen passively.

They grow *spiritually*. As the stress level of the process grows and personal interaction with congregational members increases, planning team participants find themselves surrounded by greater uncertainty and greater opportunity than they ever imagined. Prayer, Bible study, and the mutual support of other team members suddenly become more relevant.

God's vision will rarely start with them, but emerging visions are often most quickly perceived by them. The team becomes attuned to God's grace in a way that participation in a committee or official board never allowed.

What appeared at first to be a straightforward management task quickly becomes a process of constant improvisation. The planning team is always rethinking the timeline and customizing the process to fit the changing forms of congregational participation. The team is less in the background and more in the foreground of congregational life than anyone expected. They are visible to the diversity of the congregation, constantly engaged in conversation, and linked to worship as never before. Planning team members tend to assume their task will involve meetings. Instead, they discover, it involves a lifestyle.

2. Congregational Timelines

"*What should we stop doing?*" Even though the discernment process is time-limited, it still requires a significant block of time, during which congregational energies are redirected and reprioritized. Three to six months of intensive effort is not uncommon and nine months or more may be needed to give birth to vision. Clearly, the work of the discernment process cannot simply be added to the obligations and activities already scheduled. Something must be set aside for the time being. What the congregation chooses to sacrifice can be as revealing for the future discernment of core values, bedrock beliefs, motivating vision, and key mission as any of the future research and conversation.

Will the routine schedule for potluck suppers and fellowship gatherings be redirected or reduced?
Will the annual every-member financial canvass become abbreviated or eliminated?
Will the children's Christmas pageant be set aside this year?
Will Lenten activities be redirected away from the stations of the cross?
Will the number of committee meetings be reduced?
Will the project to renovate the parlor be put on hold?
Will the door-to-door visitation to community newcomers be postponed?
Will the pastor's vacation be changed to a different month?
Will the laity return from family vacations earlier than usual?

Just making time for the discernment process can reveal more about congregational core values and bedrock beliefs than many leaders might want to admit. When it comes to visioning processes, many congregations prefer the easy way out: "Just send the board and any interested volunteers away for a weekend, and we will continue as usual." Congregations tend to avoid the higher call: "Let the entire congregation devote themselves to waiting for God."

The need to reprioritize the energies of the congregation also brings stress to the daily and weekly routine of congregational life. This is experienced most severely in worship and pastoral care.

The discernment process may or may not cause the congregation to set aside the traditional Christian year for a period of time. Sometimes the symbolism of the Christian year can be adapted to facilitate the process. Epiphany, for example, might facilitate the visioning phase of the process while Pentecost might facilitate the missioning phase. Even if the congregation continues to pursue the Christian year calendar, however, the orientation of these events may dramatically shift. The discernment process recommends that the Common Lectionary be temporarily replaced by a *vision lectionary*, which leads the congregation to reflect on the great visioning stories of scripture. Worship itself often becomes increasingly dramatic, participatory, dialogical, topical, and motivational for weekly focus group participation. During the discernment process, weekly worship will simply not be the same.

The discernment process may or may not reduce the amount of time and energy devoted to one-to-one pastoral visitation, but it will certainly reorient it. As more and more people are talking with animation about values, beliefs, vision, and mission, the conversations that unfold in visitation are directed away from personal needs to personal hopes. Stress management will become a higher priority as individuals become increasingly anxious that God's vision for the church might well change the church. The various weekday groups and teams that accompany the process tend to replace some individual visitation and fulfill a pastoral care goal. They take on a function of mutual support that goes beyond mere data gathering or perspective sharing.

3. Uncertainty

"*Why are we doing this?*" Despite the promotion of the process in worship, congregational gatherings, newsletters, and so on, congregational leaders can anticipate that there will always be individuals who are continually surprised by the whole process. Even core participants will come forward long after the process has begun, puzzled about where the process came from and what it is supposed to accomplish. Aside from providing insight into the weakness of the congregational subsystem for communication, this phenomenon is usually a confirmation that the discernment process is beginning to work. People are beginning to spontaneously talk about it away from the normal church routine, and it is beginning to raise the stress level of long-standing members. Something is happening that just might change the church. It is noteworthy that anxiety here does *not* usually come from newcomers, but from the veteran members of the church.

Newcomers and visitors to worship are often quite curious and motivated to learn more about this crazy congregation that is so dedicated to learn its shared values and beliefs in order to discover God's vision, which will empower them to embark on significant mission. After all, that is precisely what many newcomers want for themselves. Newcomers tend to be unafraid of spiritual growth disciplines and tend to embrace the flow of the process.

It is among the veteran, fringe members of the church that the anxiety is greatest. These are folks who attend church irregularly, but who rely on pastoral services religiously. They are often good givers and strong committee members, and they feel very comfortable telephoning the pastor on his or her day off. For some, the anxiety simply reveals how out of touch they have allowed themselves to be from ongoing congregational life. Once the planning team interprets the process to them, they readily get on board. For others, however, the anxiety reveals a deeper need for complacency and control. Questioning the point of the process is really a way to affirm their unpreparedness for change or their unwillingness to allow others to bring change. These are the foghorns who intuitively realize that clarity and consensus about the basic umbrella of congregational life will eliminate congregational dependence on them. The best way to cope with them is to partner these foghorns with the former out-of-touch veterans who get on board. After all, they are probably already friends. The veterans who are on board need to take the foghorns to lunch. Let them put their arms around their friends' shoulders, coach them, and ease their anxiety.

4. Fear

"Are the results carved in stone?" Along with looks of surprise and questions about the point of the process, congregational leaders can anticipate participants expressing anxiety that sweeping and significant conclusions are being drawn about congregational identity in a rather short time and with at best only a significant portion of congregational participation. Some others will worry that in the years ahead the congregation might change away from the consensus identified now. Leaders will find themselves saying that the basic umbrella of congregational life must be defined, refined, and celebrated with each annual meeting. Indeed, the chief function of future annual meetings will be to intentionally reexamine and evolve this consensus.

Once again, it is noteworthy that this fear is usually expressed by core or veteran members of the church and not by marginal members or newcomers. Clarity about the future role of annual meetings does not reassure some people. The hidden reason for this fear is, not that the congregation might not have power to refine the identity of the church, but rather that power groups or influential individuals will not control the definition of the identity of the church. When a need to control lies behind the fear that results might be inflexible, the last thing controllers want to hear is that the annual meeting will be reoriented to refine, define, and celebrate the basic umbrella of congregational life. They would prefer the annual meeting to do what it did before: management. They would prefer that annual meetings take a long time, walk line-by-line through the budget, wrestle with nominations, and review every decision of the past year all over again. The real issue for some is not "Can the identity change over time?" but rather "Who has power to define the identity over time?" Leaders must be clear. Although Biblical visions are revealed to individuals (often at the fringes of congregational and public life), they must be shared, shaped, and owned by the congregation as a whole. If the vision can be controlled at all, it is not by clergy, boards, or groups, but by God and the people.

5. Cynicism

"We did this before, and it didn't work!" Many congregations have done previous work developing a mission statement, and

most leaders and participants realize that few people ever remember the mission statement. Despite the energy it took to create, it is never used in strategic planning, accountability processes, or interaction with the public. Some congregations have even had previous experiences with visioning and strategic planning. Neither activity ever seemed to lead anywhere. The visioning process may well have been a form of pipe dreaming, and the strategic planning may well have been a form of wishful thinking. The dreams and plans that emerged soon got lost in the exhausting task of simple weekly survival.

Leaders will need to stress the difference between this discernment process and previous visioning or planning experiences of the congregation. They are similar in name only. The reason that previous processes never really motivated future change was that they did not take the time; include the variety of participation; or seek the deeper clarity about values, beliefs, or vision, as the current process does. The resulting key mission in the current process is quite different from the longer, program summary previously called a mission statement. If used at all, the old mission statement was employed in never ending revisions of committee mandates and the assimilation of new members. The key mission will be used constantly to focus creative experimentation in ministry and to communicate with the unchurched public. Cynicism, however, is often deeply entrenched in the life of the congregation.

1. *Cynicism results from an inward congregational orientation.* Subsequent research and discussion about core values often reveals that the congregation celebrates quality relationships and activities of the church family but limits interaction with the public beyond the church. This inward orientation leads people to be cynical about change. Their heart is not in it because an outward orientation would beckon them to adapt themselves to strangers beyond the church rather than assume newcomers should adapt themselves to the accepted norms of church life. When this tentativeness about public interaction causes outreach programs to falter, cynicism allows the congregation to quickly conclude that change is unnecessary or impossible. "People won't come anyway (because they are sinful, indifferent, or too busy), so we may as well continue doing what we enjoy doing."

2. *Cynicism results from an ambiguity of contentment versus low corporate self-esteem.* Subsequent research and discussion about

bedrock beliefs often reveal that the beliefs held most dear tend to attract people with dysfunctional lives. They tend to be people primarily seeking help, rather than people primarily seeking fulfillment through helping others. Not only does this reinforce a dependency on salaried professionals, it also tends to reinforce a sense of corporate powerlessness and low self-esteem. Cynicism is one way that personal support for needy individuals can be maintained while at the same time allowing the self-doubts of participants to continue. Cynicism becomes a symptom for unhealthy codependency. "We poor laity are having a hard enough time trying to cope with the way things are, so we'll just have to trust our strong, healthy staff to look after the way things could be."

3. Cynicism is a way to avoid risktaking. Subsequent research and discussion about vision and mission often reveal that congregations have difficulty perceiving and grasping bold visions (what James Collins calls "Big, Hairy, Audacious Goals" in business). Even in undertaking more modest tasks for change, congregations often have difficulty following through to accomplish what they wish. Cynicism is a way to avoid taking risks, because one can declare in advance, "It is impossible" or "It will never work." The motivation to risk is missing because the congregation cannot value failure as a means to spiritual growth and fulfillment. It is not just that failure in itself is perceived as bad, nor even that failure might precipitate hard work to learn and grow, but that failure might invite an intervention of grace that will transform us into a different people. "If God really accepts us as we are, then Egypt is a better place to be than the wilderness."

The roots of cynicism will be uncovered by the process itself. However, to motivate commitment to the process, leaders will need to point out the difference between this process and those that were not effective. The planning team will need to model risk taking for others and demonstrate from their own experience how positive change can happen. The more lay leaders speak publicly and enthusiastically about the process, the less power cynicism will have to hold people back from commitment.

6. Loss

"Will clarity about identity lead to exclusiveness?" Most congregations place a very high value on quality relationships. As the

congregation struggles to survive, overlapping circles of friendship become more than sources of personal fulfillment and mutual support. They become primary vehicles for communication and the real motivation behind volunteerism. Communication is often word-of-mouth as news travels through the friendship circles, and leadership tends to be limited to an exhausted few, whose motivation is as much personal loyalty to other friends who are leaders as it is to the church itself. One fear around clarity for congregational identity is simply that current good friends might feel rejected by the congregation.

Congregational life also involves various confederations of people who share similar enthusiasms, lifestyles, or attitudes. Each group finds its place in the congregation through relationships of family connection, friendliness, or tolerance. Youth groups, for example, primarily include the children of core participants and close friends who are equally welcome in the private homes of the church families. A second fear around clarity of congregational identity is that a child, teen, parent, single adult, or grandparent might feel abandoned by the church.

Finally, congregations do take considerable pride in their ability to attract newcomers to the church (usually Sunday worship). The power to assimilate newcomers into the church depends on the potential for the newcomer to establish a friendship with someone in the congregation or establish a link with one of the confederations of shared enthusiasm, lifestyle, or attitude. If this does not happen within four weeks, the newcomer will drift away. A third fear around clarity of congregational identity is that some members of the public will never connect with the church no matter how friendly the church tries to be.

The truth is that most congregations believe themselves to be far more inclusive than they really are. This can often be demonstrated fairly easily:

1. *Congregational participation does not in fact mirror the demographic and psychographic diversity of the community.* The congregation is homogeneous in race, culture, language, age, economic background, educational background, dress, behavioral expectations, or other commonalities unconsciously modeled by the friendship circles of the church.

2. *Congregational participants are remarkably timid and selective*

when interacting with strangers. Friendliness may be a function of an office (greeter, usher, or so on) rather than a spontaneous outreach of every member. Coffee hours find people standing in their own friendship circles. Follow-up visits must be done by staff. Few strangers come to church accompanied by laity they have recently met, and little energy is given to interacting with the public unless it involves a service club, a property dispute, or a fund raiser.

3. *Congregational participants are not motivated to communicate with church dropouts or marginal members.* While the names may continue on membership and newsletter lists, visits are undertaken solely by staff or designated officers. Church insiders tend to believe that dropouts "had a problem with the church" while church outsiders tend to say that the church "had a problem with them."

4. *The number of newcomers who fail to make a lasting connection with the church is greater than the number of newcomers who stay.* Those who do stay tend to fit a limited demographic profile of acceptability. Those who do not stay are often not even remembered.

5. *The number of marginal members is growing.* Average worship attendance tends to be dropping. The number of burned out leaders who are somehow disenchanted with the church tends to be growing. It is increasingly difficult to persuade people to hold an office.

All of these are measurable signs that the church may already be more exclusive than members believe.

Clarity and consensus about the core values, bedrock beliefs, motivating vision, and key mission of the congregation will not lead to exclusivity. In fact, it will lead to a greater inclusivity than the congregation has known. That is just the problem. The real fear is, not that anyone will be rejected, but that the spiritual bond of the congregation will carry higher expectations than mere friendship—and some will choose not to meet that expectation. A breadth of shared values, a depth of spirituality, an excitement for discipleship, and an urgency for God's mission now become the bonds that hold the church together. A greater diversity of the public is apt to become involved in such a congregation. The congregation is apt to include people with whom I have nothing in common except Christ and people who may never become my close personal friends.

7. Self-centeredness

"Why should we listen to the public?" Despite the clearly expressed congregational desire to grow, leaders can anticipate discomfort with the need to include the public (or the unchurched) in the discernment process. This may be particularly apparent as the leaders seek to deploy listening-prayer triads or teams to interview and survey public opinion. It is not uncommon to hear comments like: "Why do we always have to change to accommodate *them?* Surely *they* can change enough to accommodate *us.*"

1. *Anxiety about "eavesdropping":* Some may question the ethical integrity of "eavesdropping" on the conversations of strangers. The question is a very responsible one and deserves to be taken seriously. Privacy is valued highly by all. Leaders should point out that listening-prayer triads are not asked to invade the privacy of others. They are not tape recording, intruding upon conversations that are obviously personal, or pursuing people away from the public forum in which their conversations unfolded. The triad is simply asked to keep their ears and eyes open and pay attention to what people are saying and doing in restaurants, shopping malls, sports arenas, and other public places. They seek to read between the lines of public behavior to discover the issues, concerns, questions, and problems that are foremost in the thoughts of people and then pray about them.

This simple explanation eases the minds of most folks. For others, however, the discomfort with listening-prayer triads has little to do with ethical considerations. The strategy contradicts the hidden assumption of some church insiders that the views and needs of the public are at best secondary to the views and needs of members.

2. *Anxiety about market surveys:* The discernment process requires volunteers to proactively seek the views of nonchurch members. Some may question the organizational assumptions implicit in the discernment process. The congregational agenda is decisively influenced by people beyond the congregation. It is important to clarify that the discernment process is not reviewing

denominational polity. Interviews with the public are intended to reality-test congregational perceptions about core values and bedrock beliefs. Surveys among the public are intended to identify mission gaps and mission opportunities that may have been ignored or resisted by the congregation.

For most folks, this simple clarification is enough to ease their anxiety. For others, however, concern about market surveys has little to do with ambiguities between denominational polity and business practice. This strategy simply contradicts the hidden assumption that membership is a requirement to access mission.

There is a yet deeper reason why congregations may be uncomfortable with listening to the public. They are uncertain about the source and context of divine revelation. First, congregations assume that visions are essentially creations of the congregation rather than revelations from God. They associate visioning with activities like brainstorming and dreaming rather than with processes of waiting and listening. Second, congregations assume that mission is a strategic plan for institutional growth rather than a calling to take risks for Christ. They associate mission planning with utilizing the time and talents of members effectively rather than spiritual formation that builds courage and confidence for creative outreach. The ideas that Biblical visions are always apocalyptic and that such visions most commonly emerge at the fringes of congregational and community life are both novel and frightening to churches accustomed to Christendom.

8. Untrained Small Group Leaders

"*Who am I to lead a discernment process?*" Much of the discernment process requires small group leaders, and it is not always easy to recruit these people. Initially, volunteers believe that their role will simply involve group management and data collection. It does not take long to realize, however, that the role of small group leader is really about the facilitation of personal insight and spiritual growth. Many volunteers feel inadequate for this role, often because the congregation has not emphasized adult spiritual formation disciplines in its life and mission.

Staff must resist the temptation to lead the various small groups on behalf of the congregation. Not only will groups be too few, unhealthy dependencies on clergy will simply be perpetuated. It may be that staff can model with the planning team the skills to encourage personal insight and spiritual growth, but only in the context of equipping lay volunteers for group leadership. Perhaps the most important point to recognize is that the small groups deployed in the discernment process are limited to one or two gatherings and specifically oriented to an agenda. They do not require the level of leadership skill required by more sophisticated cell group strategies. Leaders in this discernment process can often be encouraged to simply do what comes naturally to them, using the guidelines provided earlier in this resource. If they are confident in the support of the staff and the planning team, they will do just fine.

Most volunteers will find this reassuring. However, the anxiety for some lies deeper. Their worry really has nothing to do with confidence or skills but with the imperative of spiritual growth itself. This discernment process contradicts a hidden assumption that disciplined adult spiritual growth is optional. The truth is that there is no option. Disciplined spiritual growth is the only way clarity and consensus about values, beliefs, vision, and mission can be gained.

9. Fear of Leaving Anyone Behind

"How much involvement is enough?" Congregational leaders can anticipate anxiety about the size of the consensus achieved. Should every congregational participant be involved? Should participants be involved in every gathering or aspect of the process? Should every single individual have a chance to share every single thought that comes to his or her mind? How much involvement is sufficient for the process to be effective?

The planning team will undoubtedly find itself revising the timeline for the process several times. This is particularly true for the visioning phase because God's revelation, and human readiness to perceive it, cannot be packaged neatly in an agenda. On the other hand, a clear ending to the process is important. Generally, the process takes no less than three months. Momentum will build as more and more people awaken to the urgency and the opportunity, but it usually cannot be sustained longer than nine months. Always remember that the basic umbrella of congregational life will be revisited annually—and more often if congregational circumstances dramatically change.

Keep in mind that the real issue behind this anxiety may not be consensus at all. The real issue for some may be control. One way to block change is to do research forever—during which time a smaller group is allowed temporary powers to influence congregational life and mission.

Consensus means that the broadest diversity possible in the congregation will have opportunity to participate in the process. No cluster of individuals or groups will control it, but neither is it reasonable to expect that every single individual will have participated in it. The following benchmarks may help the planning team evaluate involvement.

1. Target two-thirds of the those who would normally worship during the year to grasp at least one opportunity to become involved in the process.

2. Target at least one-third of every identifiable group within the congregation to grasp at least one opportunity to participate in the process.

3. Target a random sampling of members (and former members) clearly identified to be resident in the area but inactive in the church, and deploy at least 1 interview team for every 150 members and/or adherents of the church.

4. Target places and occasions for gatherings of the public, and deploy at least 1 listening-prayer triad for every 150 members and/or adherents of the church.

5. Target the times of greatest public use of the church property, and deploy market survey teams sufficient to cover every major entry and exit at those times for at least 2 weeks.

6. Target weekly updates or summaries of the collage of information and discussion that has taken place so far in the process, and provide lay leaders with binders to organize these updates in the four phases of the process.

7. Include significant opportunities in every worship service for volunteers to share their experiences in the process and for prayerful support of the individuals involved.

In addition, the planning team members need to be prepared to reach out to any individual perceived to be anxious or uncertain about the process in order to interpret each phase and coach or encourage participation. The planning team must balance the impatience of some participants to move forward and the slowness of other participants to discover how they best can participate. Whatever the exact benchmarks you use, there will come a time when genuinely new information or perspective no longer seems to emerge, and the congregation as a whole is ready to bring closure to the process.

EXPERIENCING THE DISCERNMENT PROCESS

In my book *Kicking Habits: Welcome Relief for Addicted Churches,* I described the declining and thriving church systems by telling the stories of two congregations. St. Friendly-on-the-Hill Church lived in a declining church system. Growing anxiety had led them to learn about the thriving church system from New Hope-in-the-Heart Church. Earlier in this book, we revisited St. Friendly-on-the-Hill Church following their experience with the Congregational Mission Assessment and traced the corporate addictions that ran through all eleven subsystems of congregational life and blocked transformation. In the end, they learned . . . and changed.

Now let us revisit New Hope-in-the-Heart Church. Change for this congregation did not really begin with an assessment of eleven subsystems of congregational life. Indeed, at the time they had no idea that there were so many subsystems to congregational life! Remember what Edith (lay leader and veteran member) said in *Kicking Habits:*

> "You know," Edith says, "New Hope-in-the-Heart Church was not always this way. In fact, some years ago, it was a traditional, declining church just like St. Friendly. The congregation at that time was called 'Old Faithful Church.' Back in the forties and fifties it was a really big church, but by the eighties only about thirty people worshiped inside the big, old, beautiful building. Basically, they were great folks, who were in deep trouble. Then one day things began to change." (p. 148)

The change in Old Faithful Church was brought about by an intentional discernment process for core values, bedrock beliefs, motivating vision, and ultimately, key mission. The following things happened.

Old Faithful Church decided that they would rather change than die—even if change meant abandoning cherished traditions and risking all their assets. They had enjoyed relatively healthy, harmonious pastoral relationships for years, but the current pastor was weary of doing all the things clergy usually do and still having no real impact on the community. The lay leaders were fed up with management, operating deficits, and the never ending, fruitless quest for a youth group. They yearned to give themselves to spiritual growth. The worship participants cared about each other very much but were bored to tears. The women were tired of potluck suppers and longed to have visions. The men were tired of meetings and longed to dream dreams. And everybody wanted to do something that really mattered for a change.

Old Faithful Church was ready to sacrifice everything for the sake of a Biblical vision. "After all," they said, "what have we got to lose? If we stake everything on change and fail, we will only close the church a few years ahead of what was anticipated. We may as well have a great time! And maybe our children and grandchildren will discover some crazy new opportunities and come back to church for a while. If we are going to look like fools anyway, we would rather be fools who went looking for a Biblical vision than fools who just handed over the congregational assets to our declining denominational land bank."

The whole congregation set aside much of the routine baggage of activity they normally carried around during the Christian year and covenanted together for spiritual growth. For 52 weeks they studied the great visioning stories of the Bible—in worship, in groups, and as individuals. These stories became the topic of conversation during the Couples' Club dinners and the after-service coffee hours. They discovered that Biblical visions did not come in a vacuum but invariably came when Biblical people became clear about their real values and deepest beliefs. They designed a process of congregational gatherings and focus groups to achieve that clarity and consensus, in the belief that Biblical visions could be revealed in such fertile spiritual ground.

Of course, there were obstacles. First, Old Faithful Church had a long list of inactive voting members, many of whom were cynical. "We tried all that strategic planning stuff when we put in the new pipe organ," they said, "and it didn't get us anywhere." Others just shrugged their shoulders and refused to participate: "We're doomed anyway. The most important thing is to make sure my funeral can take place in the sanctuary where my great-grandfather's memorial window is located."

The congregation found it helpful to look beyond the periodic strategic planning attempts of the congregation and celebrate the historic transformational moments and surprising ministry breakthroughs, from their earliest mission beginnings right up to the experimental Christmas Eve service that packed the church. They refused to let the agenda of the church be manipulated to service the personal needs of a few. About half of the inactive members left the church to prearrange their funerals elsewhere, and income dipped approximately two years earlier than originally predicted. Yet it was a relief to leave the nay-sayers behind on what some called with exhilaration "the greatest church gamble in two centuries of ministry."

Second, Old Faithful Church had the honesty to recognize that not a few people were scared to death by the visioning stories of the Bible. "A Biblical vision would be wonderful," someone said, "but will I have to be touched by a burning coal or walk with a limp?" Another core leader muttered: "I'm a little old to leave Egypt and go wandering in the desert!" Even the teenagers remaining in the church were scared: "Peter had a vision on a rooftop and ended by befriending his worst enemy. Is God going to ask me to get close to that geek down the street?"

The congregation discovered that Bible study and mutual support were merging into a single activity. Reading the Bible became stressful, as well as exciting, and people needed to talk through their fears. Prayer began to have a deeper significance. People no longer prayed for things they already knew they could accept and understand; they prayed for the courage to receive things they could not accept or understand. Unlikely prayer partnerships were formed between young and old, women and men, rich and poor, well educated and poorly educated. The budget certainly was not reassuring—and they looked toward their faith.

Third, Old Faithful Church had a long tradition of avoiding public interaction, and most of the folks doubted the public had much interest in religion beyond a fascination with long center aisles for a bridal procession. "People will get mad if we start talking to them about religion," some said. Others predicted that the strangers would just laugh at them and walk away. One elderly lady mused: "Truth is, I'm not all sure I want to know what they think of us!"

The congregation was very tentative at first. They began with some very cautious surveys among groups who used their property. Congregational leaders began holding their meetings beyond the church building in public places. When public interaction brought neither anger nor indifference, the congregation become fascinated by the spiritual hunger that actually existed out there. Sometimes some of their self-perceptions were contradicted, and they winced at the real truth about their so-called friendliness. But, more often than not, congregational participants began to realize that they did have something of vital importance to share that could really benefit other people.

Finally, Old Faithful Church had a few really optimistic people who worried that if the congregation were revitalized they might just slip back into old habits again. "If it's just a numbers game," they said, "I don't want to play." Another added: "I can never go back to that pipe organ again, but am I prepared to let rap be the liturgical form of the future?"

The congregation realized that, however clear they might become about their values, beliefs, vision, and mission, they must enshrine creativity and change in the heart of congregational experience. Never again would they allow themselves to be dominated by any genre of music, be it pipe organ or electric guitar. Never again would they allow themselves to be lulled to sleep by an ecclesiastical machine that perpetuated the institution and ignored people.

Core Values

After several weeks of congregational gatherings, focus groups, and innumerable conversations, Old Faithful Church began to identify their core values. The process was a little unnerving because they realized some unpleasant truths about their behavior. Mostly, however, the process was fun. It was a joy to understand the values their closest friends held, but never really shared, and then to discover that they celebrated these values together. They also felt a little like Jacob fleeing from Esau. For decades they had used public interest in religion to aggrandize their ecclesiastical institution, had stolen the public birthright of spirituality, and had only now awakened to their authentic values to find themselves alone in the cultural desert. They now knew that:

Their Core Values were NOT:	Their Core Values REALLY WERE:
Homogeneous circles of friendliness	Deep, safe intimacy
Orderliness and structure	Personal and spiritual growth
Children and youth who perpetuate our heritage	Love for teens as teens, children as children
Membership	Generosity to total strangers
Property	Care for creation
Solemnity and duty	Joy and laughter
Tradition	Creativity
Personal sacrifice	Holistic health
Financial stability	Aggressive mission

Of course, the temptations to return to the old core values were always strong—and often very subtle! For the first time, however, they could see clearly what preference or choices they passionately wanted to make in their daily living. They realized that these were exactly the positive values they wanted to enshrine in congregational life. Even if only one newcomer were to come to their worship service all year, that newcomer needed to know that Old Faithful Church lived those values. Maybe it was too late. Maybe they had stolen their brother's birthright, and there was nothing else to expect but that their brother Esau would pursue and destroy them. But at least they knew what mattered.

Bedrock Beliefs

Now that they had built deeper confidence and trust in each other, the congregational participants of Old Faithful Church were ready to talk about their beliefs. This was a little more frightening. After years of repeating the same old creeds in church, studying the traditional catechism, and listening to the regular cycles of the lectionary, folks were apt to think of beliefs in abstract, doctrinal formulas or trite, well-worn phrases. They really hated being pushed to prioritize them, because they had been told all their lives that theology is systematic and no one belief could be more significant than another. Because most of the folks did not really understand many of the doctrines anyway, they were afraid that sharing their beliefs would only reveal how ignorant and shallow they were.

Oddly enough, feeling like Jacob fleeing from Esau actually helped them take courage to examine their bedrock beliefs. The pastor invited the people to imagine themselves in Jacob's sandals. They pictured themselves alone and frightened, vulnerable and threatened by injury or death, hungry, poor, and homeless. Then the pastor asked, "What is there in your faith to give you strength?" It was actually not hard to imagine this situation. Everyone in the congregation had experienced crises that felt like that—even the youngest. In order to stimulate the imagination, the congregation sang a great diversity of songs, viewed Christian art over the centuries, and listened to stories of faith. Not everyone found strength in faith in the same way, but the collage revealed these patterns:

This We *Really* Believe

God miraculously changes people.
God *always* forgives.

Jesus is "Summer in the Soul"
[from the song "As Comes the Breath of Spring"].

Jesus is the shepherd.

The Bible is a guide for living,
and the Gospel is welcome relief

Prayer can change fate.
Mission is a ripple effect of my spiritual growth.

Creation *must* be cherished.
Personal relationships are sacred.

Every human being is gifted by God.
Christian Maturity = Christian Ministry

Of course, individuals in the congregation believed additional things about God, life, death, destiny, and Jesus that were not included in this list. And of course, individuals all had their unique perspectives and experiences with the beliefs shared in this list. Their celebration was that this list of beliefs was shared by everyone—shared so passionately that the congregation was willing to stake its very future on them.

This shared celebration was both exciting and uncomfortable for Old Faithful Church. In the past, the congregation had occasionally been accused of being hypocritical by church outsiders because they did not behave in the way outsiders thought they must believe. Now, however, they were really vulnerable to any charge of hypocrisy, because everybody inside and outside the church knew exactly what they believed—and reasonably expected their behavior to match it! Participants swallowed hard when they realized their imperfections, and they therefore entrenched their commitment to adult spiritual disciplines even more deeply into their lifestyles.

That, of course, uncovered an even deeper anxiety for Old Faithful Church. Readiness for spiritual growth assumed that God would bless it. But what if God had already left Old Faithful Church behind? They knew that God was already out there doing divine work in the hungry world and that at best they were just trying to catch up. What if the best thing they could do for the mission of God was to just sell the building, amalgamate with some other bigger congregation, and distribute their assets? They felt like Jacob must have felt. It was midnight in the desert, and life and God's mission seemed to have vanished over their horizon, leaving them powerless and alone.

Motivating Vision

Now that they had built deeper confidence and trust in each other and identified the heartfelt beliefs that gave them strength, the participants of Old Faithful Church were ready to look for a vision. This was the most frightening thing of all! Their Bible study had taught them that authentic Biblical visions could be painful as well as joyous. If they were to receive a vision, it would come like the ladder to heaven came to Jacob. It would come in the night, startle them from contented slumber, and proceed to change their very identity. It would come in the tears and anguish of deepest yearning—at the moment when they were giving the least energy to see it—and it would change Old Faithful Church forever. Here was the paradox of any vision process: How do you gaze out of the corner of your eye? Despite their spiritual preparation, the people of Old Faithful Church still felt prey to three addictions left over from life in Christendom.

1. *Deep in their hearts, Old Faithful Church believed visions were created, not revealed.* They tried brainstorming and collected all the creative ideas every person could think, but still no vision emerged. They tried dreaming and collected all the hopes every person could imagine, but still no vision emerged. Finally, they painstakingly developed a strategic plan to modify programs, property, and staff over the next five years, but still no vision emerged. They had lots of ideas, lots of dreams, and lots of plans—but no confidence in God's blessing and no motivation to move heaven and earth to achieve them.

Finally, they stopped trying to be creative. Instead, they committed themselves to a spirituality of waiting. In personal discipline and corporate worship, they created a climate of prayer, meditation, and intense conversation. The atmosphere of the congregation's life became pregnant with expectation. All the business of the liturgical agenda, and all the crush of institutional meetings, came to a halt as the people waited with baited breath in the sacred void.

2. *Without even thinking, Old Faithful Church assumed that vision would come to the official board.* They sent the board away on weekend retreat—no vision. They elected new, more spiritual people to the official board, and sent them away on retreat—no vision. They converted the agenda of every group and committee to emphasize prayer and Bible study, and every officer covenanted to a spiritual discipline—no vision. They did have more powerful meetings. They also had leaders who were hungrier than ever before for a vision. Their leaders also felt guiltier than ever before that they had not received one.

It took a while for Old Faithful Church to accept the fact that Biblical visions usually come to individuals on the margins of community and church life and at the pioneering edges of spirituality. In the midst of the spirituality of waiting, the staff and officers were empty, but unexpected people were starting to bubble with excitement. Some were teens; others were seniors. Some were very rich, and some were very poor. Few were on the board now, but some had been on the board previously and had burned out. Many were church dropouts, marginal members, fringe community members, or core worship participants who had always resisted serving offices. Most were people linked to the church through some particular group or outreach ministry. The church began multiplying opportunities for conversation with and among these people, and soon visions were being shared, refined, and owned with passion everywhere.

3. *Old Faithful Church assumed that the old wineskins of worship still had enough flexibility to hold this new wine that was beginning to ferment in the life of the congregation.* The clergy tried putting a different slant on the exposition of the Common Lectionary—no vision. The choir introduced some more upbeat anthems, and the organist switched to the grand piano—no vision. The worship committee borrowed liturgies and prayers from a greater variety of contemporary resources—no vision. They had more people in worship than before but not the fringe people who were at the center of the fermentation process.

Finally, painfully, the worship designers threw caution to the winds. They did it with clear time limits, assuring the 30 veterans who never missed a Sunday that their tradition would return as a worship opportunity. And because the 30 veterans were as eager for a vision of Biblical proportions as everybody else, that was acceptable to them.

Throwing caution to the winds meant that experimentation became the rule in worship. The Common Lectionary was replaced with the great visioning stories of scripture. Laity and other volunteers from the fringes frequently spoke. Liturgy was reduced and spontaneity was encouraged. Drama, dance, and visual arts made worship very participatory. The choir was replaced by various ensembles, which attempted every genre of music possible; and the grand piano was moved aside to make room for keyboard and percussion. Music included everything from folk, to jazz, to Dixieland, to rock, to rap (the last two being particularly painful to the stalwart 30 veterans who placed cotton in their ears and still came every Sunday because they, too, yearned for a Biblical vision). Every prayer, every liturgy, every worship response was handcrafted by someone or some group in the church. They even rented extra cordless microphones for ushers to hand out during the service to anyone who raised a hand, amplifiers and speakers for surround-sound, and extralarge projection screens to continually display the words of songs and images of the real world that was God's mission field. The vision came. It came in the night as several people sat bolt upright in bed at 4:00 [A.M.] and immediately telephoned members of the official board. It spread like wildfire during the week. They cast the vision on Sunday morning, and the coffee hour was electric. It took a few weeks to refine it and build an ever larger team-ownership for it. When people heard the vision, their hearts leapt and their blood raced. It was audacious, urgent, and hinted toward congregational changes they could only guess at. God called them to be "Summer in the Soul" for the spiritually yearning public.

The vision of "Summer in the Soul" was clearly linked to the bedrock beliefs, which had identified the old hymn "As Comes the Breath of Spring" as a powerful source for strength in times of trouble. In fact, that very hymn had brought the congregation to its feet in tears when they sang it to open the funeral service for a young woman beloved by the church who had been killed meaninglessly by a drunk driver. Because this was a hymn from the historic past of the church, the vision clearly had continuity with the mission heritage of the congregation, and this was reassuring to the 30 church veterans. Whatever audacious change the future might hold, that continuity would be precious.

The context of the congregation was a lush, temperate climate with big trees, fantastic gardens, and weeds and wildflowers that could take over a field overnight. "Summer in the Soul" seemed to capture that sense of dynamic, healthy, uncontrollable growth that was true not only of the climate but also of the spiritual ferment of the public. This was an area receiving enormous immigration from all over the world, and it was experiencing such extraordinary growth that the social infrastructures were almost overwhelmed. The mixed cultures of the region awakened to new surprises (positive and negative) every day. The spiritual yearning and experimentation was no less dynamic. To be "Summer in the Soul" in such a context implied multicultural sensitivity; the multiplication of new shoots for spiritual growth; the splicing of branches in safe, healthy relationships; and the fruitfulness of all kinds of spontaneous ministries that cared for people and creation, all at the same time. It was a big vision. And Old Faithful

Church knew they would have to be more than old and faithful to achieve it.

Key Mission

The excitement and urgency of the vision motivated the people of Old Faithful Church to begin developing strategies and tactics to fulfill the vision as soon as possible. At the beginning, however, they wanted to declare themselves to the public. There were two reasons for this. First, the congregation wanted to celebrate the vision in a way that would capture the imagination of all the people in the wider community. This would give them an instant public recognition no matter what the ministry opportunity might be in the future. Second, the congregation wanted to involve all those people in the ongoing process of building strategies and tactics to fulfill the vision. They did not want to develop a strategic plan and then lay it on the public. They had already tried that and knew it would not work. Instead, they wanted to invite the public to help them celebrate the vision *and* actually help in developing the new ministries. They were ready to enter into creative new partnerships with religious organizations, non-profit organizations and charities, municipalities, and even corporate business.

In order to do this, the congregation chose 12 of the most creative people they could find—each of whom had strong synthesizing skills—and asked them to ponder the core values, bedrock beliefs, and motivating vision of the congregation and distill the mission statement of the church. In the end, this team did more than that.

1. *The first thing they recommended was that the name of the congregation be changed.* The vision had, indeed, changed the very identity of the congregation. Just as God changed Jacob's name after the vision of the ladder to heaven, so also God would change the name of the congregation to reflect the new identity that the vision had given to them. The congregation was renamed New Hope-in-the-Heart Church.

2. *The mission statement to be developed needed to be sufficiently brief to be printed on the side of a bus, a pencil, or a business card.* They considered printing it on a match cover but decided the association of matches with smoking would contradict their core

value to care for creation. Using a variety of startling graphics, the mission statement became:

They used this mission statement on every document and in all publicity. Eventually, it would be illuminated on billboards at the corners of the church property and sewn as patches on to the sleeves of every volunteer in every ministry. The phrase was already used in a closing song regularly used during worship, which congregational participants had also identified as powerfully emotional and motivating.

3. *Finally, the visual metaphor implied by the vision "Summer in the Soul" gave the congregation a general marketing strategy.* The cry would be: "Everything organic!" The congregation would create T-shirts with an almost jungle-like picture on the front and use many other pictures of gardens, forests, and grain fields—all with the slogan "Summer in the Soul!"—to be given away to newcomers. They would be cotton, of course, not synthetic. If the sacrament of communion was served during one of the worship options, neither the wine nor the bread would contain preservatives. Eventually, the worship center and property would be filled with real, growing vegetation. Indeed, during a later property expansion, the congregation abandoned old ecclesiastical plans and incorporated the organic architectural insights of Frank Lloyd Wright.

It was not hard to imagine strategies and tactics for ministry springing from such a vision and mission. The imaginations of the participants of New Hope-in-the-Heart Church went wild. Could there be worship options reflecting the ethnic heritage and music of every new immigration community in the region? Could there be new partnerships for community service and advocacy with native Indians or First Nations? Could there be an explosion of affinity groups building healthy, safe relationships? Could there be social service opportunities to assist the currently over-whelmed regional infrastructure? Could a single facility include holistic health opportunities that included gardens for Tai Chi, aerobic workout centers, parlors for intimate discussion, safe havens for private prayer, and hi-tech worship centers for corporate celebration so that under a single vision of Christian health body, mind, heart, and spirit could all be addressed? The opportunities for a community with clarity and consensus about its core values, bedrock beliefs, motivating vision, and key mission were endless.

— PART IV —

DRAWING A NEW MINISTRY MAP!

— 15 —
DRAWING A NEW
MINISTRY MAP

The congregational mission assessment and the discernment of the basic boundaries of congregational life together lay a foundation for future planning. Not only can the congregation make plans but they can make plans . . .

- that target systemic weaknesses, build on systemic strengths, and avoid self-defeating behavior patterns;
- with confidence that the congregation will truly be motivated to follow through with even the most ambitious plans; and
- with maximum energy for creativity and experimentation because every congregational leader and group knows clearly the boundaries beyond which they cannot go.

The long-range planning done during the last gasps of Christendom in the twentieth century usually failed to be effective. This was because Christendom congregations tended to think *programmatically*, rather than *systemically*, and failed to identify corporate addictions that would sabotage their best-laid plans. These congregations also tended to assume a clarity about congregational identity that did not exist. Congregational identity tended to be blended with denominational identity. The result was low motivation and an inability to enthusiastically follow planning with action. Finally, Christendom congregations tended to simply repeat well-worn and ineffective paths of ministry because their obsessions with control hindered any serious experimentation and creativity. The Pre-Christian era of the twenty-first century demands a more comprehensive, more entrepreneurial, and more flexible process for church development.

THE INADEQUACY OF STRATEGIC PLANNING

Traditional strategic planning is being replaced in growing churches with a more effective process, which I call *ministry mapping*. Here is the difference:

STRATEGIC PLANNING	MINISTRY MAPPING
Long Distance	On Site
Linear	Omnidirectional
Uniform	Contextual
Performed by Technicians	Performed by Explorers
Relies on Property and Programs	Relies on Spiritual Disciplines and Activities
Follows a Chain of Command	Follows Individual Initiative
Allows Little Deviation	Expects Constant Deviation

1. *Strategic planning was deliberately done from a distance, usually from a national or judicatory office.* This supposedly gave planning greater objectivity, freeing the process from the personal perspectives or leadership styles of local people. It also allowed the greater resources of the denomination to be used in a controlled environment, so that finances could be allocated with all the clarity of a bird's eye view. Demographic statistics and trends gathered by telephone or mail—or by relative strangers temporarily imported into the neighborhood—were the primary foundation of planning.

In contrast, *ministry mapping is deliberately done on site* by the same people who will live or die by the implementation of the plan. Ministry mapping celebrates a subjectivity that is directly linked to the intuitions and experiences of local people. While the generic mission funds of the denomination can be important, it is the entrepreneurship and creativity of the growing congregation itself that is the real resource. They would rather be cash-poor and creative than debt-free and stagnant. Clarity in mission comes from recognition of the minute details of local needs as perceived by the people who live there.

2. *Strategic planning in the age of Christendom was linear.* It assumed change would occur through a continuous series of actions and consequences that could be reasonably predicted.

Planners would project a five-year plan or a ten-year plan and prescribe a series of specific actions that, done in the proper order, would inevitably lead to a vibrant church. The plan worked independent of anything but the most dramatic changing circumstances.

In contrast, *ministry mapping in the Pre-Christian era is omnidirectional*. It assumes change will only occur through the combination of a variety of influences happening simultaneously and that the end result is rarely predictable. At any given time, the local planners cannot know exactly what the ministry will be like two years away. As mission unfolds, planners do not repeatedly refer to a timeline. They prepare themselves for the unexpected. They seize opportunities as they emerge. Even the smallest nuance of change will impact the emerging map of ministry.

3. *Strategic planning assumed contextual uniformity.* People were essentially the same, their needs were the same, and their cultural forms of experience were essentially the same. Architectural designs, organizational structures, and worship services could simply be borrowed from one place to another. One church of a given denominational brand name looked remarkably like every other. Continuity in planning was a higher value than sensitivity to context.

In contrast, *ministry mapping assumes contextual diversity*. People, their needs, and their cultural forms of experience are not the same. Architecture, organization, and worship must all be significantly adapted to the local realities. Ethnic or cultural orientation will be far more decisive than denominational continuity. The ministry map in one congregation will be dramatically different from another.

4. *Strategic planning in Christendom was performed by technicians.* These experts, sometimes called church planters or church developers, were essentially interim leaders appointed because of their expertise and then rotated to another church once they had worked their magic. They had most of the church growth tactics already in their toolbox and industriously created an ecclesiastical machine.

In contrast, *ministry mapping in the Pre-Christian era is performed by explorers*. These leaders are always amateurs, no matter how long they have been involved in church growth. They explore the contextual territory thoroughly before ever proposing change for the church. They have no well-stocked toolbox of proven tactics that simply can be deployed. They are committed to long-term ministry, knowing that a percentage of all experiments will inevitably fail and that they will need to learn from their mistakes, customize every strategy, and try again. They will nurture what Bill Easum and I have described as a "Spiritual Redwood."

5. *Strategic planning has traditionally relied on property and program as the keys for church development.* Property was the primary vehicle of mission. Its space would be used both by the church community and rented to the public, and the mission goal was to bring as many people inside as possible. The architecture would articulate the faith. Programs would be the other significant vehicle of mission. They would be led by professionals (who all needed offices) and supported by volunteer managers and fund raisers (who all cherished the property as the foundation for all mission). The property became a constant in the planning process, and programming was adapted to it.

In contrast, *ministry mapping relies on spiritual disciplines and activities as the keys for church growth.* Spiritual discipline is the primary vehicle of mission. The development of people precedes the development of property. The people articulate the faith, and the goal is to get as many of them out among the public as possible. Their activities may be organized or spontaneous—and may involve individuals or groups—but all are self-directed and occur anywhere in the community. Emerging mission becomes the constant in the planning process, and property is either reshaped, relocated, or set aside altogether to facilitate it.

6. *Strategic planning in Christendom followed a chain of command.* A clear hierarchy of authority implemented and monitored the strategic plan so that the proper sequence of actions and consequences could not be intentionally or unintentionally subverted. Strategic plans required control. Clergy and elected officers controlled what was done, when it was done, and how it was done. Endless reports and liaison relationships ensured that no part of the strategic plan interfered with another part of the strategic plan and that the sequence of actions and consequences unfolded as predicted.

In contrast, *ministry mapping in the Pre-Christian era follows individual initiative.* Consensus and clarity about values, beliefs, vision, and mission allow individuals or teams to do whatever they feel called to do. Ministry maps require freedom. Leadership equips for excellence and then gets out of the way. Networks of communication help people learn from each other's mistakes (and successes). Although it is important to know what is going on and what possibilities are emerging, the choices will be made out of the spiritual growth of individuals.

7. *Strategic planning allowed little deviation from the plan.* This is why they rarely work in the rapidly changing environment of the twenty-first century. By the time the organization has reached the second year in a five-year plan, the world is a different place and the plan is obsolete. Nevertheless, the strategic plan has a life of its own. It seeks to impose itself, sometimes by sheer brute force, on congregational life. What most people believe to be their denominational tradition or their congregational heritage is really just a strategic plan from a decade or so ago that continues to dominate the agenda.

In contrast, *ministry mapping* not only allows deviation, it *expects constant deviation.* Even the smallest change in the cultural environment will reshape the map of ministry because mission must be effective above all. Ministry maps do not have a life outside the changing context of congregation and community life. Explorers are constantly being deployed to perceive the shifts and changes happening among the people of the community. Sometimes old initiatives will be terminated (no matter how sacred), and sometimes new initiatives will be started (no matter how risky), but most often, options will simply be multiplied to mirror the increasingly diverse community.

THE EMERGENCE OF MINISTRY MAPPING

The strategic planning of Christendom can be described as the science of controlling one's own destiny in a Christian society. The ministry mapping of the emerging Pre-Christian era is the art of finding your way in a chaos of cultures.

I use the metaphor of topographic cartography to describe this form of planning. Today's satellites can map the landscape of the planet to an accuracy of inches. Ministry mapping, however, resembles the adventure of cartography in humbler days. These were the days when cartographers were also explorers risking their lives in the unknown wilderness. Ministry mappers today must risk themselves for every mile measured and risk the properties and pension plans for every hill explored. Every nuance of culture, every change in regional infrastructure, every opportunity to benefit humankind, and every pathway to grace must be investigated, correlated with the other features of the cultural landscape, and plotted on the spiritual map. And, since the cultural wilderness continues to run wild, this must be done over and over again. For every path to a safe haven or breathtaking ministry, there are ten dead ends that will need to be explored.

Ministry mapping is not about tactical tips and programs that can be implemented in proper order and inevitably result in positive church growth. It is about principles, orientations, and flexible strategies that result in multiple options for mission. It equips leaders to learn from mistakes, experiment with possibilities, and move through the cultural chaos with the conviction that nothing is sacred except the transforming power of God and their daily walk with Jesus.

— 16 —
DRAWING THE MAP

CALIBRATE YOUR COMPASS

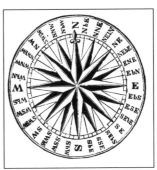

The basic boundaries of congregational life, which together form the congregation's identity, function as a sophisticated compass for future exploration and planning. Congregational leaders must know their limits of creativity. Remember that this is not a prescriptive list of everything congregational leaders can do. This is a proscriptive boundary beyond which congregational leaders cannot go—but within which they are free to explore wherever they wish. The more deeply they penetrate the cultural wilderness, the more important it will be to have clarity about the core values, bedrock beliefs, motivating vision, and key mission that are their orientation in personal and corporate life.

You may wish to refer to the discernment process described in chapter 8 and to the foundation questions of the congregational mission assessment in chapter 4 (especially questions 4-7, 10-16, 25-27, 38-45, and, from chapter 6, 261-66).

Picture the essential identity of the congregation as an umbrella that is held over the heads of a diverse people by visionary, motivating leaders with a simple, flexible organization. Identify the key elements in each aspect of the picture. Identify the song in the heart that expresses the vision and the key mission to which all activities are directed. List the core values and bedrock beliefs that are the consensus of the congregation. Describe the organizational principles that allow the umbrella to bend, rather than break. Identify the leaders whose primary purpose is to articulate the basic boundaries of congregational life over and over again.

MOTIVATING VISION
KEY MISSION

CORE
VALUES

BEDROCK
BELIEFS

PERMISSION
GIVING
ORGANIZATION

LEADERSHIP

Once you have completed the picture, answer the following questions by listing strategies and identifying gaps in communication:

1. How do people within the congregation clearly perceive and celebrate this umbrella? and what groups have the most difficulty perceiving and celebrating the umbrella?
2. How do the people beyond the congregation recognize this umbrella? and what groups have the most difficulty recognizing the umbrella?
3. How do congregational leaders clearly and effectively extend this umbrella over their daily lives and the daily life of the congregation? and is any activity taking place beyond the umbrella?

Rank in order of urgency the aspects of the umbrella that require the prayerful attention and intense dialogue of the annual congregational meeting or annual congregational leadership summit:

	Define	Refine	Celebrate
Motivating Vision	____	____	____
Key Mission	____	____	____
Core Values	____	____	____
Bedrock Beliefs	____	____	____
Organizational Flexibility	____	____	____
Leadership Roles	____	____	____

Finally, regularly review the key mission of the congregation in every congregational gathering or leadership training event: *In 15 words or less this is the message every person in the world needs to hear from us right now.*

IDENTIFY THE TOPOGRAPHY

An initial survey of the landscape will immediately reveal dominant features that will determine the choices for future exploration. These mountains and valleys, lakes, rivers, or deserts will not only need to be incorporated into the map, they will shape future exploration and settlement. In the same way, the ministry map must immediately recognize the dominant features and trends of the cultural landscape. Any ministry will need to be customized to fit into the local context. Why deploy ministries suitable for Caucasian populations when the landscape is clearly Asian? Why laboriously build a road to import a new ministry into the cultural landscape when it could be more easily transported by canoe with the help of a few local friends?

Ministry mapping gives special attention to the identification of trends and the recognition of potential partners who are already working in the region. You may wish to refer to the feedback from the listening-prayer triads (described in the discernment process in chapter 9) and the following questions from the congregational mission assessment in Part 2: All Systems Go!: 18-23, 192-97, 204, 216-19, 229-30, and 262.

Trends

The cultural landscape is dynamic and changing with greater rapidity than ever before. Congregational leadership will need to be continually deployed to observe the changing publics of the region. Research will need to gather data from municipal, business, social service, and nonprofit-charity planners. Community experience is not segmented anymore into sacred and secular, and all data must be welcomed and compared.

The following charts invite comparison not only between different cultural trends but between the patterns of change within the congregation and those beyond the congregation. List the key trends.

A. Demographic Trends: (changes in race, culture, language, age, wealth, and living conditions)

Community	Congregation
1.	
2.	
3.	
4.	

Population segments involved in our church:

Population segments not involved in our church:

B. Psychographic Trends: (changes in attitudes, lifestyles, tastes, and political perspectives)

Community	Congregation
1.	
2.	

3.

4.

Population segments involved in our church:

Population segments not involved in our church:

    C. Geographic Trends: (changes in zoning, utilities, construction, environment, and traffic patterns)

Community   Congregation
1.
2.
3.
4.

Emerging geographic obstacles to ministry:

Emerging geographic opportunities for ministry:

    D. Behavioral Trends: (Changes in racial integration, shopping, crisis management, and crime rates)

Community   Congregation
1.
2.
3.
4.

    E. Spiritual Trends: (topical interests, media priorities, moral ambiguities, and spiritual hunger)

Community   Congregation
1.
2.
3.
4.

Partnerships

The cultural landscape already includes individuals, groups, or organizations that are interacting with the above trends and doing important work. In the era of Christendom, when society was essentially Christian, culturally homogeneous, and evolving slowly, strategic planners could afford to be competitive for a share of a large religious market. In the Pre-Christian era, however, when society is spiritually and culturally diverse and change is revolutionary, ministry mappers must be committed to conversation and cooperation.

Identify the potential partners that already exist, or are emerging, in the cultural chaos of the region. Be sure to consider church, parachurch, government, social service, nonprofit, business, and informal social movements.

POTENTIAL PARTNER	Core Values We Share	Bedrock Beliefs We Share	Motivating Vision We Share	Key Mission We Share

IDENTIFY THE BENCHMARKS

In order to draw future contour lines to reflect the topography of the landscape, cartographers must carefully fix specific key elevations to be points of reference. These benchmarks are often physically marked by a cairn or tower visible from miles away. Not only can the explorers orient themselves on their journey through the wilderness, they can do this with remarkable precision and evaluate how far above or below the benchmark they might be.

In the same way, ministry mappers must define the benchmarks within both the cultural landscape and their own congregation. These benchmarks will be the institutions or activities that: (1) set the standards for quality to which everything will be compared and (2) determine the pace of change for everything that happens. A benchmark on a ministry map identifies those community or congregational realities around which everything else will orient itself. You may wish to refer to the following questions from the pentagon model in the congregational mission assessment in Part 2: All Systems Go!:

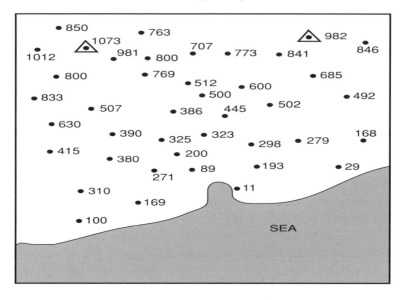

- Experiencing God, questions 56, 64, and 75;
- Growing in God, questions 93-94, 99-101, and 103-5;
- Listening to God, questions 121-22, 125, and 130-32;
- Serving God, questions 144-45, 148-51, and 158-59; and
- Sharing God, questions 170-72, and 177-81.

The following charts help you identify the nature of the benchmarks for your context.

COMMUNITY		
Institution or Activity	Standard of Quality	Pace of Change

CONGREGATION		
Institution or Activity	Standard of Quality	Pace of Change

These benchmarks in the community and the congregation now become your reference points for the development of every creative ministry in the congregation. Every ministry will strive to achieve these standards of quality; and the development of every ministry will need to be paced by, and related to, the development of each of these benchmark institutions or activities.

MARK THE HAZARDS

Once the benchmarks have been set, cartographers will seek to identify significant hazards in the landscape. These are areas that

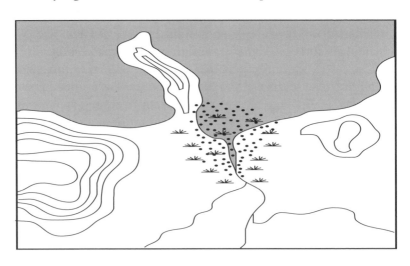

are dangerous or will likely be unsuitable for human habitation and travel. Such hazards include swamps and bogs, geysers and hot springs, steep slopes with potential for rock slides and avalanche, or deserts with no stable source of water. The identification of hazards is not an end in itself. It helps the explorers plot their course for the future process of mapping. It is always helpful to know where the quicksand is before risking an expedition!

In the same way, ministry mappers need to identify the hazards in the cultural landscape and the corporate addictions within their congregation. Hazards will include issues and activities that will be particularly challenging or difficult in the unique context of the community. For example, building a credible marriage enrichment ministry in a community whose history includes several clergy found guilty of sexual indiscretions could become a long and challenging task. Initiating any residential ministry to house a special group (a home for seniors or the physically impaired, a halfway house, or other ministry) in a context with particularly complex municipal codes or bureaucratic barriers could become a costly endeavor.

Addictions are the self-defeating behavior patterns, which congregations chronically deny, that you have identified in the congregational mission assessment. The fact that you have identified them does not mean that they do not still have power in your congregational life and mission. For example, a congregation addicted to patterns of clergy dependency and staff conflict can expect that marriage enrichment ministry to become even more challenging. A congregation addicted to traditional Sunday schools and organ music may find that residential housing project for seniors to be an activity that reinforces addiction rather than maximizes mission.

These examples hint at the real danger of hidden hazards on the cultural map of the community. Community hazards and congregational addictions are each bad on their own, but they often seem to attract each other. It is as if congregations are compelled to enter the swamp! The self-defeating behavior pattern seeks out the hazard so that the congregation can more easily be defeated! Congregations tend to be drawn into activities for which they are systemically weakest! In the game of golf, it really does not matter where you hit the ball in the fairway—just do not hit it into the sandtrap! And those who repeatedly hit it into the sandtrap cannot blame the golf course; they must blame their golf swing!

I do not suggest that congregations must avoid cultural hazards at all costs. Even swamps have been transformed into residential estates, and geysers can become opportunities for tourism! I am suggesting that a congregation will need to prepare itself in advance. Ministry among the cultural hazards on the map will require even more intentional spiritual discipline. The congregation will need to exercise itself and perhaps receive special coaching to overcome its addictions before attempting such daunting tasks.

You will want to refer to the addictive behavior patterns that you have traced through all eleven subsystems of congregational life using the congregational mission assessment. You may also wish to refer to the following questions:

- Congregational Mission, questions 18-19, and 22-24;
- Congregational Organization, questions 38-44;
- Experiencing God, questions 60, 70-73;
- Growing in God, questions 94-95;
- Listening to God, questions 127-32;
- Serving God, 148-50; and
- Sharing God, questions 179-81.

The following charts will help you identify cultural hazards and congregational addictions, explore the potential negative links between them, and identify the spiritual exercise or coaching required before the congregation tries to do ministry in the midst of such hazards.

COMMUNITY

HAZARD Issue or Activity	Link to Addictive Behavior	Spiritual Exercise Required	Possible Coaching Needed

CONGREGATION

ADDICTION Self-Defeating Pattern	Link to Hazard of Issue or Activity	Spiritual Exercise Required	Possible Coaching Needed

DRAW THE CONTOUR LINES

The most visible features on a topographic map are the contour lines. These curving lines mark the varying elevations that are the hills, mountains, slopes, and valleys of the landscape. The space between each contour line marks a specific number of feet higher or lower than the next line. Contour lines that are close together reveal a steep slope, and contour lines that are widely spaced mark a gentle hill or plain. The curves of the lines indicate peaks and valleys, hills and depressions in the landscape, and they therefore also reveal the degree of difficulty any explorer might experience traveling across the land.

Contour lines are not roads or highways. They are the contours of the land. Roads sometimes follow these contours, but more often than not they cut across the natural contours of the landscape. Roads are a product of civilization. Contours are a product of nature.

Contour lines are drawn by taking a seemingly endless series of sightings and elevations. The sightings compare any given spot in the landscape with a fixed benchmark in the distance. Contour lines represent the subtle or dramatic differences in elevation from one spot to the next. Therefore, contour lines can only be drawn by explorers in constant contact with the land. They are perpetually tramping, climbing, and scrambling over the terrain, taking their measurements and gazing intently about them.

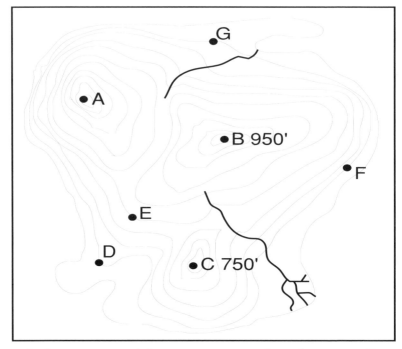

In the same way, ministry mappers must draw the contour lines of culture in order to plot the most effective course of ministry for the future. They must endlessly tramp, climb, and scramble over the social terrain, taking measurements and gazing intently about them. Notice that they are not building roads. That would be the strategic planning activity that was only possible in the days when the cultural landscape had been civilized by Christendom. In those days, the society had been tamed, and both resources and motivation existed to allow the church to cut across the natural curves of culture and impose artificial structures. Only in Christendom could magnificent downtown cathedrals be built in the midst of relative poverty. No, ministry mappers are not building roads. They are exploring a post-Christendom landscape that is now virgin territory. In order to arrive at their destination, they will need to follow the natural contours of the cultural landscape.

This means that ministry mapping is more than just identifying a social need and filling it. Many congregations see needs and even attempt to address them, but because they have not perceived the subtle links between the need and other aspects of culture, they fail. Ministry mapping is also more than just identifying the weaknesses in congregational programming and addressing them. Many congregations perceive weaknesses in programming and prioritize budget or hire staff to correct the weakness, but because they have not traced the connections between the program need and the systems of congregational life, they fail. Ministry mapping is all about finding an opportunity—a pathway into culture, if you will—and then exhausting the possibilities. If the contour line drawn by a ministry mapper is not clearly filled with potential, then no matter how urgent the social need might be, the congregation will wait until they find a better way to address it. Ministry mappers know that there are more ways than one to get from A to B.

The following chart helps ministry mappers draw the contour lines of culture. These contour lines will link emerging patterns, potential partnerships with others already working in the midst of these trends, the benchmarks of quality and change, and the systemic weaknesses and strengths of the congregation. As the contour lines are drawn, gaps may emerge:

• between emerging needs or opportunities and existing community and congregational resources.
• between emerging needs or opportunities and possible partnerships for intervention or initiative.
• between congregational systemic strengths and benchmarks for quality and speed.

These gaps may require some intermediate action that will maximize the possibilities for mission. These are not ends in themselves but necessary bridges to allow an ultimate opportunity to be seized. Finally, the clearly drawn contour line helps the ministry mappers understand the opportunity that is before them; link the opportunity to their core values, beliefs, vision, and mission; and develop specific tactics to follow the pathway and explore all its possibilities. Ministry mappers are opportunists, but they are never reckless.

The chart represents a flow of energy that moves from prayerful perception to tactics for change. Within this river of movement there are important currents. Note, for example, the following:

• The flow of energy begins with clear perceptions of the community, the world beyond the congregation where God is already working, and not with the congregation itself.

CONTOURS of OPPORTUNITY

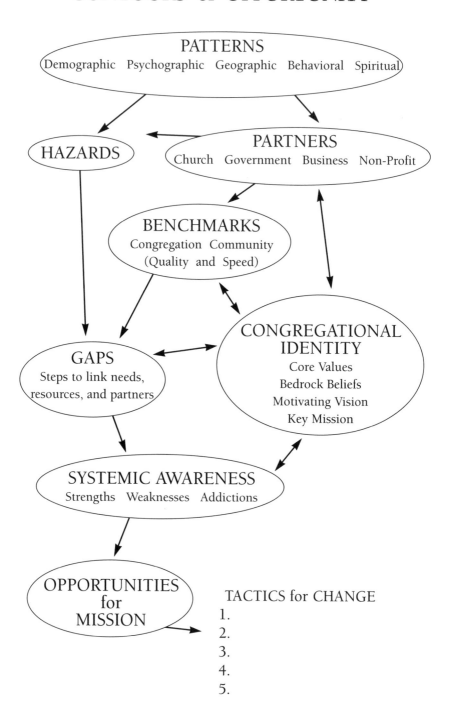

• Congregational perceptions of the hazards for mission are not discerned by the congregation alone (and therefore subject to the individual fears or dreams of congregational participants) but are discerned through partners working in the world and through clear benchmarks for quality and speed, both of which realistically test the boundaries of what is truly possible.

• All currents of energy that touch congregational identity flow both ways because identity will not only influence but also be influenced by evolving partnerships, emerging benchmarks and gaps, and growing awareness of the systems of congregational life.

• There is no direct connection between congregational identity and tactics for change because tactics will emerge only from interaction of cultural change and spiritual growth, which is the flow of the energy.

The flow of energy is itself a kind of chaos of constant interaction. Unlike strategic planning, ministry mapping is not linear. It is a constant interaction of spiritual growth and long-range planning that ultimately results in concrete tactics for change. Congregations that leap immediately from congregational identity to tactical planning will almost inevitably fail to achieve their goals. Congregations that first leap into the raging river that is the interface of cultural change and congregational mission will have the wisdom and courage to pursue their goals to the end.

Develop Exploration Teams

In ministry mapping, drawing the contour lines that connect culture and Christian mission is as much art as science, and it is as much intuition as research. Like so many of the great explorers of the North American wilderness (and one thinks of people like Lewis and Clark, Coronado, or McKenzie), the really effective ministry mappers are more than researchers. They are leaders.

The explorers who will be deployed by the congregation to seize opportunities for mission emerging in the midst of culture will reflect the new leadership that I described in the first chapter of this book in connection with the transformation of clergy. The distinction between clergy and laity is vanishing in the twenty-first century. Explorers who lead every distinct ministry of the congregation need to have the same spiritual authenticity, dedication, and skill once associated solely with the office-holding clergy, and clergy who seek to lead a congregation need to have the same worldly perceptiveness, enthusiasm, and flexibility once associated solely with volunteers.

The foundation for leadership in strategic planning processes was an ability to manipulate data and coordinate resources. Strategic planning required management skills. However, the foundation for leadership in ministry mapping is spiritual authenticity. It is the ability to interact with the public out of one's own experience of life struggle and spiritual victory. Therefore, leaders must answer the key question, which I have repeated from my previous books: What is it about my experience with Jesus that this community cannot live without? The translation of this spiritual question into cultural terminology is: What is that fundamental goal, the achievement of which is my whole purpose for living? This goal is larger than any particular mission and greater than any specific opportunity for ministry. In a sense, that entire chart of the contours of opportunity, complex and chaotic as it may be, is itself incorporated into the heart of the explorer.

WHAT IS THAT FUNDAMENTAL GOAL, THE ACHIEVEMENT OF WHICH IS MY WHOLE PURPOSE FOR LIVING??

Of course, the great explorers of North America were not only entrepreneurs. They were great team leaders. Strategic planning requires committees, but ministry mapping requires teams. These teams resemble the cartographic teams sent out from the base camp of an expedition into the unknown. They have an ultimate purpose to discover and seize opportunities for mission, but they have no clear idea where they might wander or what obstacles they might have to overcome to do it. They are a unique combination of technicians (performing repetitive tasks with dedication and skill) and buccaneers (weighing risks and seizing opportunities).

I am indebted to the excellent book *The Wisdom of Teams* by Katzenbach and Smith (Boston: Harvard Business School Press, 1993) for a definition and model that can be adapted so readily to the task of ministry mapping. They describe a team as "a small number of people with complementary skills, committed to a common purpose, performance goals, and approach for which they hold themselves mutually accountable" (p. 45). I have adapted the diagram on the next page for the church.

Ministry mappers create effective teams by developing partnerships for mutual support in spiritual growth, shared skills, and profound trust that combines a common thirst for quality and commitment to integrity. At the same time, each team is intentionally linked to the larger flow of mission energy around them. The collective abilities of the team are linked to the greater partnerships between the congregation and other organizations. The spiritual growth of team participants is linked to the larger interface between cultural change and congregational mission. Finally, the mission results of teamwork can be measured or evaluated in reference to the emerging patterns of change that are continually monitored by congregational leaders.

LOCATE BASE CAMP

Once the contour lines have been drawn on the topographic map, permanent structures can be located on the map. The word "permanent" is always a relative term because these structures (communities, roads, railroads, mining camps, and other structures made by human hands) are probably the least permanent features on the map! It is the landscape that is more enduring! In

MISSION TEAMS
Effective Ministry Partnerships

Learning
Disciplines

Mission
Results

Mutual Respect for Mission-
related Competencies
SKILLS

Mutual Respect for Mission-
related Energy and Integrity
ACCOUNTABILITY

TEAM

Collective
Ministries

Spiritual
Growth

COMMITMENT
Group ownership of
property and purpose.

Community
Partnerships

Congregational
Worship

the same way, once the contour lines of opportunity have been drawn on the ministry map, the location and design of the base camp and mission units can be identified with precision. These locations will identify the geographical region of activity, the property used for mission, or the actual facility that houses the ministry.

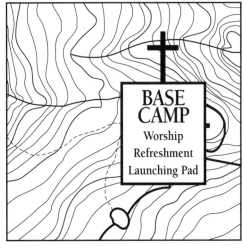

Strategic planning tended to locate these structures first and then extend ministry from these fixed points. The structures became the benchmarks of long-range planning. Ministry mappers, however, locate these structures last, making sure that such structures are precisely placed in the center of mission activity. Their benchmarks are features of the cultural landscape. The structures produced by strategic planning tended to be clearly ecclesiastical and timeless. They were fixed points, around which the neighborhood and the world were expected to rotate. The structures produced by ministry mapping, however, are always clearly marketable and changeable. Ministry mappers anticipate in advance the inevitable need to sell property and relocate wherever the emerging mission opportunity has moved, and they are prepared to radically change property in order maximize ministry amid the changing culture.

Because Christendom congregations are chronically addicted to property, those who wish to learn the art of ministry mapping will need to understand this phenomenon fully. The facilities of the Christendom era were built on the assumption that uniformity, agreement, and control were virtues in congregational life.

Uniformity

Uniformity meant that worship services and sacramental celebrations would be essentially the same, regardless of how many times during the week they happened. Music would rely on the same instrumentation (organ or piano), with the same musical strategies (large massed choirs with occasional soloists). Liturgies would require uniform movement, multiple copies of the same books, and dialogue between a single speaker and a group responding in unison. Not only would worship in a given church be essentially the same, but worship among churches of a given denomination would be the same. It was considered a virtue that a person could enter any church, anywhere, and expect to have basically the same experience.

Therefore, church facilities looked alike. Decorations and embellishments aside, a church facility was always designed for observation of activities presented at the front of the room. Chancel furniture was intended to be fixed because it was not desirable to rearrange the floor plan. Fixed pews forced people to move together, and provided racks for multiple print resources. Significant floor space was provided for massed choirs; the chancel area was elevated and sometimes guarded by a railing. The pulpit kept the preacher from moving around, and only one or two microphone jacks and fixed spotlights were needed. A long, wide center aisle encouraged pageantry, just as narrow pews encouraged passivity.

Agreement

Agreement meant that congregational participants would all assent to the same principles and that they would always take action with at least a majority vote. Spontaneity and individuality were discouraged. Individual disagreement or creativity would be tested through consultation with the entire group, and policy changes and permissions would only be granted with as near a unanimous opinion as possible. Groups were almost always large groups, and the success of a group would be measured by the number of people who participated. Women's groups, men's groups, and youth groups all sought to include as many people as possible, organizing them in a parliamentary procedure parallel to the consensus management of the church as a whole. It was considered to be a virtue that every individual should be a part of a group because of his or her identity rather than decision.

Therefore, church facilities were designed for large groups and parliamentary procedure. Large gymnasiums, halls, classrooms, and parlors permitted a maximum number of people to gather with unobstructed hearing and sight. Even meeting rooms needed to be large because consensus management demanded the largest representative church board possible. Such groups learned best through lecture-listen methodologies, so rooms would be designed for speeches or presentations, with little dialogue. Since church participants prided themselves on their reasoned commitment to a wider agreement of doctrine, polity, and practice, dogma and ritual would be fixed to walls or enshrined in permanent stained-glass windows.

Control

Control meant that the conformity and assent of the congregation needed to be guarded, and that the united congregational body needed to be protected from intentional or unintentional disgrace. The congregation needed to ensure that participants truly understood and fulfilled their commitments as expressed through baptismal or membership vows. Elders, stewards, deacons, and other church officers formed a middle management of oversight for all church activities. Church constitutions were carefully crafted, and committees followed mandates and reported to the board and the congregation. Clergy wore vestments to symbolize their authority. Information would be distributed only by monthly newsletter, Sunday bulletin, or meeting minutes—all of which were carefully supervised.

Therefore, church facilities were designed to maximize control in the church. Pulpits were large, impressive, and centered in the front of the sanctuary. Sanctuary lighting was dim, and the atmosphere solemn, discouraging spontaneous outbursts. Memorial windows, books, and plaques constantly reminded people of the heritage they were bound in honor to preserve. The two control rooms of the building (the office and the kitchen) were carefully located and guarded. In the church office, seating capacity was often reduced to avoid idle conversation or eavesdropping. In the kitchen, cupboards would be locked and printed instructions for use clearly posted. Governors would be placed on the telephones and photocopiers. Access into the building would be restricted by locked doors, and access to the offices of clergy would be gained only through the church office. Outdoor signs, hourly chimes, and night lighting supported the church's claim to be the moral and spiritual conscience of the community.

Generally speaking, church facilities of the Christendom era proclaimed their assumptions about uniformity, agreement, and control through ecclesiastical architecture. Such architecture did not need to be Gothic, but it was always identifiably churchy. There was never any doubt that the building was a church because no other community organization would choose to be housed in such a building. In a sense, Christendom churches deliberately chose not to own marketable properties because they assumed their organizations would never die and that their ministries would never become irrelevant. They lay claim to being the center of spiritual and moral life in the community, regardless of subsequent demographic shifts. Ecclesiastical architecture, by its very nature, proclaims the belief of the church that people will and must come to them in the end.

These assumptions lead Christendom leaders to treat long-range planning like a road map. Structures were fixed features on the map, and roads were simply carved through the cultural landscape to connect them. As Bill Easum and I pointed out in *Growing Spiritual Redwoods*, Christendom planners perceived themselves in confrontation with culture and simply imposed an ecclesiastical grid over a tamed and civilized society. Just as roads ignored the contours of the land, so also the formation of multipoint pastoral charges ignored the cultural differences between communities, and the geographical boundaries of ecclesiastical judicatories ignored the evolution of urban growth or rural decline. The demographic realities have changed, but churches continue to plan as if the road maps of the nineteenth century were still valid. Indeed, they assume that paving ecclesiastical highways through strategic planning still works in the Pre-Christian world.

In order to understand the changes that are happening in twenty-first century church facilities, we must understand that Christendom is dead. Churches no longer can assume that uniformity, agreement, and control are virtues. These are no longer values in contemporary society, and these values are no longer perceived to be essential to authentic spirituality. People do not have to come to the church in the end. The church will have to go to them or provide opportunities for personal and community health that they can find nowhere else with such quality.

The church facilities located on ministry maps follow the cultural landscape and blend with the contours of opportunity that are ever changing. These facilities are no more, and no less, than base camps from which explorers and their ministry teams will be released into the unknown cultural landscape. Construction of these base camps will follow assumptions very different from those of Christendom.

Diversity

Diversity means that worship services vary in both cultural form and missional purpose. Each service targets a different segment of the population, uses the indigenous cultural forms that are familiar to that public, and addresses the spiritual yearning that is most urgent to that public. Worship services will use amplified, contemporary instruments for rock, new country, jazz, and blues and will specifically aim to heal or transform lives, coach people through ambiguities, celebrate spiritual victories, or cherish eternal truths. Sensory experience, rather than the spoken word, will communicate meaning. Spontaneity will be welcomed, just as individual discovery will be encouraged. It will be considered a virtue that a person can select the church, and the specific worship or growth experience within that church, that helps him or her the most at any specific time in life.

Therefore, church facilities will need to maximize options. Sanctuaries will resemble activity centers with excellent acoustics. Seating will be individual and movable. Stages will be portable and incremental. Access in and out of the worship space will be unrestricted—and will usually open to a refreshment area. Electrical outlets and microphone jacks will be everywhere. Large television screens (or future holographic imaging sites) will allow subgroups to gather, ebb, and flow at the discretion of participants. Such flexibility will allow the floor plan to be easily adjusted to suit the missional purpose of the worship experience. Small rooms adjacent to the worship space will facilitate intimate conversation or private meditation.

Creativity

Creativity means that congregational participants are bound together by a common experience, but not necessarily by common assent to dogmas or practices. People will actually be encouraged to question, converse, debate, and discuss the ideas and feelings that are shared. Small groups will become more important than large groups, and group participation will be determined by decision rather than identity. Yes, there will be consensus about the core values, bedrock beliefs, and motivating vision, but within this umbrella of congregational life there will be instant freedom to explore and discover.

Therefore, church facilities must be endlessly adaptable for programs and ministries yet to be imagined. Movable chairs, removable walls, wide doorways, and the fewest possible stairways typify the facility that can be easily customized for any use. There will be multiple small-group rooms, equipped with comfortable seating and refreshment cupboards. Multiple units of video and audio equipment will service simultaneous gatherings, and pull-down projection screens and computer terminals will be available in most rooms. Floor and wall coverings will require low maintenance, withstand hard use, and encourage arts and crafts.

Initiative

Initiative means that congregational participants take risks and church programming encourages experimentation. Processes for rapid feedback, which helps spiritual pioneers learn from their mistakes, are built into all aspects of congregational life. Christian development emphasizes the discernment of personal spiritual gifts and callings rather than the dissemination of politically correct or doctrinally pure information. Within the broad boundaries of core values, bedrock beliefs, and motivating vision, participants can initiate any activity they wish, and they can do it with excellence. Coaching support is always available, and information about individual or group ministries is constantly being shared and supported by prayer.

Therefore, church facilities must be designed to encourage personal initiative and provide the tools necessary for quality ministries. Communications will be enhanced with multiple bulletin boards, email bulletins, automated fax, or even congregational Web pages so that any and all information can be instantly accessible for any person in the church. Church offices become multiple work stations in which secretaries serve as coachs and trainers. Church kitchens are supplemented by multiple refreshment areas in the building, and the kitchen itself makes utensils and dinnerware available to all (with coaches and trainers available). Access to the building is increased and made easier. Outdoor signs communicate congregational vision and personal opportunities. Nighttime lighting has less to do with illuminating windows and architecture and more to do with personal security.

Generally speaking, church facilities of the Pre-Christian Era proclaim a bias for diversity, creativity, and initiative through utilitarian architecture. There is nothing churchy about them. This is not to say that they will not be attractive. Indeed, beauty in building design and landscaping is vital. Nor is this to say that Christian symbolism will not be vital—it will simply be portable. Church facilities will above all be useful, adaptable, . . . and marketable. In the Pre-Christian Era, the church will not expect people to come to them but will be prepared to go to the people. They will be ready to sell their property, carry their symbols with them, and relocate to a more effective place of ministry. In the twenty-first century, architecture and tradition are secondary. All that matters is the Gospel—and nothing else!

A base camp for cartographers exploring unknown territory is designed with three features in mind: purposefulness, usefulness, and safety. It will be purposeful in that even the smallest detail of the camp will have a clear connection with that fundamental goal, the achievement of which is the whole purpose of living for the explorers who reside in the camp. It will be useful in that the design of the camp can be quickly adapted to meet any need or accomplish any task demanded by the mission. It will be safe, so that explorers who take daring risks beyond the camp can be confident that life within the camp will be as worry-free as humanly possible. In the same way, church facilities of the future will be designed with three features in mind.

1. *Symbolism, vision, and mission:* The primary symbolism (exterior and interior) will be neither generic (such as a cross)

nor denominational (such as an ecclesiastical crest). Symbols will communicate to the public everything they need to know about this particular congregation in a simple graphic or a well-chosen phrase. Even the smallest detail of the facility will immediately link to the present purpose of the congregation. The accumulation of baggage (artifacts, memorials, old curricula, and objects that have outlived their usefulness for contemporary mission) will be severely restricted. Any detail that will not immediately link a visitor from the cultural forest with the single-minded purpose of the congregation will be left behind.

2. *Multiple options supported by up-to-date technologies:* The church facility will be easily adapted to any emerging need or task—and to simultaneous, distinct tasks. In order to do this, church facilities will be oriented around three basic circles of space:

• *Worship Center: Versatile space for drama and dance, small and large groups, and music and movement. Supported by surround-sound, abundant microphones, computer terminals, video screens, and adjustable lighting. Open to fresh air and natural light.*

• *Conversation Court: Immediately adjacent to, and half the size of, the worship center. With no steps or narrow doors. Includes a refreshment center with multiple choices for popular foods, a resource center to purchase spiritual growth resources in all media, a prayer center that allows confidential and intimate sharing, and a personal support center storing wheelchairs and other helps for those who are physically challenged. Volunteers are available at all times.*

• *Child care Center: Immediately adjacent the conversation court, with no steps. Has security access. Divided for infants and toddlers, and equipped with the same standards of quality as the best day care in the community. Video/audio links to the worship center and pagers available for parents.*

These base camps of the future will have additional space for education, sports, small groups, food preparation, and other activities, which will constantly be reshaped to support the changing ministries on the ministry map.

3. *Personal security, safety, and accessibility.* The church facility will exceed the municipal codes for accessibility and safety. All

areas indoors and outdoors will be brightly illuminated and free from hazards. The church office will be able to monitor access to the building. Rooms will have appropriate locks and visible alarms. Volunteers will be readily available to assist people on and off the property.

The base camp will be linked by computer to other facilities pertaining to mission units elsewhere in the cultural landscape. As the ministry teams move ever forward exploring the cultural landscape, the base camp will be readily relocated to be central to the mission field.

LOCATE MISSION UNITS

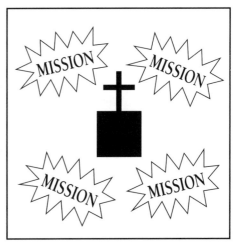

Cartographers exploring unknown territory will establish a series of temporary camps wherever their explorations take them. In the same way, ministry mappers will establish mission units, with or without facilities, wherever opportunities arise. The location of these specific mission units is perhaps the one way in which traditional strategic planning continues to have value for the church of the future. Even then, it is not so much strategic planning that is helpful but rather a research and marketing strategy that helps ministry mappers prioritize and locate mission units. This work is generally described by Norman Shawchuck and colleagues in *Marketing for Congregations* (Nashville: Abingdon, 1992) and reflects the practices of profit and nonprofit organizations already at work amid rapidly changing culture. There are three basic tasks:

1. Discerning Call

The priorities for mission opportunities are evaluated using seven criteria. Mission units must be:

a. *Clearly Christian:* Which opportunities are clearly in keeping with the life, mission, and teachings of Jesus?

b. *Clearly Mission Fulfilling:* Which opportunities clearly advance the congregation toward that fundamental goal that is its purpose for living?

c. *Clearly Congregational:* Which opportunities clearly express the core values, bedrock beliefs, motivating vision, and key mission that together form the identity of the congregation?

d. *Clearly Distinctive:* Which opportunities are not only necessary but visibly unique and obviously linked to the local cultural context?

e. *Clearly Feasible:* Which opportunities can be shared with existing or potential partners; are manageable within realistic timelines; and use actual, trainable, or obtainable resources and leadership?

f. *Clearly Motivational:* Which opportunities excite the emotions of the congregational participants, fire the imaginations of community members, and can be readily celebrated as enhancing the experience of Christ?

Note that discernment of call precedes the assessment of risks and that the degree of challenge or the audacity of the call is not a criteria used in prioritizing mission opportunities. If a mission opportunity does not clearly reflect these criteria, then no matter how socially beneficial, popular, or financially rewarding it might be, the congregation will not do it.

2. Measuring Risk

The priorities for mission opportunities are tested using six criteria, in the following order:

a. *Heritage Costs:* Identify what must change or be intentionally maintained in the self-understanding of the congregation, or the preservation of structures or traditions, for the new opportunity to flourish.

b. *Attitude Costs:* Identify what must change or be intentionally emphasized in the behavior patterns and lifestyles of congregational participants, or the assumptions they hold about the future, for the new opportunity to flourish.

c. *Leadership Costs:* Identify how leadership roles must change, what leadership skills must be gained, what new expertise must be obtained, or what boundaries for creativity must be established for the new opportunity to flourish.

d. *Organization Costs:* Identify what structures must change, what communications systems will need to be enhanced, or what key policies must be revised for the new opportunity to flourish.

e. *Property Costs:* Identify what must change or be intentionally preserved in the location or status of present facilities (including staff accommodation) for the new opportunity to flourish.

f. *Financial Costs:* Identify the sources of lost revenue and potential income, the costs for continuing education for clergy and laity, and the capital requirements for renovation or property acquisition (including risk management) for the new opportunity to flourish.

Note that financial costs are the last to be considered. The truth is, if the congregation is able to meet all the previous costs, then the financial cost will probably be the least significant obstacle. If the costs of mission opportunity can be faced in every other way, then financial challenge will *not* be a barrier for implementation. It may take a while, but the congregation will eventually implement the mission.

3. Planning Ministry

The planning for mission opportunities can now be done by answering five key strategic questions. In a sense, these key questions represent the residual effectiveness of traditional strategic planning. Once again, the order in which these questions are asked and answered is important. The sequence of priority is mission, people, tasks, timing, and method.

a. *Why?* How does this mission unit advance the congregation toward its vision and mission?

b. *Who?* What publics within the community will be involved in the mission; and what combination of spiritual and physical, emotional, or relational needs will be met?

c. *What?* What measurable, beneficial impact will the mission have on the cultural context of the community, region, or world?

   If the primary impact is in faith witness, what will be the simultaneous social benefit? and if the primary impact is social service, what will be the simultaneous faith witness?

d. *When?* How urgent is the implementation of the mission, and what extra degree of risk is implied by this urgency?

   When will the mission be implemented, how frequently will the selected public interact with the mission, and when will the mission close?

e. *How?* What skilled leadership will be required, and how much will it cost to train them for excellence and deploy them?

   What vehicles of ministry will be required (such as property or technology), and what will it cost to acquire and upgrade these vehicles?

   How will the congregation learn from inevitable, occasional failure?

You will note that there are several peculiar features about these five keys to strategic planning. First, vision comes first. Nothing happens unless it links the congregation to its deep sense of unique purpose. Second, the spiritual aspects of mission are always combined with every other aspect of mission. Mission is never merely philanthropic but always intended to communicate Christian faith. Third, every mission is a unity of social service and soul care. No faith witness is ever offered unless accompanied by actions of practical benefit to the well-being of other human beings, and no beneficial action happens that does not explain clearly its faith motivation. Fourth, the timetable is always urgent. Assurance of success is important, but always secondary. Finally, quality is built into every tactic. Property and technology must be the best and most useful that can be obtained, and it must be upgradeable or replaceable. Nothing is sacred—only the vision.

As you reflect back on these three basic tasks for locating mission units on the ministry map, you will notice several important differences from traditional strategic planning. First, the location of the mission unit on the ministry map arises from the spiritual formation of the people. It does not arise from the happy coincidence of superfluous congregational resources, nor does it arise from the community requests for action. It is neither reactive nor proactive, but vision directed. Mission results from spiritual discernment.

Second, the location of the mission unit on the ministry map accepts the reality of gaps in ministry. Just as cartographers cannot cover the entire landscape with surveyors, so also the congregation cannot do everything, for everyone, all the time. There is no guilt about this, nor do they allow themselves to be manipulated by those beyond the church to address the agenda of those who do not share their vision. The gaps will be filled in God's time, as mission is evoked from the spiritual growth of the people.

Third, the location of the mission unit on the ministry map celebrates redundancy. Just as cartographers may do the same repetitive actions in several places at once, so also the congregation may do the same mission in several places at once. Redundancy is not bad and does not imply duplication of effort or competition for turf. Redundancy is good because the units can learn for each other and multiply the benefits of any given mission one hundredfold.

Fourth, the location of the mission unit on the ministry map recognizes the inevitably of occasional failure. As soon as urgency and quality are introduced into the plan for mission, the possibilities for moving too quickly or too slowly are multiplied. Some failure must be anticipated. The key is that no failure will happen without subsequent learning.

Planning of any kind requires organizational principles in order to be effectively implemented. In ministry mapping, the organizational principles that lie behind the exploration of the unknown include the following:

Motivation: The profound calling that drives core leaders to take great risks.

Unity: The wholehearted endorsement of the basic umbrella of congregational life.

Ownership: The passionate partnerships of cell groups to pursue contextual opportunities.

Freedom: The permission extended to leadership and cell groups for creative experiments.

Integrity: The personal and spiritual maturity that is fed by disciplined growth.

Learning: The corporate, courageous strategies to learn from inevitable failures.

Many congregations of the Christendom era are obsessed with control. The strategic planning that they undertake is as much an effort to maintain central control through a complex system of hierarchical accountability as it is an effort to determine future directions for action. The real issue for such strategic planning is not what ministries will be done but, rather, who will control them. For every 10 words used to describe the potential mission, there will be 50 words used to define who can exercise control for the course of that mission.

Ministry mapping reverses that obsession with control and concentrates on mission. Ultimately, nothing matters but the Gospel: not property, not finances, not traditions, not offices, not denominational ethos, not liturgies, not even past success. Everything can be shaped, changed, renovated, and relocated for the sake of mission. This does not mean that ministry mapping is not disciplined and intentional but that the heart of discipline lies in personal spiritual growth and that the seriousness of intentionality lies in the identity and calling of the congregation itself.

CONSENSUS ———— CONTROL

Congregational > Congregational > Strategies > Tactics
Identity   Policy

PERMISSION ———— PARTNERSHIP

Many congregations of Christendom want to impose consensus on management. That is, they want to control the implementation of mission and completely ignore the need for clarity about calling and identity, which will help them shape the governance policies. In ministry mapping, the emphases are different:

Consensus is crucial to:	*congregational calling and identity and ownership of the basic umbrella of congregational life.*
Permission is crucial to:	*strategies and tactics that lead to creative partnerships and experimentation in ministry.*

Adult spiritual formation is crucial to the whole because without it neither integrity nor learning can be accomplished. Consensus requires disciplined spiritual growth, not membership privileges and majority voting. Permission requires disciplined spiritual growth, not nominations or bureaucracy.

The cartographic expedition enters the unknown with clarity and unity of purpose, and they will release a multitude of survey teams into the landscape, confident in their ability for independent action. They know that their survey teams may well be out of touch with base camp for extended periods of time, and they will be required to make instant decisions and take urgent actions in the field in order to do the work. In the same way, the twenty-first century congregation enters the new cultural wilderness with clarity and unity of purpose, and they will release a multitude of ministry teams into the cultural landscape, confident in their ability for independent action. This confidence is not based on complex, bureaucratic lines of reporting and accountability but, rather, on trust that ministry teams share the core values, beliefs, vision, and mission of the congregation and that they are all committed to disciplined spiritual growth. When the cartographers return to base camp, they will join other teams to assess their successes and failures and continue to refine the topographic map. When the ministry teams reunite with the congregation, they will assess their successes and failures and continue to refine the ministry map.

Therefore, your ministry map is now completed—just in time for you to begin revising it again! This is not a strategic plan. It cannot be enshrined in the congregational agenda for five or more years and implemented in predictable, incremental stages. The ministry map will require continuous revision. It will be redrawn again and again as the cultural context changes. Once the congregation has gone this far, there are no blueprints for action. Experimentation is everything. You will forever be moving off the map . . . drawing a new map . . . and moving off it again.

This returns us to the place where we began in this field guide. The future of the church in the twenty-first century will not be determined by planning. It will be determined by leadership development. These leaders may be clergy or laity, and they will probably not care about the designation. They will be risk-takers and adventurers. They will always be wondering what opportunity lies over the next cultural hill. They will be explorers of the unknown. They will be you.